KT-525-976

 TEACH YOURSELF

A CONCISE DICTIONARY OF
PHRASE
& FABLE

B. A. Phythian

Hodder & Stoughton
LONDON SYDNEY AUCKLAND

A CIP catalogue record for this book
is available from the British Library

ISBN 0 340 55633 1

First published 1993

Typeset by Rowland Phototypesetting Ltd,
Bury St Edmunds, Suffolk
Printed in Great Britain for the educational publishing
division of Hodder & Stoughton Ltd, Mill Road, Dunton Green,
Sevenoaks, Kent by Clays Ltd, St Ives plc

PREFACE

Why are bats in the belfry, the cuckoo in the nest, the albatross round one's neck, the fly in the ointment, the flea in the ear, the cat out of the bag and the dog in the manger? Who were Fred Karno's Army, the real McCoy, peeping Tom, Aunt Sally and Uncle Sam, Gordon Bennett, the Bill, Sweet Fanny Adams and jack of all trades? What are apple-pie order, a banana republic, the grapevine, an olive branch and limelight—and why take two bites of the cherry or blow a raspberry? Where are cloud-cuckoo-land, the land of Nod, Liberty Hall, Utopia, Armageddon and Marathon, not to mention limbo and bunkum? Why are people at sixes and sevens, one over the eight, dressed to the nines at the eleventh hour, talking nineteen to the dozen or having forty winks? What precisely are loggerheads, fleshpots, shambles, digs, claptrap, flying colours, gobbledegook and short shrift? Who were Maverick, Biro, Silhouette, Lynch, Shrapnel, Boycott and Jumbo? And why is pie in the sky, the skeleton in the cupboard, the thorn in the flesh, the writing on the wall, the bolt from the blue and the chip on the shoulder?

These are just a few of the 1,500 everyday words and expressions for which this dictionary supplies an explanation in terms of their origins and development. It is an exploration through mythology, folklore, literature, religion, science, history, superstition, proverb, slang, popular metaphor and daily life. It shows how some of our most common words and phrases go back to the earliest civilisations, and how our daily English draws from the language and culture of India and Africa, the Far East and North America, from languages and customs long since dead as well as from the events of our own day.

I hope that this book will add to the reader's understanding and enjoyment of the richness of the English language, and also help the foreign reader to gain an insight into some of its apparent eccentricities.

Brian Phythian
London, 1992

A

A1 • *in first-class condition*

A borrowing from the *Register of Shipping* maintained by Lloyd's of London, the insurance market, from the eighteenth century onwards. The quality of a ship's hull is denoted by a letter and that of its equipment by a number. 'A1' therefore indicates the best quality in all respects. The term is now normally used of someone's health.

aback, be taken • *be startled*

Aback is found only with the verb *take*. The expression is one of many that have passed from nautical into general use. A ship was said to be taken aback if the wind pressed its sails back against its mast, preventing forward movement.

Abandon hope, all ye who enter here

The common but inaccurate version of a famous line from Dante's *Divina Commedia* (*Inferno*, iii 9), more correctly translated as 'All hope abandon, ye who enter here'. In the poem the words are inscribed over the entrance to hell.

above board: see *board*

abracadabra • *gibberish*

Also a magician's spell or incantation and a mystic word used as a charm against aches and pains. It made its appearance in a Latin poem (second century AD) by Q. Severus Sammonicus and has been said to comprise the initials of the Hebrew words for 'Father, Son and Holy Ghost', but is more likely to be related to a Greek word for a deity.

Absence makes the heart grow fonder

A catch-phrase quoting a line in an anonymous song from *Davison's Poetical Rhapsody* (1602) later popularised by the much ridiculed society poet T. H. Bayly (1797–1839) in his song *Isle of Beauty*.

Academe, groves of • *places of learning, especially universities; academic circles*

The first Academy, from which the modern 'academy' derives its meaning, was the garden near Athens where Plato taught; it took its name from Akademos, a mythological hero. Plato's Academy lasted nearly a thousand years: it was the forerunner of the modern university and exercised considerable influence over centuries of subsequent thinking throughout Europe.

Shakespeare coined *Academe* as a poetic name for this Academy (*Love's Labours Lost*, I, 1, line 13) in about 1595. Some 75 years later Milton embroidered the idea into 'the olive groves of Academe,/ Plato's retirement', recalling the original garden setting (*Paradise Regained*, Book 4, lines 244–5). This is the origin of the modern expression, now used playfully—or even with slight mockery to imply the remoteness of Academe from the practicalities of daily life.

ace

An ace was originally the side of a dice that was marked with a single pip, counting one. The term was later extended to a playing card similarly marked, and has long been used figuratively to denote any very small amount: a person who *comes within an ace* of doing something fails to do it by only a very narrow margin.

As well as signifying something insignificant, *ace* can—rather confusingly—stand for something important, because in some card games an ace is a powerful card. A person who succeeds by a master-stroke may be said to have *played his or her ace*, i.e.

produced, perhaps unexpectedly, a winning tactic. If he has *an ace up his sleeve* his advantage is not only powerful but also hidden, as a conjurer may conceal a playing card.

This meaning of the word accounts for the development in First Word War slang of *ace* to denote a person, usually an airman, who was expert or showy. The word is still in use, rather informally, with the first of these meanings.

The use of *ace* as a slang exclamation or adjective expressing pleasure, usually by young people, is a more modern and obviously related development of this.

Achilles' heel or tendon

In Homer's *Iliad* (probably eighth century BC), the story of the siege of Troy, Achilles is the great Greek hero whose principal exploit is the killing of Hector, commander of the Trojan army. According to legend he was as an infant immersed by his mother Thetis in the Styx, a river of the underworld, to make him invulnerable. However, the heel by which she held him was untouched by the waters and remained vulnerable. Paris, the Trojan prince, knew this and so was able to kill him at the siege by shooting him in the heel with a poisoned arrow (though this part of the story is not in Homer).

A person's *Achilles' heel* is therefore his vulnerable spot or fatal weakness—his only one, strictly speaking. The *Achilles' tendon*, between heel and calf, is often strained by athletes and takes its name from its position and this vulnerability.

acid test   • *crucial test that determines worth, truth, reliability, etc.*

In former days nitric acid was used to test the genuineness of gold, which remains unaffected by the action of other acids, to assist in making valuations when buying or selling. The *acid test*—the name goes back to the Middle Ages—was accepted as definitive and, in its more general modern sense, still is.

Adam

In the Bible story of the creation of the world (*Genesis*, 1–3) Adam was the first man, created by God from the dust of the earth, and therefore the progenitor of the human race. He and Eve, who was formed from his rib, lived in innocence in the Garden of Eden

3

until Eve succumbed to temptation by the serpent and ate the fruit (commonly said to be an apple, though not identified as such in the Bible) of the tree of the knowledge of good and evil, contrary to the command God had given Adam. She gave Adam some to eat. In punishment for their disobedience, which gave them knowledge of their sexuality, God banished them from the Garden and condemned Adam to work.

These events have given rise to such expressions as *the Fall* or *fall of man* (the lapse of Adam and Eve and thus of humanity into a sinful state) or *fall from grace* (originally, from God's favour; now any loss of favour) into *original sin*, said to be the innate depravity of man, inherited from Adam. The *old Adam* is man's fallen nature, so called from St Paul's contrast between the 'first Adam', destined to die, and the 'last Adam', man redeemed by Christ (*I Corinthians*, 15: 45).

The *Adam's apple* at the front of the throat takes its name from the supposition that a piece of the *forbidden fruit* stuck in Adam's throat. *Adam's ale* is a fanciful name for water, presumably the only strong drink available in the Garden of Eden.

add insult to injury: see *insult to injury*

Adonis　　• *exceptionally handsome young man*

Adonis was a Phoenician deity in classical mythology, a beautiful youth loved by Aphrodite, Greek goddess of love. He was killed by a boar or bear while hunting, a pastime which Aphrodite had tried to discourage as she feared that a tragic fate would befall him.

adrenalin

A hormone secreted in response to stress, it increases the heart and pulse rate, constricts the blood vessels and relaxes muscle. *The adrenalin is flowing* is a rather extravagant—and hackneyed— explanation for the state of controlled excitement experienced by successful public performers, athletes, etc., on special occasions.

aegis of, under the　　• *under the sponsorship or protection of*

The original *aegis* was the shield of Zeus, king of the gods in Greek mythology. It took its name from the Greek word for goatskin: as a child Zeus had been suckled by a goat, Amalthea, and as a man he carried a shield covered with its skin. The aegis therefore symbolised divine protection—a far cry from its usually humdrum modern use.

Aladdin

The story of Aladdin is an oriental one of the type found in the *Arabian Nights*, a collection of popular tales from Indian, Persian and Arabian sources first published in England in the early eighteenth century. He is the son of a poor tailor in China; sent by a sorcerer to obtain a magic lamp from a cave, he keeps it for himself and through it amasses great wealth. He marries the Sultan's daughter and with the help of the genie or spirit of the lamp builds a fine palace. The sorcerer, disguised as a trader offering 'new lamps for old', acquires Aladdin's lamp and takes his palace and princess to Africa, but Aladdin pursues and kills him, returning to China with his wife and home.

Two aspects of the story have entered the language of popular English metaphor: *Aladdin's cave* as a storehouse of fabulous treasure (not necessarily material treasure) and *Aladdin's lamp* as a means of access to power or good fortune.

albatross round one's neck   • *encumbering, inescapable liability*

In Coleridge's *The Rime of the Ancient Mariner* (1798) the mariner tells of an occasion when his ship became ice-bound and was visited by an albatross, greeted as a bird of good omen. The ship was freed from the ice but for some unknown reason the mariner shot the albatross. A curse fell on the ship, the dead albatross was hung round his neck as punishment and the rest of the crew died. While watching beautiful watersnakes around the ship the mariner found himself blessing them; the albatross fell from his neck, the ship was no longer becalmed and his life was saved. He must wander the earth telling his tale and teaching reverence for God's creation, 'All things both great and small'.

In the metaphorical expression to which this story has given rise the albatross is, strictly speaking, a symbol of personal guilt from which freedom has to be earned. In practice it is used of any oppressive influence that is difficult to escape from.

Alice in Wonderland

This shortening of the title of Lewis Carroll's story for children *Alice's Adventures in Wonderland* (1865) is sometimes used to describe any situation that is bizarre, topsy-turvy, more like the fantastical world of wild imagination than the real one. In the story Alice dreams that she pursues a White Rabbit down a rabbit-hole into a surreal world of strange animals and people such as the Cheshire Cat, the Mad Hatter and the King and Queen of Hearts. The writing is characterised by whimsical humour, nonsense verses and inverted logic.

all good things come to an end: see *end*

all hell broke loose: see *hell broke loose*

all my eye: see *eye*

all that glitters is not gold: see *gold*

all things to all men, is

Normally a criticism levelled at someone who lacks firmness of purpose or belief, goes along with whatever is put to him or her and is therefore guilty of inconsistency if not dishonesty. The original is more reputable: 'I am made all things to all men, that I might by all means save some' (1 *Corinthians*, 9: 22). St Paul is explaining that in preaching the **gospel** he seeks to make converts by appealing to different people in ways appropriate to their differences.

all to pot: see *pot*

alpha and omega   ● *the beginning and the end (i.e. everything)*

Literally these are the first and last letters of the Greek alphabet. They are used to signify God's eternity in 'I am Alpha and Omega, the beginning and the ending, saith the Lord, which is, and which was, and which is to come, the Almighty' (*Revelation*, 1: 8). From this quotation comes the modern non-theological use to denote anything all-embracing.

also-ran ● *loser*

A horse-racing term for a runner that fails to gain a place among the first three. It originates in the way in which racing results are normally published in newspapers: the first, second and third horses are specified because they are the ones on which bets are payable; the remainder are merely listed with an introductory 'Also ran:'.

amazon ● *woman who is physically strong, aggressive or virile*

The original Amazons were a mythical people of female warriors from the Caucasus who settled south of the Black Sea in Cappadocia and founded a state to which men were not admitted. Once a year they visited a neighbouring state to become pregnant, but only baby girls were retained and brought up to hunt and make war. The ancient Greeks gave them their name from two Greek words which appear to mean 'lacking a breast', explaining that the Amazons removed their right breasts so as to be able to draw a bow more easily. Curiously, neither they nor their great goddess Artemis have ever been depicted in Greek art with such mutilations, and it could be that their name really means 'large breast' or comes from a foreign word. They were famed for their ferocity in war, and in Greek mythology appear in many notable encounters including the Trojan War.

The River Amazon in South America was so named by its Spanish explorer because he found a tribe of warlike women in the region.

ambrosia ● *delicious food*

In Greek mythology the food of the gods, from a Greek adjective meaning 'immortal'.

angels, on the side of ● *on the side of virtue (and usually of tradition)*

Coined by Benjamin Disraeli in a speech of 1864 during the bitter controversy over Darwin's theory of the origin of species which contradicted the biblical version of how man was created (see **Adam**): 'Is man an ape or an angel? Now I am on the side of the angels.'

7

annus mirabilis • *year of wonders*

Now a rather high-faluting term for a special year in a field of activity or in one person's success, it was originally applied to 1666—the year of the Great Fire of London, the plague and victories over the Dutch—by John Dryden in his poem of 1667 to which he gave the modern Latin title *Annus Mirabilis*.

anything for a quiet life

A catch-phrase expressing a resigned willingness to do anything to secure freedom from trouble. It first appears as the title of a play by John Middleton first performed in about 1621.

apocalypse • *event of great moment and disaster, comparable to the end of the world*

Literally, a revelation or uncovering. The word (from Greek) was originally a theological term for the revelation of the future granted in prophetic visions to St John the Divine on the island of Patmos and set out by him in *Revelation* (about 97 AD), the final book in the Bible and sometimes called the Apocalypse. The modern meaning comes from the fact that the book describes the final great battle between good and evil in the world, with visions of the Last Judgement of humanity by God.

Apollo

Sometimes used as a high-sounding or literary epithet for a handsome young man or for one who represents the perfection of young manhood. In Greek mythology Apollo was among the chief gods, son of Zeus, a pastoral and sun deity, and god of music, prophecy, archery and healing. He was represented in art as a youth of idealised beauty and worshipped at Delphi, the most celebrated of shrines. See **Delphic**.

apostle • *ardent leader or early advocate of a cause, movement or new principle; reformer, pioneer*

Although now in everyday use, this was originally an exclusively theological word (from the Greek for 'one sent') for one of the twelve disciples of Jesus, then for anyone resembling them, especially as a missionary responsible for first implanting Christianity in a region. In the Roman Catholic church the *apostolic succession* is the line believed to stretch in unbroken continuity from St Peter through all popes, thus conferring authority.

apple

The *apple of one's eye* is a specially cherished person or thing. It originally meant the pupil of the eye, thought to be globular and solid like an apple, and acquired its present metaphorical sense because of the special preciousness of the pupil and the need to protect it. This sense is first found in the Bible in several places, e.g. 'he led him about, he instructed him, he kept him as the apple of his eye' (*Deuteronomy*, 32: 10).

To *upset the apple-cart* is to cause confusion in plans, circumstances, etc. Despite suggestions that *apple-cart* was eighteenth-century slang for the human body it is more likely that the phrase was originally American, referring simply to a commonplace rural accident or the upsetting of a vendor's stall by traffic in a crowded market.

Apple-pie order is complete and perfect order. Several old military expressions are French, and in the sixteenth century a familiar one was *cap-à-pie*, meaning 'from head to foot'. The ghost of Hamlet's father is 'Armed at point exactly, cap-à-pie' (I, 2, line 200). If this term was pronounced as spelt it could well have become corrupted to *apple-pie* (i.e. complete) in jocular military slang, or it could simply have been consistently misspelt.

The *apple of discord* (subject of dissention) comes from a story in Greek mythology. When the gods and goddesses assembled for a wedding, Eris (Discord) arrived uninvited and threw on the table a golden apple for the most beautiful woman present. Hera, Aphrodite and Athene contended for it; Paris, as umpire, awarded it to Aphrodite who had promised him the love of Helen, the most beautiful woman in the world. As Paris was a Trojan prince and Helen a Greek queen, this judgement led to the Trojan War.

For *Adam's apple* see **Adam.**

arcadian ● *simply and innocently pleasurable, in a way associated with idyllic rural surroundings*

Arcadia is actually a rather bleak mountainous area of the Peloponnese, the peninsula forming the southern part of Greece, but it was celebrated by the Latin poet Virgil (first century BC) in his *Eclogues* as the location of his idealised world of shepherds, sunshine, love and song. This type of writing became very popular and influential in later English literature, such as Sir Philip Sidney's prose romance *The Arcadia* (1581–4), so much so that the adjective *arcadian* has now lost its geographical particularity and therefore its original capital letter.

Argus-eyed   ● *vigilant, observant*

Argus, the all-seeing giant of Greek mythology, had 100 eyes of which 50 remained opened while the other 50 were closed in sleep. He was employed by the goddess Hera to spy on her husband Zeus. After his death Hera distributed his eyes in the tail feathers of the peacock, her favourite bird.

ark

Anything which *came out of the ark* is very old. The allusion is to Noah's Ark, a large wooden structure that held Noah's family and representative animals when God flooded the earth in punishment for mankind's disregard; Noah was spared because of his goodness, and his family repopulated the earth with God's blessing. Traces of a prehistoric flood have been found in Mesopotamia (modern-day Iraq), and stories about a great deluge appear in the literatures of several ancient civilisations as well as in the Bible (*Genesis*, 6–8).

The *Ark of the Covenant* was a box containing the tablets of the law given by God to Moses. It was carried by the Israelites to the **Promised Land** and ultimately disappeared from Solomon's temple at Jerusalem at the time of the Babylonian captivity. The term is sometimes irreverently used in modern speech or writing to denote any unchangeable set of rules, regulations, conventions or beliefs, especially mysterious or time-honoured ones.

armada   ● *large number of ships*

A Spanish word meaning a fleet of warships, best known from the 'invincible armada' of 130 ships sent by Philip of Spain to invade England in 1588. It was routed by the English fleet under Howard and Drake, but chiefly by the weather. Because of the power of Spain and the magnitude of its threat, this success was greeted by the first great outpouring of a sense of English nationhood and marks the birth of the English naval tradition, which is why an unnecessary foreign word entered the language.

Armageddon • *catastrophic and decisive conflict*

Often applied to a large-scale nuclear war with the power to destroy civilisation. It is a Hebrew word for the site of the final great battle between the forces of good and evil at the end of the world, according to biblical prophecy in *Revelation*, 16: 16.

arrant • *extreme*

Found only with 'nonsense' and one or two other nouns expressive of contempt, this word has a curious history. It is a variant of *errant* (i.e. wandering, as in 'knight errant') and because of its frequent use in *arrant thief* (i.e. a thief who wandered about the country) it was wrongly assumed to mean 'out-and-out, thorough, complete'. This is the meaning it now has, and the original one has dropped away.

artful dodger • *crafty person, especially one engaged in criminal or sharp practice*

This may also be spelt with capital letters as it is in the original nickname of Jack Dawkins, a young and expert pickpocket in the gang of thieves headed by Fagin, in Charles Dickens' *Oliver Twist* (1837–8).

assassin • *murderer, especially of public figure or for political reasons*

From an Arabic word meaning *hashish-eater*, applied in the time of the Crusades to a set of fanatical Muslims dispatched by their leader to murder the Christians; they first intoxicated themselves by eating hashish (Indian hemp). The Assassins were founded in Persia (modern day Iran) in the eleventh century and extended their influence through what is now Iraq and Syria before their destruction by the Mongols in the thirteenth century.

assurance doubly sure, make　　● *give oneself security twice over*

Macbeth actually said 'double sure' (IV, 1, line 83), but the popular misquotation is well established.

atlas　　● *book of maps*

In Greek mythology Atlas was one of the **Titans**. He was punished for his part in their revolt against Zeus, king of the gods, by being condemned to support the world on his shoulders. A drawing of him in this posture appeared on the title page of a collection of maps by Mercator in 1595 and his name thus began its passage into everyday use.

Attila the Hun

Used in comparisons with any person in authority who behaves brutally and insensitively.

The Huns were a ferocious nomadic people from central Asia against whom the Chinese emperors built the Great Wall. They invaded the Balkans and central Europe and helped to bring about the final disintegration of the Roman Empire. Their king, Attila, sometimes called 'the scourge of God', brought them to the height of their power in the fifth century AD, but then led them to defeat by the Visigoths in France (451) after which they ceased to have any importance.

Though not particularly more expansionist and inhumane than other powerful forces in early European history, the Huns entered popular vocabulary when the German emperor, angered by Chinese atrocities against Europeans, instructed his contingent in the international force mustered against the Chinese Boxer Rebellion (1900) to behave 'like Huns'. As a result of this the German forces were called Huns, often for propaganda purposes, during the two World Wars of the twentieth century.

Augean stables, (clean the)　　● *(sweep away) a state of extreme corruption, immorality, illegality, etc.*

Augeus, a Greek king of mythology, owned countless herds of cattle whose foul stables were heaped with 30 years' accumulation of manure. As one of his labours, Hercules cleaned them in a single day by breaching their walls and diverting two rivers through them. See **Herculean**.

augury   ● *omen, portent*

Literally, the art of an augur, a priest of ancient Rome whose duty was to interpret signs to determine the will of the gods. By observing such things as the flight, singing or feeding of birds, or the entrails of sacrificed animals, the augur was held to be able to say whether or not the gods approved of a proposed course of action. His predecessor was the auspex (see **auspices**). In modern use *augury* is a secular word.

Aunt Sally   ● *target for abuse, ridicule, criticism or opposition*

From the name of an old fairground game in which sticks were thrown at the figure of an old woman, or of her head, with a pipe in its mouth, the object being to break the pipe. *Aunt* used to be a familiar form of address to any old lady. *Sally* may have been chosen at random, or as a pun on *sally* meaning 'attack'.

auspices of, under the   ● *with the help or protection of*

In ancient Rome the forerunner of the augur (see **augury**) was the Auspex, literally the bird-watcher, who observed the flight of birds as an omen. If his *auspice*, i.e. observation, was favourable he would advise that the signs indicated divine approval for a course of action. The modern expression which comes from this carries no such supernatural implication.

axe to grind   ● *ulterior and selfish motive; private grievance; pet subject*

The second and third meanings have developed from the first, which comes from the language of US politics, which in turn found it in *Too Much for your Whistle* by the self-educated writer, scientist and statesman Benjamin Franklin (1706–90). It tells how, as a young man, he had obligingly turned a heavy grindstone after a man had flattered him into doing so; in reality the man merely wished to sharpen his axe, after which his attitude changed. From this, Franklin learned to be cautious about the motives behind people's smooth talk: perhaps they merely had another axe to grind.

B

Babel, (tower of)   ● *(scene of) confusion of sounds, especially voices*

An allusion to a story told in *Genesis*, 11: 1–9. At a time when people all spoke the same language, they set about building a city with a tower that would reach as high as heaven. To punish them for this presumption God confounded their efforts by putting different languages into their mouths so that they could not understand each other. He also scattered them all over the world. *Babel* is Hebrew for **Babylon**.

Babylon

The splendid and wealthy capital of the Chaldee Empire, in what is now Iraq, but also in the Bible the place of the Jewish captivity in the fifth century BC and in the New Testament *Revelation* an image of sin and depravity destroyed by God for its worldliness. It is this last sense, combined with the richness and grandeur of the original city, that occurs in modern references to corrupt materialism, sometimes in the expression *a modern Babylon*.

bacchanalia   ● *wild drunken revelry or orgy*

So called, sometimes with a capital B, from Bacchus, the Roman name for the Greek god Dionysus, the god of wine and pleasures, who was exuberantly celebrated with drinking, feasting, music, dancing and general licentiousness.

back to square one: see *square one*

back up, get one's   ● *make one angry*

From the action of a cat, which arches its back when angry.

backstairs   ● *surreptitious (influence, methods, etc.)*

A palace or large house of the kind owned by important people would have not only a main staircase but also backstairs, a simpler set of stairs at the back of the house for the use of servants so that their toings and froings could be kept separate from the more dignified business of the house. The backstairs would also be useful for people not wishing to be seen using the main staircase because their business with the owner was private or underhand. This accounts for the metaphorical meaning of *backstairs*.

Backstairs gossip is, however, a contemptuous term, meaning the sort of unreliable tittle-tattle thought to be typical of servants.

bacon

To *save one's bacon* is to escape from danger. Originally it meant to escape injury to one's body, especially to one's back where one was likely to be beaten. Both *bacon* and *back* are related to the same Old Teutonic word, and this is more likely to account for the expression than the burning of heretics or the preservation of meat from hungry dogs during winter in the days before refrigerators, as some have suggested.

To *bring home the bacon* is to have a success. This may refer to winning a pig as a prize at a bowling competition or at a fair, where catching a greased pig was a traditional sport; the winner kept it. There may also be a connection with the Dunmow Flitch, a gammon of bacon which could be claimed at Dunmow, Essex, by anyone swearing to have lived for a year and a day without a household quarrel or a desire to be unmarried; a version of this well-known tradition, established in 1111, still continues. However, the expression came into use only in the twentieth century and therefore is more likely to be a simple development or new version of *save one's bacon*.

bad books, in one's: see *black books*

bad odour, in: see *odour of sanctity*

badger   ● *pester, harass*

From badger-baiting. Because of their fierceness in defending their burrows against attack, captured badgers were formerly used in sport: a badger was placed in an artificial burrow, such as a kennel made out of a tub, and dogs were set on it in turn to see which could draw it out.

bag

Anything which is *in the bag* is (virtually) certain to be arranged or obtained or to succeed. The bag may be the one behind the Speaker's chair in the House of Commons for the receipt of petitions to Parliament, but is more likely to be the one in which game is carried after it has been shot: the origin of the expression seems to be in military slang, which contains a certain amount of hunting metaphor.

Bag and baggage also started life as a military term. To march out (with) bag and baggage was to march away intact without surrendering any equipment. It now means 'entirely' though it is still normally used to express the completeness of a departure.

See **cat out of the bag, let the**.

baker's dozen, a   ● *thirteen*

This has been explained as originating in the thirteenth century when the price and weight of bread were regulated and the penalties for giving short weight were heavy. Bakers, it is said, used to add an extra loaf to every batch of twelve to make sure that they stayed on the right side of the law.

This explanation overlooks the problem that few people were ever likely to buy that sort of quantity. A better explanation, dating from 1419, is that dealers and street vendors were given thirteen loaves for the price of twelve, this being an arrangement with the baker to regulate the extent of the middleman's profit or commission.

balaclava   • *close-fitting woollen covering for head and neck*

Named from the village of Balaclava in the Ukraine where a famous battle (1854) took place, involving the charge of the Light Brigade, during the Crimean War. The balaclava hat/helmet was not invented until much later, in the 1890s, and was so called because of the protection it offered against bitterly cold weather of the kind experienced by troops in the Crimea. See also **cardigan**.

bald-headed, go   • *act impetuously, without restraint*

The colourful story of the Marquis of Granby who led a cavalry charge at Warburg (1760) despite having lost his wig—or, better still, incensed at having it shot off—may well be true but it is unlikely to be responsible for this expression, which is not recorded until nearly a century later. It is an Americanism originating in the rather more mundane idea of a person acting in unseemly haste by rushing out of the house without even putting a hat on—an unusual breach of etiquette in former times.

ball

A football player is said to be *on the ball* when having control of the ball and looking for a scoring opportunity or someone to pass to. Thus *on the ball* has come to mean alert, efficient, etc. A less common version of the same idea is *have the ball at one's feet* (be in control), which dates from the middle of the sixteenth century. To *start the ball rolling* (begin a process) is also from games-playing, probably football, but if *the ball is in one's court* (the initiative or responsibility has passed over to one) the allusion is to tennis, in which one can only strike the ball if it is in one's own half of the court. See also **play ball**.

ball-game, whole new   • *completely different situation*

A term first used by radio commentators on American football and baseball matches, known as ball-games in that country, when a score or succession of scores transformed the fortunes of one of the teams.

ballot: see *blackball*

balloon goes up   • *action (especially trouble) begins*

The expression dates from the First World War when observation balloons were hoisted close to the trench-lines so that the enemy positions and movements could be watched; observers were also used to help range their own artillery before a bombardment. The hoisting of balloons was often, for the infantry, a sign that a major attack was imminent, though nowadays 'What time does the balloon go up?' can simply mean 'What time does it start?'.

ballpark figure   • *realistic estimate*

Ballpark is the American term for the playing area of a baseball match. The idea behind a *ballpark figure* is that of a ball being hit within the playing area where it can be seen, as distinct from being hit out of the ballpark—both out of sight and high-scoring.

Because of ignorance of baseball among the British, and their willingness to adopt Americanisms without understanding them (see **rain-check**), this expression is frequently used to mean no more than a very vague estimate.

ballyhoo   • *noisy publicity*

From the language of the American circus or carnival. The ballyhoo was a short free exhibition or sample of a sideshow given on a small stage, called the bally stand, in front of the sideshow tent. It was accompanied by raucous commentary by the owner to attract spectators and lure them inside as customers for the whole show. Perhaps the word comes from 'hullabaloo', which is a rhyming duplication of 'halloo', a shout to call attention.

baloney   • *nonsense, rubbish*

Initially the colloquial American pronunciation of the Italian 'bologna'; the Italian pronunciation does not sound the g, as may be seen from an earlier English spelling, 'bolonia'. It is short for Bologna sausage, named after the Italian city where it originated as a large spicy sausage of mixed meat. Judging by the modern meaning it did not find favour among Americans—apart, one assumes, from Italian immigrants—and seems to have suffered the same fate as the English 'tripe'.

banana republic   • *small country, politically unstable, dependent on limited agriculture, ruled by small, wealthy and corrupt clique*

Coined by O. Henry (real name W. S. Porter, 1862–1910), the American humorist and short-story writer, with reference to the Honduras. *Republic* is often a euphemism for dictatorship. *Banana* implies an easy reliance on basic agriculture and backwardness in the development of modern industrial technology.

bandwagon   • *movement that seems likely to succeed*

First used in American circus slang for the large, high and ornamented wagon which had seats for musicians and was used in circus parades advertising the circus's arrival. It was also often used as stationary seating for the band during performances. The word then came to be applied figuratively to a politician's election campaign, presumably because of its likeness to a circus. From that developed the idea of *jumping on to a bandwagon*, joining an apparently winning side, popular tide of opinion, fashion, etc. The term still has a touch of showbusiness about it: there is a sense that a bandwagon may have more style than substance and that those who join one do so for personal glorification or because they lack independent judgement or ideas.

baptism of fire   • *first painful experience*

Initially this meant the grace of the Holy Spirit imparted by baptism: 'he [Jesus] shall baptise you with the Holy Ghost, and with fire' (*Matthew*, 3: 11) is one of many biblical metaphors comparing the action of God with that of fire in refining and purifying (especially metals) or destroying.

Later the expression was used, again theologically, of martyrdom by fire as an equivalent to baptism (in securing admission to salvation). Finally it was applied to a soldier's first experience of being under fire in battle. This last sense gave rise to the modern usage.

barbarous   • *uncultured, savage*

Like other words beginning with the same two syllables this comes from a Greek word which originally meant 'foreign', i.e. non-Greek, hence outlandish, uncivilised. The Greek word was

19

invented to signify stammering, meaningless speech, its first two syllables echoing the babbling sound of the foreigner.

barge-pole, not touch with   • *refuse to have anything to do with*

On a canal a barge-pole could be used either to propel a barge or to stave off collision with the bank. For either purpose it had to be long. To refuse to touch something even with a barge-pole (sometimes spelt without the hyphen) is to keep well away from it.

bark up the wrong tree: see *tree*

barmy   • *crazy*

Barm is not only yeast but also the froth that forms on the top of fermenting malt liquors. From this latter meaning it is easy to see how *barmy* came to be applied to a person who had a frothy top in the form of insubstantial brains.

barnstorming   • *(of a performance) enjoying huge popular success*

The original barn-stormers were strolling players who acted in barns, usually the largest available spaces in small centres of population, and whose style of performance was stormy or ranting, either because they were not very good actors or because they performed popular pieces such as melodramas requiring an exaggerated style. The term was later applied to American politicians on campaign tours in rural areas, presumably delivering rousing speeches in a similar style.

barrack   • *shout derisively (at person)*

Originally Australian, from an Aboriginal word meaning 'chaff' or 'banter'. It became known in England only in the early part of the twentieth century from newspaper reports by cricket correspondents accompanying English touring teams in Australia. Spectators at matches, notably in Sydney and Melbourne, expressed their feelings noisily, in sharp contrast to the sedate behaviour of contemporary English crowds. The experience of visiting English teams was such that the word became synonymous with derision, though in Australia and New Zealand it retains its original wider meaning, including that of expressing friendly support.

bat, off one's own   ● *on one's own initiative*

A reference to using one's bat to score runs in cricket. It is rather a tautologous term as there are few other methods of scoring.

For *old bat* see **bats**.

bats, batty   ● *crazy*

From the fuller *have bats in the belfry* (be crazy). The comparison is between the head and the upper part of a church: the belfry is the brain; the bats clutter it up or flutter around when disturbed by the bell, like confused thoughts in a disordered mind.

The derisory term *old bat* for a mad old woman comes from the same idea.

battle royal   ● *violent struggle*

A term originally used in cock-fighting for the sort of contest in which a number of birds were pitted together and left to fight among themselves until only one survived, or for a knockout competition beginning with sixteen birds fighting in pairs. Presumably these variations on the more normal single combat were thought to provide first-rate or 'royal' entertainment.

See **pitched battle**.

battle-axe   ● *belligerent old woman*

The word has been in English since at least the fourteenth century but acquired this sense only in the late nineteenth. The explanation seems to be that the word was given a new lease of life during hostilities between American settlers and Indians, whose tomahawks were called 'war-hatchets' or 'battle-axes'. It then came into metaphorical use from *The Battle Axe*, the name of an American women's rights magazine whose writers and readers were presumed to be belligerent and probably elderly spinsters with nothing better to do.

batty: see *bats*

21

be-all and end-all   ● *essential element; entire purpose; supreme issue*

Shakespeare invented the phrase but meant something slightly different. His Macbeth appears willing to kill the king as long as the murder 'Might be the be-all and the end-all here' (I, 7, line 5), i.e. if it could be complete in itself, without any consequences.

beam-ends, on one's   ● *almost penniless; destitute*

On a wooden ship the beams were the horizontal transverse timbers holding it together. A ship was said to be on its beam-ends if it rolled violently to one side so that these beams became almost vertical, as if the ship were lying on their ends. In that position it was of course in danger of capsizing, a desperate plight echoed in the metaphorical meaning of the expression.

bean, beans

A *bean-feast* used to be an annual dinner given by an employer to his staff and was so called because beans, or more likely bean-goose, were served. Often shortened to *beano*, it now means any jollification.

Full of beans means full of energy, of which beans are providers.

The Americanism *spill the beans* (reveal information or a secret) may come from *bean* as US slang for 'head' (spill or let slip what is in one's head). More likely it comes from *know one's beans* (know what's what); this is clearly related to the early seventeenth-century English saying *know how many beans make five*, which has the same meaning. It is a short step from knowing one's beans to spilling them, i.e. telling what one knows. Certainly, and despite what some authorities say, the expression has nothing to do with the disclosure of a secret ballot, from the ancient Greeks' use of beans as tokens when voting for candidates for public office; it did not enter the language until the twentieth century.

bear-garden   ● *scene of uproar*

Originally a place for the baiting of bears; they were chained to a post and attacked by dogs. The pastime was notorious for rowdiness and bad language among the rabble who enjoyed it.

beard the lion (in his den)   • *confront a dangerous adversary (on his own ground)*

Two distinct ideas are run together here. The first is from the words of the young David explaining why he should be allowed to fight Goliath: when he was a shepherd 'there came a lion . . . I caught him by his beard, and smote him, and slew him' (*I Samuel*, 17: 34–5). The second, which is first found added on in Walter Scott's poem *Marmion* (1808), is a borrowing from a different story, that of **Daniel in the lion's den**.

beat, beaten

Beat a retreat (depart) is from the military *beat retreat*, beat a drum as a signal for retreat. In *beat hollow* (vanquish completely), 'hollow' is probably a corruption of 'wholly'. In *off the beaten track* (remotely situated; unusual), 'beaten' is used in its old sense of 'well-trodden', i.e. beaten by feet.

See also **bush, beat about the**.

beauty and the beast

Now a jocular catch-phrase for two sharply contrasting people or things, this is originally the title of a fairy-tale introduced into European literature in Straparola's *Pleasant Nights* (1550–3) and in a better-known French version by Villeneuve in 1740–1. To save the life of her father, his youngest daughter Beauty agrees to live with the Beast, an ugly monster; filled with pity and affection she finally agrees to marry him, whereupon he turns into a handsome prince, released from a cruel spell by her virtue.

beaver

The animal is remarkable for its industry (and skill) in constructing its habitation and creating dams to preserve its water supply. This has given rise to the verb *beaver away* (work assiduously) and to the faintly derogatory *eager beaver* for a person who is keen to succeed.

bed of roses: see *roses*

bed on the wrong side, has got out of   • *is irritable*

Strictly speaking, 'has got out of bed on the left-hand side', having put the left foot on the floor first. This was unlucky according to an old superstition, one of many having to do with preferring right to left.

bedlam   • *(place of) loud uproar and confusion*

A contraction of *Bethlem*, from the priory of St Mary of Bethlehem in London (1247). It later cared for the insane, then became a hospital for lunatics, and finally transferred to Moorfields (now the Imperial War Museum) where it became a popular resort for sightseers; admission tickets were sold so that people could watch the behaviour of inmates. Its name used to be synonymous with human degradation and callous indifference to it. Since 1931, as the Bethlem Royal Hospital, it has been at Beckenham, Kent. The modern meaning of *bedlam* reflects conditions in earlier times.

bedpost: see *gatepost*

bee in one's bonnet   • *obsession*

An alliterative refinement of an earlier expression 'his head is full of bees', i.e. he is scatterbrained, unable to think straight, as if he has bees buzzing around inside his head. The notion of having a bee in one's bonnet implies an inability to concentrate on anything else.

bee's knees, the   • *the height of perfection*

A more intelligible piece of slang, 'no bigger than a bee's knee', is recorded from the late eighteenth century onwards. This might, or might not, have been transmogrified into the present expression by the bright young things of the 1920s, when not only language, but music, dancing, dress and social behaviour were frantically valued—in the wake of the First World War—for their breaking of convention. *Bee's knees*, like the equally improbable *cat's pyjamas* and its variant *the cat's whiskers*—all three mean the same—belongs to that period and has survived because of an engaging idiocy reinforced by rhyme.

beef   • *grouse*

An Americanism, probably from the moaning sound made by a 'beef', the American name for a cow, bull, etc.

beggar description, belief, etc.   • *to be beyond description, belief, etc.*

This use of beggar to mean 'exhaust the resources of' dates from Shakespeare's *Antony and Cleopatra*: 'For her own person,/It beggared all description' (II, 2, lines 197–8).

behemoth   • *gigantic thing (or animal or person)*

An approximation to a Hebrew word, perhaps meaning 'hippopotamus', first used in Wyclif's translation of the Bible (1380) probably because he was not sure of the English meaning, and later adopted by the translators of the Authorised Version. It occurs in *Job*, 40: 15, as an illustration of the greatness of God's creation.

belt, below the   • *unfair; unscrupulous*

The rules for the previously unregulated sport of boxing were drawn up by the Marquess of Queensberry in 1867 and prohibited any blow delivered to the body below the line of the belt (now waistband) because of the special vulnerability of the groin, etc.

bend over backwards   • *try very hard, especially to help*

The implication is that one puts oneself out in doing so.

This curious American expression seems to have originated simply as the opposite of the notion of leaning towards or bending over someone in solicitude or friendship. In other words it means making a special effort even if that entails acting against one's inclination and going to the opposite extreme in an attempt to show no bias.

berserk, go   • *become frenzied*

A *berserk(er)*—there are various other spellings—was a Norse warrior renowned for the fury of his fighting. His name came from an Icelandic word probably signifying the bear-skin (*bear-sark*) or coat he wore; he was reputed to fight without armour. The word is now usually an adjective.

berth, give a wide   ● *avoid; keep at a safe distance*

A metaphor from seamanship. A berth is, among other things, a place where a ship is at anchor or at a wharf. A *wide berth* is plenty of room, especially important in former days for a ship swinging at anchor.

best laid plans of mice and men (go oft astray)

In his poem *To a Mouse*, subtitled 'On turning her up in her nest with the plough, November 1785', Robert Burns expresses sorrow for destroying the mouse's carefully constructed shelter and muses on the lot of man and animal. It is in this context that these words first occur, except that in the original they are in dialect and that Burns actually wrote 'schemes' not 'plans'.

better or worse, for   ● *whatever the outcome*

A variant of 'for better, for worse' from the part of the Christian Prayer Book marriage service where the bride and groom take each other as man and wife until separated by death, whatever life may bring them.

between you and me: see *gatepost*

beware Greeks: see *Greek(s)*

beyond the pale: see *pale*

bib and tucker, best   ● *one's best clothes*

Sometimes used of formal dress. Originally used only of women's clothes: a bib was a piece of cloth, like the upper part of an apron, worn between throat and waist; a tucker was a frill of lace or muslin covering the neck and shoulders. The phrase dates from the seventeenth century and has gradually been adopted, originally jocularly, to apply to men's clothes as well.

Big Brother (is watching you)

Said jocularly, ironically or more seriously of a person or organisation, such as a government, exercising dictatorial control. The allusion is to George Orwell's prophetic novel *1984* (1949) in which Big Brother is the sinister, despotic and omnipresent figurehead of a ruthlessly repressive and dehumanising **Stalinist** state which crushes all individuality. 'Big Brother is watching you' is the slogan on huge posters showing his image, displayed everywhere in a manner still characteristic of some totalitarian regimes.

bigwig   ● *noted or important person, especially one in public position*

From the specially large wigs formerly worn by people of high station in life, now retained only by judges, the Speaker of the House of Commons and the Lord Chancellor. Slightly jocular.

bikini   ● *two-piece bathing costume for women*

First used in France in 1947; the costume was previously named—erroneously, as it turned out—*le minimum*. The new name came from the atoll of Bikini, in the Marshall Islands of the Pacific, which had been the site of US atom-bomb tests during the previous year. It is not known whether the link between garment and atoll/atom was smallness or explosiveness of effect. Probably the latter, given the reputation of the French.

bilge   ● *worthless remarks or ideas*

The bilge of a ship is the lowest internal part of the hull, where water used to collect and gradually became stale or foul until its periodical removal. This bilge-water, also known as bilge, became synonymous with rubbish and thus with nonsense.

Bill, the or (the) old Bill   ● *the police*

Formerly London slang for the Metropolitan Police but now, as a result of a popular television series, a widespread term for any police.

The best-known Old Bill is the famous character in Bruce

Bairnsfather's cartoons of trench life in the First World War, frequently reprinted and even turned into a play and a film. Attempts have been made to link him with the slang use of his name, but the origins go back very much further. Constables of the Watch—the precursors of the police force—until late in the eighteenth century carried a weapon known as a *bill*, which earlier was an infantry weapon generally consisting of a blade or axe mounted on a wooden handle, sometimes called a halberd. The most famous Shakespearean constable, Dogberry in *Much Ado About Nothing*, advises members of his Watch to 'have a care that your bills be not stolen' (III, 3, line 44). From this a watchman was sometimes called a 'billman', often abbreviated to *bill*, and this name was transferred to their successors, sometimes with the addition of a familiar or affectionate 'old'. The modern capital letter seems to have been added through a misapprehension that *bill* must be a Christian name.

bill, fill (fit) the   ● *meet the requirements*

Bill here means poster, as it often does. The whole expression originated in America, where a famous performer whose name appeared in large letters on a theatre-bill to the exclusion of all others literally 'filled' the bill. The meaning (originally, 'have importance') shifted over the years, as frequently happens, as the phrase moved from theatrical circles which understood its origins to a wider public which did not.

billy-o(h) or billio, like   ● *vigorously*

Variously identified as the zealous Joseph Billio, the first Nonconformist minister of Maldon, Essex, in the late seventeenth century; Nino Biglio, a dashing officer in Garibaldi's army, reputed to have always been urging his men to fight 'like Biglio'; the famous steam locomotive 'Puffing Billy' (1813) which was energetic by contemporary standards in mechanical engineering; and the devil, not because he was ever known as Billy but because some people may have wanted a polite alternative to 'like the devil' (vigorously) and chose *Billy* at random. The date of the expression (late nineteenth century) points to Puffing Billy as the likeliest contender: it was employed in hauling coal wagons, was more efficient than previous engines in being the first not to use cogs and rack-rails, and achieved celebrity.

bird, get or **give the**   • *receive or show derision*

From theatrical slang; originally 'get the big bird', i.e. the goose, which hisses as people do when they make a traditional sound of disapproval at a bad public performance.

bird in the hand is worth two in the bush, a   • *it is better to possess something than merely to hope for something better*

A very ancient proverb related to the activity described at **bush, beat about the**.

bird told me, a little

Catch-phrase used when refusing to disclose the source of one's information. It has gradually evolved, reaching its present form in the nineteenth century, from the Old Testament: 'Curse not the King, no not in thy thought . . . for a bird of the air shall carry the voice, and that which hath wings shall tell the matter' (*Ecclesiastes*, 10: 20).

biro

The ball-point pen is named after its inventor, the Hungarian Lazlo Biro, who patented it in 1938. It was first marketed in England towards the end of the Second World War.

birthright, sell one's   • *relinquish one's native rights*

The earliest story of the selling of birthright is in *Genesis* and is explained at **pottage**.

biscuit, take the   • *be regarded (by the speaker) as surpassing everything else*

Used in expressions of astonishment or disbelief. It is an anglicisation of the American 'take the cake' (take the prize) from the very popular parade or walk-around known as the cake-walk, a good-natured competition originating among the Afro-Americans in which the reward for the fanciest steps in style or elegance was customarily a cake.

bit between one's teeth, get the   • *act without restraint*

A metaphor from horsemanship. The bit is the mouthpiece of a horse's bridle and acts on the side of the mouth in response to the pulling of the reins. If the horse gets the bit between its teeth so that the bit can no longer hurt its mouth it becomes difficult or impossible to control.

bite at the cherry: see *cherry*

bite the bullet: see *bullet*

bite the dust: see *dust*

bite the hand that feeds one: see *hand that feeds one*

bitter end, to the   • *to the last extremity, however painful or difficult*

On old ships the bitts were the strong posts or framework on the deck to which the anchor cable was attached. The bitter end of the cable was the end nearer the bitts, as distinct from the anchor-end, and if the cable was paid out to the bitter end there was none left to go.

It is possible that this expression passed into general use, where this technical sense of 'bitter' was unknown and the expression was assumed to have a sense of painfulness not in the original. It is equally possible that the expression developed in an entirely different way and that the existence of an identical nautical term was an irrelevant coincidence. The expression does make sense in its own right. Moreover, *bitter* and *end* are in fact found together in Scripture: 'her end is bitter as wormwood' (*Proverbs*, 5: 4).

black as one is painted, not as   • *not as bad as one's reputation suggests*

From the proverbial 'The devil is not so black as he is painted', which may be a literal reference to medieval painting or a more general one to his association with the traditional colour of evil, falsehood and error.

black books, in one's   • *out of favour*

The earliest Black Books were official documents; the adjective seems to have had no other significance than to indicate the colour of the binding. For example, there were the Black Book of the Exchequer (about 1175), listing royal revenues, and the Black Book of the Admiralty, containing rules compiled in the reign of Edward III. However, a Black Book of the 1530s, during the reign of Henry VIII, lists abuses in the monasteries, which were subsequently dissolved, and it is from about this time that a black book became specifically associated with censure or punishment, as it still is.

From this sense emerged *black list*, denoting people considered disloyal, untrustworthy or deserving of punishment; *bad books* as a fairly modern variant of *black books*; and its converse, *good books*, meaning favour. These last two may also be related to two old expressions from at least 1509: *in one's book(s)* (in one's opinion) and *out of one's book* (mistaken).

black hole of Calcutta, like the

A jocular simile used of a place that is small, dark, cramped, uncomfortable or dismal. The original was a prison cell of less than 30 square yards in Fort William, Calcutta, into which 146 European prisoners were crammed overnight by the Nawab of Bengal after he had penetrated the defences under a flag of truce during his capture of the city in 1756. By the following morning all but 23 of the prisoners had suffocated. This notorious event during the struggle for India was an important factor in the establishment of British rule, as the British saw it as demonstrating the impossibility of civilised coexistence between local rulers and foreign traders.

black sheep   • *person regarded as a disgrace or failure by the standards of his or her family, group, society, etc.*

The black sheep may once have been feared because of a superstition that black was the colour of the devil; there was also a proverb to the effect that black sheep bit people. The more likely reason for disdain, however, is more pragmatic: its fleece could not be dyed and was therefore less valuable than that of its paler siblings.

31

blackball • *veto; ostracise*

As its spelling implies, a ballot was originally a small ball. It was used in a secret voting system which involved placing ballots in a box or urn; a black one was used to express an adverse vote, hence the modern meaning. This method of voting goes back to ancient Greece and Rome.

In the course of time, the word 'ballot' was used not only as the name of the ball but also as the name of the voting system, and later still of other voting systems which do not use balls.

blackguard • *scoundrel, specially one using bullying or abuse*

Originally the band of kitchen servants or other menials of the lowest rank in a household, called the 'black guard' presumably because of their dirty work or appearance and their responsibility for pots and pans, etc. The term continued in use from the sixteenth century onwards, sometimes as two words, sometimes as one, to mean a variety of people connected with low life—army **camp-followers**, vagabonds, street shoe-blacks, criminals—before emerging with its modern sense.

The -*ck* in the word is no longer pronounced.

blackleg • *person who continues to work when others are on strike or who takes over someone else's job*

The origin appears to be an ancient antipathy to the rook or crow because of its ravenousness and its feeding off cornfields. 'Rook' was initially a term of abuse or disapproval and in the sixteenth century came to mean a cheat, anyone who took advantage of others or lived on his wits. As the rook is black and has black legs, swindlers/rooks became known as *blacklegs*; it was then natural to use the same term for strike-breakers, who were believed to be cheating their fellows. This is the sense that has stuck, while the previous ones have disappeared.

The American *rookie* (novice) is someone inexperienced enough to be easily *rooked* or taken advantage of. Thus an everyday term in modern American football has its origins in the cornfields of medieval England.

blacklist: see *black books*

blackmail • *extortion (especially of money) by threats or other strong pressure*

'Mail' here is an Old English and principally Scottish word for tax, rent or tribute, and 'black' is used in its familiar figurative sense of dirty, bitter or wicked. *Black mail* originated in the borders of England and Scotland in the sixteenth century when outlaw chiefs exacted tribute from small landowners in return for immunity from plunder.

blackout • *temporary loss of memory or consciousness*

This relatively modern meaning originates, as did the Second World War *blackout* (covering of lights as an air-raid precaution), in the theatrical term for the darkening of the stage between scenes.

The earliest use of the verb *black out* meant to obliterate with black ink, notably in public libraries where racing information in newspapers used to be so treated to discourage lingering or in the interests of public morality. It finds a modern echo in *news blackout*, the suppression of news to maintain secrecy.

blank, draw a • *get no result (usually from a search, enquiry, etc.)*

From a lottery ticket which is blank and therefore not a winning one.

blarney • *cajoling, flattering, persuasive talk*

From the Blarney Stone at Blarney Castle near Cork, Ireland; if kissed, it is said to give the gift of smooth talk. The original stone is placed below the castle battlements on the south wall and can only be reached by hanging head down over the battlements, so a more accessible but allegedly efficacious substitute is now used.

The story was unknown until the eighteenth century and there is no legendary explanation of the stone's properties. Some say that it simply marks the castle's foundation in 1446, others that it more pertinently commemorates an event of 1602 when the lord of the castle agreed to surrender it to the British but managed to prolong his excuses for not actually doing so for so many months that the enemy became a laughing stock.

blast: see *full blast*

blaze a trail: see *trail, blaze a*

blazes

Used in a number of expressions to mean hell, as in *Go to blazes*. The association of hell with fire came into English through Christian theology: see for example *Matthew*, 5: 22.

Blighty   ● *England*

An approximation to the Hindi *bilayati* (foreign, far away). Although several words from, or derived from, Indian languages had previously filtered into English as a result of British rule, this one belongs to the time of the First World War. It had obviously been picked up by British regular soldiers in India, where it was presumably applied to them and thus became synonymous with their home country. They in turn passed it on to the much larger temporary army who fought alongside them in the war. A number of popular songs helped to disseminate it even more generally.

blimp, blimpish: see *Colonel Blimp*

blind eye, turn a   ● *pretend not to notice*

Lord Nelson was blinded in the right eye in Corsica during the war with France. During the first battle of Copenhagen (1801), when the admiral to whom Nelson was second in command signalled that he should break off the action, Nelson ignored the order (or, in one version, put his telescope to his blind eye), claiming that he had both a blind eye and the right to use it. To have obeyed at that time would have risked disaster because of nearby shallows.

The familiar expression came into use after his widely mourned death at Trafalgar in 1805.

blind leading the blind   ● *ignorant or incompetent people giving advice or instructions to others similarly incapacitated*

Used of misguided leadership. Originally said by Jesus in reference to the Pharisees, a sect who strictly observed the letter of religious law and claimed superior sanctity: 'They be blind leaders of the blind. And if the blind lead the blind, both shall fall into the ditch' (*Matthew*, 15: 14). See **pharisaic**.

blind man's buff

A children's game, sometimes used as a metaphor for an erratic human activity, procedure, search, etc. depending more on luck than on method. *Buff* is here an obsolete word for 'blow' or 'buffet'. In the modern version of the game a blindfolded child tries to locate and identify one of the other players who stand silently; in earlier versions the blindfolded one was pushed about or given three 'buffs' or pats when he succeeded.

blitz　　●　*sudden vigorous effort to get something done, cleared out or away, etc.*

A metaphorical use of the common abbreviation of the German word Blitzkrieg, literally meaning 'lightning war' (i.e. designed to be swift and decisive). It came into general English use when applied to the bombing of London and other cities, particularly in 1940.

blockbuster　　●　*something (occasionally somebody) outstandingly effective or forceful, especially an extravagant or highly successful film*

Originally a high-explosive bomb developed during the Second World War, capable of destroying a whole block of buildings.

blockhead　　●　*stupid person*

Originally a wooden block shaped like a head, used for making hats or wigs.

blood boil, make one's: see *cold blood*

blood is thicker than water　　●　*the tie of blood relationship is very strong*

Found in twelfth-century German but not in English until Walter Scott's novel *Guy Mannering* (1815), though there is some evidence that it was a Scottish proverb before that date.

bloody but unbowed   ● *hurt but still defiant*

From *Invictus* by W. E. Henley (1849–1903):

> Under the bludgeonings of chance
> My head is bloody, but unbowed.

bloody Mary   ● *cocktail of tomato juice and vodka*

So called because of its colour and from the nickname of Mary I (Mary Tudor, 1516–58), Queen of England and Ireland from 1553, during whose reign some 300 Protestants were put to death for heresy, including Thomas Cranmer, Archbishop of Canterbury.

bloomer(s), blooming

When *bloomer* is used to mean *mistake* (there are other meanings), it is an abbreviation of 'blooming mistake'; here *blooming* is, as so often, a polite evasion of 'bloody' as a meaningless intensive expressing dislike or anger.

Bloomers as a garment, however, take their name from the American social reformer Mrs Amelia Bloomer (1818–94) who in 1851 launched an outfit which included baggy trousers gathered at the ankles. Though this fashion did not catch on, her name has subsequently been given to various styles of baggy shorts, notably to voluminous **knickers** gathered above the knee.

blot one's copybook: see *copybook*

blotto   ● *drunk*

From the capacity of blotting-paper to absorb a different kind of liquid.

blow a raspberry: see *raspberry*

blow hot and cold: see *hot and cold*

blow one's own trumpet: see *trumpet*

blow the gaff: see *gaff*

blue moon, once in a • *extremely seldom*

A development from an earlier expression 'once in a moon', literally once a month but actually meaning very rarely. 'Blue' seems to have been added as a meaningless fanciful intensive in the eighteenth century, perhaps under the influence of the proverbial 'he thinks the moon is made of green cheese', i.e. he is a fool.

blue-blooded • *aristocratic; socially superior*

Blue blood, a direct translation of a Spanish term, was claimed by certain noble Castilian families who were of pure Spanish descent with no dark-skinned Moorish ancestry. Their claim appears to have been based on the blueness of their veins, which were not of course bluer than anyone else's: they merely showed through more clearly against fairer skin.

blue-chip • *reliable and likely to be profitable*

Mainly a financial term, applied to a stock or investment regarded as safe; originally a gambling expression, from the counters in games such as poker, the blue chips being the most valuable.

Bluebeard

Now a journalistic name for a man who murders several women or has several mistresses or wives. The original Blue Beard, found in a popular oriental tale by the French writer Charles Perrault (1628–1703) translated into English in 1729, was a wealthy man disfigured by the colour of his beard and with an evil reputation. When going away on business he enjoined his new young wife not to enter a locked turret chamber in the castle, but she disobeyed him and discovered the murdered bodies of previous wives. In her shock she dropped the key, which became bloodstained, enabling her husband to discover her disobedience on his return. He resolved to kill her but was himself killed by her brothers before he could do so.

bluestocking • *pedantic, earnest woman*

As an adjective this was applied to members of a coterie who met to hold conversations about literature at Montagu House,

London, from about 1750. One of the principal members, Benjamin Stillingfleet, habitually wore his everyday blue worsted stockings because he could not afford the black silk ones normally worn as evening dress. According to Boswell his conversation was so good that when he was absent the members felt lost 'without the blue stockings'. Admiral Boscawan, husband of one of the most successful hostesses of such gatherings, derisively dubbed them 'The Blue Stocking Society'. Men and women, including the most eminent literary and learned figures of the second half of the eighteenth century, attended these meetings in equal numbers, but 'bluestocking' became attached exclusively to the women, partly because they were instrumental in organising the evenings, partly because they were sometimes ridiculed for encroaching on matters not thought to be their concern. Though the adjective has sometimes been used playfully or affectionately it is still largely pejorative.

bluff, call one's • *challenge one to substantiate one's claims; reveal one's deception*

In poker-playing a bluff is a display of confidence (perhaps from a Dutch word for boast) such as heavy betting on one's own weak hand to deceive opponents and cause them to throw up their own stronger hands and lose their stakes. To 'call' such a bluff is to remain in play and require the bluffer finally to show what cards are held; a call is simply a demand that a player reveal his hand because his bet has been equalled.

blurb • *short promotional description of a book's contents, printed on jacket, etc.; (loosely) any piece of written explanation, instruction, description, etc.*

In 1907 the American humorist and illustrator Gelett Burgess (1866–1951) devised a comic book-jacket showing a Miss Blinda Blurb for a book of his that was to be given to booksellers at a function arranged by their trade association. The illustration was a parody of the sort of women often featured on the covers of contemporary novels. He later defined the word he had invented, which rapidly caught on in the book trade and then spread into general use, as 'self-praise, to make a noise like a publisher'.

board, above

Something that is *above board* is done honestly, without conceal-ment. 'Board' here is the old word for 'table', as in 'sideboard'. The whole expression was originally a gambling term: when playing, one was expected to keep one's hands 'above the board' to avoid suspicions of cheating.

To *sweep the board* (win comprehensively) was to clear the table by taking all the tricks and winning all the stake-money.

board, go by the • *be discarded, lost, abandoned or ignored*

Board was a nautical term for the side of a ship. Anything that went 'by the board', i.e. overboard, was therefore lost or liable to be.

Bob's your uncle • *everything is perfect*

Commonly thought to have originated as a catch-phrase after A. J. Balfour was promoted, not for the first time, by his uncle Robert (the Prime Minister, Lord Salisbury) to be Chief Secretary for Ireland in 1887. This move was widely interpreted as being the result of **nepotism**. The expression was initially an ironic or bitter comment, to the effect that everything will be all right for you if Bob is your uncle, though it has now lost this shade of meaning. Sometimes it means no more than 'that's that'.

bobby • *policeman*

Slightly old-fashioned, having been superseded by more scabrous terms. It is from the name of Sir Robert Peel, the Home Secretary who established the Metropolitan Police in 1829; Bobby is a familiar form of Robert. The first policemen were also known as Peelers, but that word is obsolete.

boff: see *boffin*

boffin • *scientific expert, especially one working in technological research and development*

The word is not as frequently encountered as it was during the Second World War, when it was particularly applied in RAF circles to scientists working on radar. It is curiously persistent in school slang in the abbreviated form *boff*, meaning a very studious pupil.

In Dickens' *Our Mutual Friend* (1864–5) Mr Boffin inherited wealth from a dust-contractor (coal-dust, etc.) and was called the Golden Dustman. From this a police fingerprint expert, who brushes dust on to surfaces to make fingerprints show up, became known as a boffin, as did any backroom police scientist, such as a pathologist. The name may have been adopted by the RAF and applied to their own scientists, though there is an alternative and simpler explanation: the name came from the habit of a chief scientist giving Dickensian nicknames to members of his team, and Boffin caught on and spread because it was unfamiliar.

bohemian ● *(typical of) person who leads a romantically vagabond or unconventional life, as sometimes favoured by artists, writers, actors, etc.*

Bohemia was a central European kingdom, formerly part of the Austrian Empire, now in Czechoslovakia. It was thought to be the original home of gypsies, people with a peripatetic and irregular lifestyle.

bold: see *brass*

boloney

A less common but more accurate spelling of **baloney**.

bolt

A *bolt from the blue* (complete surprise) is more fully 'a thunderbolt from a clear blue sky'. A thunderbolt is, in mythology, the destructive weapon wielded by several gods, notably Jove. It gets its name from the primitive superstition that a *bolt* (i.e. arrow) from the heavens was the destructive agent in a lightning-flash striking an object such as a tree during a thunderstorm. The expression implies that lightning and thunder when the sky is clear and blue would be unexpected.

Bolt upright (straight) is from the straightness of an arrow. To have *shot one's bolt* (to have done everything one can) also derives from archery.

bombast • *pompous, inflated language*

The word has its origins in the Greek for silkworm or silk. In English it used to mean raw cotton or cotton-wool used for padding, hence the figurative sense.

bone, near the: see *knuckle*

bone of contention • *subject of disagreement; cause of strife*

This seems to go back to the sixteenth-century 'cast a bone between', meaning to cause a quarrel between. The image is that of a bone thrown to dogs, causing a squabble between them. The clarifying addition 'of contention' is first recorded in 1711 and has remained attached to 'bone' ever since.

bone, to pick with someone, have a • *have something disagreeable to settle with someone*

Originally simply 'a bone to pick', i.e. pick clean. It meant something to occupy one, such as a problem, as a bone does a dog. The addition of 'have . . . with someone' was a later natural development.
   Less natural is the way the phrase has come to refer to an unpleasant matter. This presumably happened under the influence of **bone of contention** and **make no bones** (difficulties) or by analogy with the old 'have a crow to pluck' (have a fault to find).

bone up on • *study, learn*

Originally American student slang, from the Bohn of Bohn's Classical Library, a series of translations in wide use as a study aid from the middle of the nineteenth century.

bones about, make no • *admit without fuss; say or do openly, without hesitation or apology*

An odd term: people cannot normally be said to 'make bones'. The explanation is that the phrase was originally (mid-fifteenth century) 'to find bones in/about', meaning to find difficulty or an obstacle in something. This was a simple comparison with finding bones in food. The image was obviously so useful that people adapted it to express its opposite, i.e. not finding trouble but making it. By the mid-sixteenth century it had therefore become 'make bones about' (make difficulty about). In its more familiar negative form it has remained fixed in the language.

boo to a goose, would not say ● *is very timid*

Not *boo* as an expression of disapproval but as it is sometimes used when playing with a baby or in children's hide-and-seek games as an exclamation to surprise or frighten. The earliest printed version (1572) is 'say shoo to a goose', which makes better sense; 'shoo' is an exclamation used to drive away fowls or animals, and also a verb with the same meaning. Geese themselves are timid and easily shooed, as would be well known in days when they were much more commonly reared and eaten than they are now.

books: see *black books*

book at, throw the ● *punish or censure comprehensively*

This vigorous American image of a judge, magistrate or police officer throwing the full weight of the law at someone in the form of a sizeable statute-book aimed presumably at the offender's head has passed into more general use, the *book* now being any book of rules, or indeed any unwritten ways of doing things, which someone has offended against.

boot is on the other foot, the ● *the situation is now reversed*

A development from 'the boot is on the wrong leg' (that is a mistake). Literally this referred to an absent-minded oversight, or there may be something in the explanation that a pair of cheap boots used to be made in the same shape, without differentiation between right and left, so that discomfort could sometimes be removed by changing them round. In that case the expression implied a comparison between being in error and being in pain.

bootleg   • *make, transport or sell something illicit*

Although no longer confined to trade in alcohol, this term first became known in Britain during the 1920s in connection with the years of prohibition in the USA (1920–34), when illegal traffic in alcoholic liquor was an important criminal activity. The original *bootleggers*, however, were so named in the nineteenth century; they were people who illegally sold liquor to Indians, using flat bottles which they smuggled in the tops (i.e. boot-legs) of their long boots.

born with a silver spoon in one's mouth: see *silver spoon*

bottle   • *courage, nerve*

Cockney rhyming slang: bottle = bottle and glass = arse. *To lose one's bottle* = lose one's arse, i.e. bowel movement = show extreme fear = lose one's courage. Therefore to *have bottle* is to have courage; to *bottle out* is to show cowardice.

Alternatively, bottle = bottle and glass = class = merit or distinction which, in Cockney terms, would include an ability to stand up for oneself.

Those who find these explanations over-elaborate prefer to locate the origin in the bottle-holder who acted as a second for a prize-fighter, using both the contents of the bottle and other skills to keep up his man's fighting spirits during a bout.

The simplest and probably the best explanation is that *bottle* originally stood for the courage that comes out of a bottle (see **Dutch**) and has gradually come to mean genuine courage.

bottom line   • *basic and most important fact*

From accountancy: the bottom line of a set of financial accounts shows the total, usually the single most important figure.

bottomless pit: see *pit, bottomless*

bowdlerise   • *censor (book etc.) by removing what is held to be indecent*

From the name of Thomas Bowdler (1754–1825) who published in 1818 what was to become an extremely successful expurgated edition of Shakespeare's works, omitting everything 'which cannot with propriety be read aloud in a family'. In consequence 'God' as an expletive was always replaced by 'Heaven', some speeches lost between a half and two thirds of their lines, and in one play an entire character disappeared. The verb derived from his name now implies prudish or excessive censorship.

box and cox   • *alternate; (loosely) make shift to fit in something extra*

J. M. Morton's farce *Box and Cox* (1847), adapted from a French original, centres on two men of this name who are rented the same room, one by night and the other by day, by an opportunist lodging-house keeper. As *Cox and Box* (1867) it was also a popular operetta with music by Arthur Sullivan, but it is the earlier title which has passed into more general use.

boycott   • *refuse to take part in or deal with, often as a protest*

From the name of Captain Boycott (1832–97), who was treated in this way by tenants he was responsible for in County Mayo, Ireland, during the latter part of the nineteenth century. He was a retired British cavalry officer who was employed as agent on estates in Ireland at a time when the whole country was ruled from London and absentee landlords were common. His treatment of tenants was uncompromising; in retaliation, and encouraged by the Irish Land League, they ceased to do any work for him. Following their refusal to harvest his crop, and the refusal of others to buy it, he was ruined and forced to return to England.

Brahmin   • *intellectually or socially cultivated but aloof person*

The older spelling of 'Brahman', a member of the highest or priestly caste in the Hindu system.

brand-new   • *perfectly new*

Brand is an old word for fire. Anything metal that was *brand-new* had just come out of the forge.

brass, bold as • *totally unabashed; with great effrontery*

The simile draws a comparison between confidence of behaviour and the hardness of brass. Similarly *brass neck* for impudence.

brass tacks, get down to • *deal with basic realities, hard facts or details of immediate practical importance*

Door-knockers, drawer-handles and other fittings on wooden furniture are often made of brass because of its strength and good appearance. In fabric shops a strip of this metal, a yard or metre in length, is often set along the edge of the counter so that material can easily be measured. An alternative to this used to be—and sometimes still is—two brass nails set a certain distance apart. After a customer had selected a fabric the sales assistant would suggest getting down (one version of the phrase has 'coming down') to the brass tacks to work out the practical details of measurement and price.

There have been other explanations, the most plausible of which refers to the use of brass tacks in the final stage of upholstering furniture, but a high-street shopkeeper's phrase is more likely to have passed into general use than a specialist craftsman's.

brass, top • *most important people in an organisation*

An adaptation of 'brass hats', service slang for high-ranking officers, derived from the gold braid on the peaks of their hats.

brave new world

In Shakespeare's *The Tempest* Miranda has been brought up as a castaway on a desert island with only her father as adult company. When other castaways arrive, including younger men, she expresses her amazement:

How many goodly creatures are there here!
How beauteous mankind is! O brave new world,
That has such people in't!

Her wonderment and optimism are reflected in some modern uses of the quotation to denote an ideal future state achieved by social improvements. However, since Aldous Huxley

(1894–1963) chose *Brave New World* as the ironic title of his sombre futuristic novel (1932) Shakespeare's phrase has been more often used to imply the incompatibility of human freedom with social planning.

bread and circuses

A literal translation of *panem et circenses*, more accurately 'bread and [Roman] circus-games', i.e. food and entertainment at public expense. The words are from the *Satires* (X.80) of Juvenal (AD c. 60–130) who cynically claims that this is the way for those in authority to keep the masses docile.

breadline, on the   ● *impoverished*

Line is the American word for the British 'queue'. A breadline is therefore a queue of poor people waiting for free food to be handed out.

break

Break new ground (do something for the first time) is from the digging or ploughing of land previously uncultivated. *Break the ice* (get through initial coldness or restraint at a meeting) is not from taking the plunge but from taking a necessary step to draw water from a frozen source, such as a well. Both expressions are from early rural life, though there is an alternative explanation of *break the ice* in seamanship: it was sometimes necessary to break the ice on rivers, lakes, etc. to make a passage for boats. This practice has given rise to *cut no ice* (make no impression on a person).

For *break one's duck* see **duck, score a**.

brick, drop a   ● *blunder (especially by tactless remark or action)*

Despite the attractiveness of the 1903 story of the Cambridge University Volunteers' route march along Trumpington Road, their indiscipline, the alarming voice of their sergeant-major and its effect on nearby builders, who were startled into dropping their bricks, the expression is more likely to have originated less specifically in the more humdrum accident of dropping a brick on one's own or someone else's toe.

bricks without straw, make   • *accomplish something without the*
proper means

During their servitude in Egypt the Israelites were punished by
the Pharoah because Moses had asked for permission for them to
worship: 'Pharoah commanded the same day the taskmasters of
the people . . . Ye shall no more give the people straw to make
brick, as heretofore: let them go and gather straw for themselves'
(*Exodus*, 5: 6–7). At the same time he insisted that there should be
no reduction in the quota of bricks being produced.

The Israelites were not in fact expected to *make bricks without
straw*; this would have been impossible because straw was essential as a binding element. What they were required to do was
collect it, instead of having it brought to them, and at the same
time to keep up the same rate of brick-production. The whole
incident therefore demonstrates the harshness of expecting people to do something without sufficient resources (of raw materials, time, etc.).

In other words, the meaning of the expression is true to the
biblical original, but the expression itself is a rather misleading
approximation to it.

bring home the bacon: see *bacon*

Bristol fashion: see *ship*

broken reed   • *person who cannot be counted on for support*

Threatened by the army of Assyria in the seventh century BC,
King Hezekiah of Jerusalem hoped for help from Egypt. The
Assyrians sent him a discouraging message: 'thou trustest in the
staff [i.e. walking-stick giving support] of this broken reed, on
Egypt; whereon if a man leans, it will go into his hand and pierce
it: so is Pharoah King of Egypt to all that trust in him' (*Isaiah*, 36:
6). Reeds, a variety of cane, grew in profusion in the Jordan valley
and were broken off to be used as walking-staffs because of their
straight stems, but they were clearly unsuitable for putting much
weight on.

brother's keeper, my

'I know not. Am I my brother's keeper?' was the petulant reply of **Cain** when God asked him about the whereabouts of Abel, whom he had just murdered (*Genesis*, 4: 9). With *brother* in the sense of fellow-creature, the expression is now used of one's responsibility for another or for other people in general.

browned off: see *cheesed off*

buck, pass the   • *shift responsibility to someone else*

A term from poker originating in the USA. A knife with a buckhorn handle, abbreviated to *buck*, was put in the jackpot; some other handy object could be used but it was still called 'the buck'. It was temporarily held by the winner of the jackpot, but when the deal reached him a new jackpot had to be made and the responsibility of holding the buck was passed on. One version of poker was called *pass the buck*.

In other versions the buck is placed on the table to indicate who the dealer is or whose turn it is to put an agreed sum into the pool. In either case the buck is then passed on clockwise.

Harry S. Truman, President of the USA from 1945–53 and a keen poker-player, had a sign on his desk 'The buck stops here'. *Passing the buck* had by this time come to signify an evasion or denial of responsibility. Originally it simply meant a passing on of accountability by rotation.

buck the system   • *resist or refuse to comply with prescribed or normal arrangements*

From the action of a bucking horse trying to unseat its rider or refusing to act tamely.

bucket, kick the   • *die*

In addition to the familiar meanings that it retains, a *bucket* was a beam from which things could be hung, including slaughtered pigs strung up by their hind legs to bleed after their throats had been cut or to facilitate butchery. In struggling vainly they would *kick the bucket* and this (probably) led to the slang expression.

buff, blind man's: see *blind man's buff*

bugbear   • *something or somebody causing irritation, anxiety, dislike or fear*

Bug is an obsolete word for a hobgoblin or ghost and survives only in this word, though 'bog(e)y' is related. *Bugbear* is a later development in folklore and is a hobgoblin—perhaps in the shape of a bear—supposed to eat naughty children. It was therefore employed in threats to encourage improved behaviour and later came to mean any object of terror. The modern meaning is a dilution of this.

Buggins' turn   • *appointment of person by rotation, or promotion as a result of mere length of service, rather than on merit*

The earliest recorded use of this expression is by Admiral Fisher, later First Sea Lord, in 1901. It is not known whether he invented it or was merely the first to write down and make public, in disparaging terms, an existing piece of private Civil Service jocularity. Certainly the Buggins principle was deeply embedded, and perhaps still is, in the higher ranks of the Civil Service and the armed forces.

The surname Buggins was probably chosen because it was thought to be appropriately nondescript.

bull by the horns, take the   • *confront a difficulty boldy*

From a Spanish proverb 'Take a bull by the horn and a man at his word', known in England since the mid-seventeenth century. The general sense, which is that one should not run away from a threat, is plain enough without resorting, as some commentators do, to an explanation derived from bull-fighting or from American cowboys enjoying wrestling with steers.

bulldog breed   • *the English represented as a nation of people with obstinate courage*

The bulldog got is name either from the shape of its head or from its common use in bull-baiting because of its strength and tenacity; its flat muzzle also enabled it to breathe without letting go of the bull. It achieved symbolic national status by being represented as the companion of **John Bull**. The identification of the British as 'the bulldog breed' first occurs in 1857 in Charles Kingsley's historical novel *Two Years Ago*.

bulldozer

An Americanism from cattle-rearing, having to do with the severe 'dose' of bull-whip needed to control a bull. Bulldozers (the spelling with z was common from the beginning) came to prominence as gangs of men hired to intimidate. They were used to prevent slaves from stealing the cotton crop, for instance, and to coerce voters by violence. From this sense of flattening opposition it is easy to see how the name came to be given to the now-familiar machine.

Both *bulldozer* and its verb *bulldoze* can be used to describe the metaphorical as well as the literal flattening of obstructions.

bullet, bite the • *bravely face up to something unpleasant*

Said to refer to the practice of giving soldiers or sailors a bullet to clench between their teeth during amputation or other surgery in the days before anaesthetics. This may have been so, though a piece of wood or cloth would have been equally handy, more suitable for biting and less likely to be swallowed. A better explanation is that soldiers in battle placed bullets between their teeth so that they could reload more quickly; to be ready to 'bite the bullet' was therefore to be ready for battle.

bum's rush • *peremptory expulsion or dismissal*

In the USA a *bum* is a vagrant; the *rush* is his rapid movement as he is ejected from a place where he is unwanted. *Bum* in this sense appears to be an abbreviation of the German *Bummler* (loafer), exemplifying the absorption of immigrant languages into American colloquialism.

bumf • *paperwork, especially in bureaucratic excess*

Short for 'bum-fodder', originally schoolboy and military slang for lavatory paper, then for paper in general. During the First World War it became a disparaging term for documentation, often trivial or routine, sent to the front from the safety of headquarters.

bunk, bunkum, debunk

Bunk is short for *bunkum*, which is a simplification of Buncombe, a county in North Carolina, USA. After a memorably empty, flowery and irrelevant speech in the House of Representatives in 1820, Felix Walker explained, 'I was not speaking to the House but to Buncombe'—his constituency which he wished to impress. To speak to Buncombe thus became synonymous with talking claptrap or nonsense. For example, Thomas Carlyle (1795–1881) was able to write of 'a Parliament speaking through reporters to Buncombe and the twenty-seven millions mostly fools' of England (*Latter-day Pamphlets*, 1850) in some expectation of being understood.

Another version of the story has the Congressman explaining apologetically that he was speaking 'for Buncombe', though this does not affect the meaning.

Debunk (expose as nonsense) was coined by William Woodward in his *Bunk* (1923), a book about Henry Ford (1863–1947), who had said 'History is more or less bunk' in an interview with a newspaper reporter in 1916.

burn one's boats or bridges ● *stake everything on success*

Or, more accurately, destroy one's own means of retreat should a venture fail—an occasional practice of some Roman generals to stiffen the resolve of their troops against the possibility of any such failure. Curiously, both expressions are recorded in English no earlier than the last twenty years of the nineteenth century.

burn the candle at both ends ● *exhaust oneself (often by working hard during the day and staying up late at night to enjoy oneself)*

In the days when candles were a customary form of lighting, burning them at both ends was synonymous with wastefulness. The modern meaning is milder; in some contexts it implies anxiety for someone's state of health rather than criticism of his or her extravagance.

burn the midnight oil ● *sit up or work late, especially to study*

Midnight oil appears to have been coined by Francis Quarles (1592–1644) in his successful and popular *Emblems* (1635):

> We spend our midday sweat, our midnight oil,
> We tire the night in thought, the day in toil.

Other verbs besides 'spend' were subsequently used in adaptations of the quotation, but 'burn' has been invariable since the latter part of the nineteenth century.

The expression may owe something to an earlier one of the sixteenth century: something was said to 'smell of the oil' if it bore the marks of laborious study, i.e. of working long into the night by the light of an oil-lamp.

Burton, gone for a   • *ruined, destroyed*

Generally agreed to have been RAF slang for 'dead' or 'missing', to have originated in the Second World War, and to refer to Burton's beer. The simplest explanation is that to go for a Burton was, first of all, no more than to go for a drink, and that it was later used as an understatement when someone was killed or failed to return from a flying mission. The fact that many airmen crashed in the sea, known as 'the drink', may give this explanation added point. The current and more general meaning emerged later from this sense of loss.

There was a postwar advertisement for Burton's beer showing a football team photograph with one player missing and a caption explaining that he had gone for a Burton. If this advertisement also appeared prewar it was almost certainly the origin of the RAF usage which has led to the modern meaning. If not, it was merely capitalising on what had by then become a well-known phrase, which is now used of things as well as people.

bury one's head in the sand: see *ostrich-like*

bury the hatchet: see *hatchet*

bus, miss the: see *miss the bus*

bush, beat about the   • *show unnecessary caution, hesitation or delay*

Beat the bush dates from about 1300 and is found in the fourteenth-century proverb 'One beats the bush, another takes the bird', meaning that one person works and another, the master, profits. The reference is to hunting for game-birds: the beater disturbs it and the hunter ensnares it as it flies from cover. Nowadays game-birds are more likely to be shot in flight; before the invention of gunpowder more caution was needed to get near the bird before hunting could start. This sense of slow approach attached itself to the metaphorical meaning of the current phrase.

bush, good wine needs no • *something that is good does not need to be advertised*

The *bush* in this sense of 'advertisement' is the bunch of ivy that used to be hung up as a sign outside a wine-seller's. The Greek god of wine, Dionysius (see **baccanalia**), was specially associated with ivy and is often portrayed in art and literature wearing an ivy-wreath. According to mythology his mother, while pregnant with him, was visited by Zeus and consumed by the flames emanating from the deity; the baby was preserved because a thick shoot of ivy suddenly appeared and wound itself into a screen that protected him from the heat.

Both this symbolism and the practice of hanging out shop signs, the vestiges of which still include the barber's pole, were introduced to Britain by the Romans.

bushel, hide one's light under a • *modestly conceal one's talent*

Bushel is an obsolete word for both a fixed measure (eight gallons and about 2,200 cubic inches) and for the solid container of pottery or wood used to measure it. A candle or other light placed under a bushel would of course be invisible. The whole phrase is an allusion to Christ's Sermon on the Mount: 'Neither do men light a candle, and put it under a bushel, but on a candle-stick; and it giveth light unto all that are in the house' (*Matthew*, 5: 15). This is part of an encouragement to Christ's followers to demonstrate their faith, though in common use the expression now has no spiritual significance.

busman's holiday • *leisure time or holiday spent doing what one normally does for a living*

Said to originate in the days of horse-drawn buses when certain drivers became so attached to their horses that on their days off they spent their time travelling as passengers on their own buses in order to keep them company.

buttonhole • *detain (person) in talk*

The implication is that the detained person is held against his or her will.

The original verb was 'button-hold', which makes better sense. Perhaps the reason for the change is that people used 'button-hold' as a lazy past tense instead of 'button-held'; in time this was assumed to be spelt 'button-holed', past tense of the (non-existent) verb 'button-hole', which then had to be invented to match the original error. Whatever the reason, *buttonhole* is now standard.

by and large • *generally speaking*

Originally nautical jargon from the days of sailing ships. To steer a course 'by and large' was to keep slightly off the line of the wind when steering into it so that there was less need for constant adjustment to slight changes in its direction and less chance of being taken **aback**. In general terms the expression implied freedom from special alertness and exactitude, and this is its sense in modern use.

by hook or by crook: see *hook*

by-law • *law made by a local authority and applicable only to the area over which that authority has jurisdiction*

The *by* here is from an Old Norse word for town or village.

Byzantine

Sometimes used journalistically of anything labyrinthine, mysterious and even disreputable in its political complexity, the adjective owes more to traditional suspicion of things oriental than to historical reality. Byzantium, subsequently Constantinople and now Istanbul, was the capital of a rich and culturally distinguished Greek empire from 396 BC until its capture by the Turks in 1453. Its politics were sometimes devious but no more deserving of stigma than those of other great civilisations.

C

cabal • *(conspiracy of) small group of secret intriguers, usually political and sinister*

Although specially applied to the small Privy Council committee (1667–73) and predecessor of the modern Cabinet in Charles II's reign—the initials of its members' surnames happened to be C,A,B,A and L—this is in fact an older word from a Hebrew one related to a mystical system of interpreting Jewish scripture. The famous Cabal, which secretly signed the Treaty of Alliance with France in 1672, popularised and gave a political flavour to this word, which was rooted in theology, metaphysics and magic and meant a small, sinister group or the activity that brought it together.

Cabinet • *committee of senior government ministers*

Originally a diminutive of 'cabin', i.e. a small cabin. From that it came to mean a small private room, and this sense lies behind the modern Cabinet, a small number of people meeting privately in a room.

In a separate development the same basic idea of privacy gave rise to the name for a piece of furniture in which things are stored away.

caboodle, the whole • *the whole lot*

There are two similar but slightly earlier American expressions with the same meaning—'the whole boodle' and 'the whole kit and boodle'—in which 'boodle' seems to be from a Dutch word meaning goods or possessions. The prefix 'ca-' is found in a number of American words, usually to convey the idea of impact or sound but sometimes, as here, as just a meaningless emphasis.

Caesar, Caesarean

Caesar's wife must be above suspicion is the drift of what Julius Caesar is reported to have said in 62 BC on divorcing his wife Pompeia, who was rumoured to have committed adultery. The story is recorded in *Lives of the Caesars* by the Roman historian Suetonius (AD c. 70–140) but became better known in English from its translation in Plutarch's *Lives* (1579), one of the sources for some of Shakespeare's plays.

It is a different Caesar, Augustus, who is referred to in 'Render therefore unto Caesar the things which are Caesar's; and unto God the things that are God's' (*Matthew*, 22: 21), Christ's reply to those who asked if it was right to pay taxes to the Roman occupants of their country. This is alluded to in *Give Caesar his due* and *render unto Caesar*, catch-phrases sometimes used of the relative status of secular authority and moral conviction.

A *Caesarean operation/section* was so named in the seventeenth century after Julius Caesar, either because he was said to have been born by this method or because the Roman Caesarean Law had originally dignified the method by enjoining that a child should be so delivered if the mother died. The former is the more likely and certainly the more popular explanation. It is irrelevant to argue, as some have done, that for all sorts of good reasons Caesar was unlikely to have been born by this method. What matters is that he was believed to have been at the time the expression was coined.

The *Caesar salad*, ubiquitous in the USA in all sorts of guises, was invented by Caesar Gardini, a restauranteur in Mexico, said to have first improvised one when an unexpected number of diners arrived.

Cain and Abel

The sons of **Adam** and Eve. Cain, the elder, killed his brother out of jealousy that God seemed to favour him more. The two are therefore the archetype of brotherly discord, and Cain appears throughout literature as the personification of the original sin of murder. The *mark/brand of Cain*, though placed on him by God to protect him (*Genesis*, 4: 5), is now used to mean an identifying stigma. To *raise Cain* is to create a great disturbance, as if raising up or evoking the turbulent spirit of the first murderer.

calf: see *fatted calf, kill the*

Caligula

Sometimes referred to in political allusions as the epitome of vicious dictatorship. Caligula was emperor of Rome (AD 37–41) during one of its most corrupt periods and was both mentally and emotionally unstable: his behaviour was cruel, indecisive and wayward, and he had exaggerated ideas of personal divinity. His excesses ranged from incest to mad projects such as a planned invasion of Britain, and he is quoted as saying 'Remember that I can do anything to anybody'. Caligula was a sardonically beguiling nickname referring to the little military sandals he wore as a child; a rough translation would be Bootees or Bootikins.

call one's bluff: see *bluff*

call the tune   ● *be in control*: see *pays the piper*

Calvary   ● *place, period or experience of extremely painful punishment, often preceding demise or death*

The allusion is to the place of Christ's crucifixion, a hill just outside Jerusalem said to be the present site of the Church of the Holy Sepulchre. The name is ultimately Hebrew for skull; according to legend the skull of **Adam** was preserved there, though the more likely reason for the name was the hill's shape.

Calvinist(ic)

Loosely used to mean 'rigid and severe in morality'. Strictly speaking, it means 'conforming with the austere theology of John Calvin' (1509–64), the French Protestant reformer whose orthodoxy, challenging Roman Catholic supremacy, emphasised the sovereignty of God and the Bible, the depravity of humankind, justification by faith alone, and the notion of predestination, i.e. that some people were chosen by God for salvation before the world began.

Camelot

Now used of a place, period or elite noted for a refined ideal of cultured civility, especially associated with youth, beauty and the arts. It is actually the site—thought to be Cadbury Castle, Somerset—of the court of King Arthur, embodiment of the perfect Christian knight, the romantic spirit of chivalry, and courtly manners. See **round table**.

camp-follower   ● *adherent or supporter of a group, though not a member*

A slightly derogatory term, sometimes meaning no more than a hanger-on. In former times, before the establishment of modern standards of organisation, discipline and self-sufficiency, armies in camp or on the move were accompanied by large numbers of vagabonds and other civilians who provided services as prostitutes, washerwomen, sellers of food and drink, etc. These were the original camp-followers.

can, carry the   ● *take the blame (for another's error); take responsibility, often unpleasant or unwanted*

Usually said to originate from the beer-can which one soldier, probably the newest recruit, carried for all his companions. Another version of the expression is 'carry the can back', which implies the additional menial task of taking the empty can back to the quartermaster's stores.

This explanation leaves unanswered some obvious questions about the availability of strong drink to men in military service. A better if less colourful explanation may lie in a dialect word 'cag' (bad temper), which became corrupted to 'keg' and in turn to *can*; 'carry (on) the cag/keg/can' (sulk) may have changed its meaning as time went by.

can of worms, (open a)   ● *(venture into a) complicated and potentially unsavoury situation or course of action*

An Americanism: a can of fishing-worms to be used as bait.

candle

Someone who is *not fit to hold a candle to* a person is much inferior to or not to be compared with him or her. The phrase originated at a time when holding a candle to (i.e. for) a person was the task of a servant, lighting the house-holder's way from one part of the residence to another, for instance. Hence the modern sense of inferiority.

A *game not worth the candle* is an activity not worth the trouble or cost. The original reference was to a card-game or other pastime that was just not worth the price of the candle needed to provide illumination for it.

See also **burn the candle at both ends**.

canter, (win) at a   ● *(succeed) easily, without much effort*

An abbreviation of 'at a Canterbury pace, rate, trot, etc.', originally horse-riding terms making jocular reference to the decorous progress of mounted pilgrims on their way to the much-visited shrine of Thomas à Becket at Canterbury. The verb *canter* (gallop at moderate speed) has the same origin.

Canute

Sometimes called Cnut, a Danish prince who became king of England (1016–35), Denmark, Norway and other lands. He is reputed to have sat on the seashore surrounded by his flatterers and forbidden the tide to come in. He did this to demonstrate that he was not superhuman, though he is now more often said to have done so to provide an arrogant and foredoomed demonstration of his power. Time and time again a person who tries to prevent the inevitable is still said to be behaving like King Canute. He is not: Canute showed wisdom and humility, not brainless optimism or delusions of grandeur.

card up one's sleeve   ● *plan or course of action kept in reserve (or secret) until the appropriate moment*

There is no suggestion of dishonesty here even though the origin of the expression probably has to do with cheating at cards. Alternatively it may derive from conjuring.

cardigan   • *woollen waistcoat with long sleeves*

Named after the Earl of Cardigan, who led the charge of the Light Brigade in 1854. He is said to have worn such a garment of his own design, perhaps having anticipated the extreme cold of the Crimean campaign. It is doubtful if he had sufficient wit to do either; anyhow, during much of the war he preferred to live on his private yacht rather than share the privations of his troops. His name was probably applied to the garment by traders with an eye to the main chance during the postwar period when he enjoyed a reputation—not fully deserved—as a national hero. See also **balaclava**.

cards, on the   • *possible*

From the use of playing-cards in fortune-telling.

carpet   • *reprimand*

Also *on the carpet* (called in to be reprimanded). From the idea that people in authority enjoy the luxury of having carpets in their offices, a reflection of earlier times when carpets were a sign of wealth and far less commonplace in houses than they are today.

carpet-bagger   • *person who goes to a place with which he has no connection, for political or other ends; (loosely) opportunist*

A scornful Americanism originally applied to Northerners, usually but not always politicians, who travelled to the southern states after the Civil War ended in 1865 to try to win support from the newly enfranchised black voters or in search of personal gain during the period of reconstruction. They were named from their carpet-bags—travelling bags made of carpet material, common in the nineteenth century—in which they carried all their possessions and which became a symbol of their rootlessness.

carry coals to Newcastle: see *coals*

carry the can: see *can*

cart

In the cart (in trouble) most likely refers to the cart in which condemned people used to be taken to public execution or from which they were hanged, the noose being placed around their necks as they stood in the cart, which was then driven off.

To *put the cart before the horse* (reverse the correct order of things) can be traced back to *Ayenbite of Inwit*, an English devotional manual of 1340 translated from a French work of 1279, but it is found in several other European languages, including Greek and Latin, making it one of the oldest and most widespread sayings.

carte blanche   ● *full discretionary power*

French terms have persisted in the language of diplomacy—*chargé d'affaires*, *attaché*, *communiqué*, for example. *Carte blanche* is one that has gained wider currency: it originally meant a blank sheet of paper offered to someone so that they could write down their own terms or conditions, as distinct from having to accept those that were negotiated or dictated. There may have been an earlier military original referring to unconditional surrender, i.e. one without any terms or conditions at all.

Casanova   ● *womaniser*

Giacomo Casanova (1725–98) wrote a number of historical works in his native Italian during his adventurous and peripatetic life in the capitals of western Europe, but his reputation as a philanderer comes from his posthumously published *Mémoires* (1826–38) which describe a succession of sexual exploits thought at the time to be scandalous even by continental standards. He knew many of the most important people of his day and certainly seems to have had an extraordinary capacity for disguise and for making and losing fortunes, though some later commentators have cast doubt on his veracity, suggesting that he was more successful as a confidence-trickster than as a lover.

Cassandra   ● *prophet of doom*

In Greek legend Cassandra was the daughter of Priam and Hecuba who was given the gift of foretelling the future by Apollo, the sun god, who fell in love with her. When she resisted his advances he took his revenge by removing from her the power of persuasion, with the result that her prophecies were never believed.

She is normally thought of as someone who foretold disaster, which is why a person, male or female, who does the same is still sometimes dismissed as a Cassandra, the implication being that he or she is merely a pessimist who can be safely ignored. However, this is to overlook an important point, which is that the original Cassandra was invariably right. A Cassandra, strictly speaking, is ignored at one's peril.

cast the first stone: see *stone, cast the first*

cat

Put the cat among the pigeons (cause disturbance) was originally an expression about a cat in the dove-house and would have made better sense when dovecotes were common because of the popularity of pigeons as food. Also more explicit than its modern version was 'no more chance than a cat in hell without claws', now shortened to the more puzzling *not a cat in hell's chance* (no chance at all). *Like a cat on hot bricks* used to be ' . . . on a hot bakestone', the stone top of an oven. The proverb that *a cat has nine lives* is an obvious reference to its survivability, especially its ability always to fall on its feet, and may be related to superstitions that cats were associated with the supernatural as one of the forms taken by the devil and as witches' familiar spirits. See also **nine**.

See also below and **Cheshire cat, rain cats and dogs**.

cat out of the bag, let the   ● *disclose a secret*

A dishonest farmer, claiming to be selling a young pig, might substitute a cat or some other valueless animal in a tied bag. A circumspect buyer would examine the purchase on the spot; an unwary one would not do so until it was too late. Either way the cat would then be out of the bag and the truth would be known.

The best explanation of how this practice originated dates it from the eighth century, when southern Europe was invaded by Muslims, who held that pork was unclean and prohibited its sale. Any traffic in pigs among non-Muslims had therefore to be secret, which lends some credibility to the idea of animals being sold in sacks. If transactions additionally had to take place at night it would be easier for swindlers to make a surreptitious switch of animals, even after a sale had been agreed.

The phrase has also been explained by reference to sharp practice at English country fairs. There might well have been cheating of this kind on those occasions, but the lack of any conditions requiring secrecy makes this explanation less persuasive.

To be *sold a pup* (swindled) is a variant of this expression; perhaps some tricksters used a dog instead of a cat. A *pig in a poke* is obviously related; *poke* is an old word for a small sack and the whole expression means 'something bought or received without prior examination or knowledge'.

cat, not room to swing a   ● *insufficient space; crowded conditions*

The cat here is the cat o' nine tails formerly used to administer corporal punishment on board ship. It had nine lengths of knotted cord, each about 18 inches long, fixed to the end of a short length of thicker rope acting as a handle. Ample space was needed if this was to be swung with maximum effect. Perhaps its name came from the scratch-like weals it left.

cat's pyjamas or **whiskers**: see *bee's knees*

cat's-paw   ● *somebody used by another for the latter's own ends*

An allusion to the fable of the clever monkey (or fox) which used the foot or paw of a cat to take roasted chestnuts out of burning coals.

Catch-22   ● *deadlock consisting of two mutually exclusive conditions*

Joseph Heller's surreal comic novel *Catch-22* (1961) describes the exploits of US airmen in the Mediterranean sector during the Second World War. One of the rules, defined by the author as 'catches' or drawbacks, under which they operated was Catch-22, which specified that concern for one's safety in the face of real and immediate danger showed a rational mind. A pilot who was insane qualified for grounding, but if he asked to be grounded because he was insane he was certified sane and required to fly because his request demonstrated that he had a rational mind.

catch out   • *detect or expose (person) in a mistake or deception*

From cricket, in which a player is out if he hits a ball which is then caught by a member of the other side before it touches the ground.

caucus   • *small like-minded inner group of members of a larger group, especially political party, formed to define policy or exert influence, usually secretly, sometimes improperly*

Captain John Smith's *Travels in Virginia* (1606) refers to the Chickhamanians 'who are governed by the priests and their assistants or their elders, called cawcawwassoughes'; this is thought to be the origin of the modern word, a simplified version of the Algonquin.

Indian names were often used by clubs and secret associations in New England, where the modern word arose. In eighteenth-century American politics it came to mean a private gathering of party members belonging to a legislature and meeting to determine policy, select candidates and the like. When it reached England it was used as a pejorative term; it was first applied in 1878 to the organisation of Birmingham Liberals, which was thought to demonstrate the introduction of American-style politics into England and thus deserve the stigma of an equally outlandish American name. Its current sense implies a lack of democratic openness.

caviare to the general   • *not to the taste of the general public*

A quotation from Shakespeare: 'the play, I remember, pleased not the million; 'twas caviare to the general' (*Hamlet*, II, 2, line 430). Caviare was a novel delicacy at the end of the sixteenth century, and Hamlet implies that it was unpalatable to those who had not acquired a taste for it.

chain reaction • *succession of events, each one of which is the (sometimes unexpected) result of the previous one*

The scientific original—the concept that the explosion following the splitting of an atom by a neutron might lead to an indefinite series of further reactions and explosions—is reliably said to have occurred to the Hungarian physicist Leo Szilard in London in 1934 while he was waiting for some traffic lights to change.

chalk up • *record, register, score*

Often used of success and derived from the old custom—still found in pub darts matches, for instance—of using a blackboard and chalk to keep score.

The phrase can also mean 'charge to one's account'; in some pubs the number of drinks ordered but not paid for at the time was also recorded by chalking on a board, with a view to settlement at the end of the evening.

The same practice has also given rise to *by a long chalk* or *by long chalks*, meaning 'by a great degree or amount'. The greater one's score—or consumption of drinks—the longer would be the line of one's chalk marks.

See also **slate**.

chance one's arm • *take a risk*

Among soldiers this meant taking a chance—breaking regulations, for example—that might lead to punishment, demotion and the consequent loss of one's stripes of rank, worn on the arm; hence the phrase. It may have entered army slang from an earlier use in boxing circles, where it meant exposing oneself to risk by extending one's arm in a punch, leaving part of the body undefended.

change or swap horses in midstream: see *horses*

changes: see *ring the changes*

chapter and verse   • *detailed information, especially the authoritative and precise source of a piece of information*

A reference to the Bible and its authority. Verses are the numbered subdivisions of its chapters, according to the style introduced in 1551.

chauvinism   • *excessive or blind devotion to one's country or to a cause*

Nicholas Chauvin, a French soldier during the Revolution and subsequently under Napoleon, was notable for the number of wounds he sustained and for his exaggerated and naive devotion to Napoleon, military glory and all things French. He later became a figure of fun in contemporary satire as the archetype of dotty patriotism: a popular play of 1831 which had a character called Chauvin, a foolish soldier, made the name a household word. *Chauvinism* entered English vocabulary in about 1870 as a word for simple-minded and bellicose nationalism.

The word achieved special popularity, notably in *male chauvinism/-ist*, in the second half of the twentieth century when it was adopted by the women's liberation movement to characterise what was held to be men's unreasonable and aggressive belief in their own superiority. It is therefore sometimes applied to a similar belief in any cause, but it is always derogatory, implying unthinking, exaggerated and rather absurb fanaticism. It does not mean the same as patriotism.

cheap-jack   • *(person who sells goods which are) cheap, shoddy or inferior*: see *jack*.

cheek, turn the other   • *respond to violence or unkindness with patience; offer no retaliation*

Based on a text from the Sermon on the Mount: 'resist not evil: but whosoever shall smite thee on the right cheek, turn to him the other also' (*Matthew*, 5:39).

cheesed off   • *bored, disgruntled, disgusted*

The earlier expression 'browned off', which meant the same, was RAF slang originally used of metalwork that was becoming rusty;

it was later applied figuratively to human degeneration. *Cheesed off* may be an elaboration of this, in reference to the browning of cheese when cooked, or a quite different allusion to the sourness associated with cheese going bad.

cherry, two bites at the (same) • *two attempts to do something; more than one's fair share of something*

This meaning sometimes implies good fortune and sometimes an act of effrontery giving rise to surprise or disapproval. It is a curious development from the original meaning, which implied over-fussiness, squeamishness or even hypocrisy. A *cherry* is of course easily taken into the mouth and needs no bites at all; to take *two bites* at it was to display an excessive fastidiousness or even a false show of good breeding.

Cheshire cat, grin like a

The simile existed long before it was popularised by *Alice's Adventures in Wonderland* (1865) in which Alice asks why the Duchess's cat is grinning and is told 'It's a Cheshire cat, that's why'. Explanations of it are too numerous to mention, but do not appear to have included the most obvious one: that a cat which lives in a notable cheese-making county is bound to grin at the thought that there will never be any shortage of milk.

chestnut, old • *story, joke or excuse often repeated*

This seems to originate in William Dimond's melodrama *The Broken Sword* (1816) in which a captain tells an unlikely story about a chestnut tree time and time again until he is shown to be romancing when he inadvertently changes the chestnut tree into a different type of tree.

chestnuts out of the fire, pull one's • *do someone else's work; salvage some success from a misfortune*

The first meaning is from the story described at **cat's-paw**. The second is more common and draws a slightly different moral from the same story.

chew the fat ● *chat (or grumble) at length*

A comparison between using one's mouth for a long period and the action of chewing the fat of meat, which usually takes longer to masticate than lean meat does. There are other explanations but this one is the most obvious.

chew the rag ● *grumble, argue*

Rag, earlier 'red rag', is old slang for the tongue. *Chew* implies using it at length. The same meaning of *rag* is found in *lose one's rag* (lose one's temper, i.e. control of one's tongue).

chicken feed ● *a trifling amount (usually of money) or matter*

From the idea that the best corn is to be used for human food and what is left over—the smaller and less valuable grains—is for the chickens. The slightly contemptuous rural expression passed into wider use as a term for the equally second-rate small change in one's pocket. This financial meaning still exists, but the expression has now further broadened its use to include other sorts of trivia.

chickens will come home to roost, one's ● *one's (misguided) actions will recoil on oneself*

This is the modern version, sometimes in the shortened form *come home to roost*, of the proverbial saying 'Curses, like chickens, come home to roost'—i.e. as automatically as chickens come back to the hen-house at night in order to perch, the evil you wish on somebody in a curse will come back to trouble you. The actual words are usually attributed to Robert Southey (1774–1843) who wrote in the motto to his long poem *The Curse of Kehama* (1810) 'Curses are like young chickens; they always come home to roost'. The idea, however, though differently expressed, occurs as early as Chaucer's *Canterbury Tales* in about 1387.

chimera ● *terror or wild fancy in the mind or imagination*

A borrowing from Greek mythology: the Chimaera (a spelling still sometimes found) was a fire-breathing monster with a lion's head, goat's body and dragon's tail. She was the personification of the storm-cloud and was killed by Bellerophon, hero of Corinth, on his horse Pegasus: he stuffed her jaws with lead which melted in the flames of her mouth.

chin up, keep one's: see *pecker*

chip

There is an unusual degree of unanimity about the provenance of *have a chip on one's shoulder* (bear a grudge; behave anti-socially). Unlikely as it may seem, the reference is to a custom originating in the USA, but also known in Canada, in which a person who was looking for a fight carried a chip of wood on his shoulder and invited people to knock it off; anyone who did so was agreeing to fight. Perhaps the custom made better sense in pioneering days when chips of wood were litter as common as pieces of paper today, and fighting for its own sake was equally common.

A *chip off the old block* is literally a chip from a block of wood and therefore a piece of the same kind of wood. It is said of a person having the same characteristics as one of his or her parents or, more generally, having the good old-fashioned virtues of an older generation.

To *chip in* (make a contribution; interrupt) is from poker, where it is a request to place one's chip, representing money, in the pot or kitty during play. See also **chips**.

chips

Used in poker as replacements for money. *When the chips are down* is a time of crisis when there is no going back or room for manoeuvre and something is about to happen. In poker it means that money has been put down on the table, decisions have been taken and the crucial part of the game has been reached.

Similarly the rather dated *have one's chips* (be defeated or finished) is from the idea of giving up one's chips at the end of unsuccessful play.

See also **chip**.

chivvy   ● *harass, usually by persistent nagging to get something done*

From the title of the popular fifteenth-century *Ballad of Chevy Chase*, once said to be the favourite ballad of the common people in all England. It describes a famous running dispute and battle in the England–Scotland border country of the Cheviot Hills, from which it gets its title. From this came the noun chevy or chivy for any hunt or pursuit, and finally the familiar verb with its milder modern sense.

chock-a-block; chock-full   ● *crammed full*

Chock is probably an old variant of 'choked'. Something *chock-full* is so full that it is as if the throat is choked or stopped up.

   Chock-a-block was a nautical term for a position when two blocks of a tackle came together so that no further movement was possible—again like choking.

choke off   ● *discourage; get rid of (person)*

As if by throttling, as a dog can be made to loosen its hold by choking it.

chop and change   ● *keep making alterations or changing one's mind*

This has nothing to do with chopping in the sense of cutting. The expression dates from the fifteenth century, when *chop* meant barter (in its primary sense 'of trade by exchanging goods or services rather than money') and *change* meant 'make an exchange with'. In other words it was a repetitive expression, the two verbs meaning roughly the same.

   Over the years *chop* has lost this sense but the whole expression has remained in use with the same basic meaning of exchanging one thing for another.

church mouse, poor as a   ● *very poor*

Because there is no food stored or cooked in a church.

Churchillian   ● *characteristic of Sir Winston Churchill (1874– 65), war-leader, statesman, historian and orator*

Remembered as a national hero, Churchill had so long, full and varied a life that the use of a single adjective may be distorting. In rough terms it is applied to a type of oratory (grand, dramatic, inspiring, sonorous), prose (rather sweeping, florid, wordy) and stance (patriotic, defiant, warlike).

Cinderella   ● *person or thing undeservedly neglected, poorly re- garded or unsuccessful*

Cinderella is the heroine of the popular fairy-tale found in the French collection by Charles Perrault (1697), translated into Eng- lish in 1729, but similar to stories in the folklore of other countries, notably Germany. Treated as a drudge by her stepmother and stepsisters, she takes her name from the cinders of the hearth beside which she spends much of her time, and is left at home when the others go to the prince's ball. By her fairy godmother's intervention, however, Cinderella is able to go, and finally mar- ries the prince.

In everyday use her name as both noun and adjective implies lowly status, not her happier destiny.

claptrap   ● *(pretentious, often insincere) nonsense*

An old theatrical term for any device, trick or use of language designed to capture (trap) the audience's applause (clapping).

clean as a whistle   ● *very clean(ly)*

The whistle here is the formerly common tin or penny whistle, a simple musical instrument, which will not make notes if the holes or tube are clogged.

clean bill of health   ● *doctor's advice that there are no medical problems*

Formerly a nautical term for a certificate (i.e. bill) given to the captain of a ship sailing from a port which was liable to infection. A 'clean' bill stated that there was no infection in the port or on the ship at the time of sailing. The certificate would be needed for presentation at the next port of call before docking would be allowed.

clean sweep

Adapted from the proverb 'A new broom sweeps clean', this originally meant a complete change: see **new broom**. Now it also means an overwhelming victory, a sense which developed from the earlier one and its implication that something unwanted was being vanquished.

cleanliness is next to godliness

Although often thought to be biblical, this saying comes from a sermon by John Wesley (1703–91) referring to neatness of dress: 'Cleanliness is indeed next to godliness'. In the published sermon the words are put in inverted commas, implying an existing saying. The sentiment is certainly an old one, probably ancient Hebrew, but the familiar wording dates from Wesley.

cleanse the stables: see *Augean*

clear the decks (for action)   ● *make preparations to do something*

A nautical term meaning to get ready for military action by clearing from the decks everything that it is in the way.

cliffhanger   ● *situation, especially contest, of which the outcome is excitingly uncertain*

A forerunner of the television serial and **soap opera** was the film serial, invented in the earliest days of the silent film. It was shown in weekly parts and was usually adventurous or melodramatic. Each instalment ended in a suspense designed to make the audience come back the following week to find out what happened next. To leave the heroine perilously dangling from the edge of a cliff was one such device, and it has given the language this useful word.

clink, in   ● *in prison*

The Clink was a prison in Southwark, London, dating from the twelfth century, when it formed part of the Bishop of Winchester's palace and was used to house offenders against ecclesiastical codes. It was burned down in 1780 by the Gordon rioters. During its varied history it was also a debtors' prison and the local gaol for Southwark. Its name seems to come from a Middle English word which has also given us 'clinch' and 'clench': the underlying sense is that of secure fastening. The word passed from being the name of one particular prison to being a general name for any prison, though it is now rather dated slang.

clip one's wings: see *wing(s)*

cloak-and-dagger   ● *underhand, secret; characteristic of spying and plotting*

A development from the earlier 'cloak and sword', a translation of a Spanish literary term for a type of fiction and drama of romance, intrigue and melodrama in which the main characters are from the ranks of society which formerly wore cloaks and swords.

cloud has a silver lining, every   ● *every misfortune brings some benefit or gives way to something better*

Adapted from John Milton's *Comus* (1634), lines 221–2:

Was I deceived, or did a sable cloud
Turn forth her silver lining on the night?

cloud nine, on   ● *ecstatically happy*

Said to be from the terminology of the US Weather Bureau. Just as wind may be force five or an earthquake measure seven on the Richter scale, cloud nine is that which reaches to 30,000–40,000 feet, i.e. very high. The idea of being on a cloud comes from the traditional association of the sky with heaven, the place of supreme bliss.

Another explanation is that the expression is merely an intensification of the earlier 'cloud seven', an Americanism for **seventh heaven**.

cloud-cuckoo-land   ● *impossibly and foolish idealistic world; crazy, impractical scheme*

The English translation of a Greek word in Aristophanes' satirical comedy *The Birds* (414 BC). It is the name of a city built by birds in the clouds, between Athens and the heavens, under the persuasion of two Athenians who are disillusioned with city life.

Classicists have complained that its comparatively recent vogue as a derogatory metaphor is ignorant misuse because the original is actually a successful and desirable place to live. They are unlikely to have any more success than historians and ornithologists struggling to correct the popular reputation of **Canute** and the **ostrich**.

clue   • *something that leads towards the solution of a mystery*

Originally 'clew', a ball of string or yarn. In Greek mythology Theseus set himself the task of killing the Minotaur, a Cretan monster kept in a labyrinth and fed with an annual tribute of seven virgins and seven young men from Athens. He unwound a clew as he made his way through the labyrinth and, after killing the monster, found his way back by following the thread. This explains the metaphorical meaning of *clue* (the normal spelling for several centuries), which has now supplanted the original literal one.

clutch at straws: see *straws, clutch at*

coals

To *heap coals of fire* (on someone's head) is to make her or him feel remorse. The scriptural origin is an injunction to do good to one's enemies to make them feel embarrassment or contrition: 'If thine enemy be hungry, give him bread to eat; and if he be thirsty, give him water to drink: For thou shalt heap coals of fire upon his head, and the Lord shall reward thee' (*Proverbs*, 25: 21–2, cited as good doctrine in the New Testament in *Romans*, 12: 20). Here 'coals of fire', an old way of saying burning coals, is a metaphor of extreme discomfort. To *heap coals of fire on one's own head* is to make difficulties for oneself or do something one is later going to be sorry for.

Haul over the coals (reprimand severely) is from the torture of suspected heretics in the Middle Ages. They were literally hauled over a bed of burning coals, being pronounced innocent if they survived and guilty if they did not.

Carrying coals to Newcastle—coals is an obsolete plural—is doing something foolishly superfluous: when the expression came into being, Newcastle had been an important coalport (supplying London, for instance) since the thirteenth century, and no one needed to take coal there.

coast is clear, the   ● *there is no one about; there is no obstacle or danger in the way*

Originally a military term having to do with the literal clearing away of an enemy from a coast, for example as a preliminary to a safe invasion.

cobbler should stick to his last, the   ● *one should do the work one is expert at and not try to do or interfere in that of others*

Apelles, the great Greek painter of the fourth century BC, is reputed to have changed a detail of the painting of a shoe on one of his works when a cobbler pointed out a fault. When the cobbler then went on to criticise the painting of a leg the artist told him to stick to his trade.

The proverb is found in Pliny (first century AD) and in English from the early sixteenth century.

cock and bull story   ● *concocted, incredible tale, especially an obviously untrue one*

From an early fable, now lost, in which one of the characters appears to have been a cock and a bull metamorphosed into a single animal.

cock-a-hoop   ● *in very high spirits, sometimes boastfully*

Most of the earliest versions of this expression occur in contexts having to do with drinking, which suggests that the original form may have been 'set the cock [i.e. tap] on the hoop [of the barrel, i.e. on top of the barrel]'. In other words, 'take the tap off and allow the contents to flow freely', which would certainly be conducive to high spirits.

An alternative explanation, which lacks the same sense of abandon, is that the *cock* is the bird and *hoop* an old word for a measure of grain; the whole expression therefore means that the

75

cock—proverbially exultant and cocksure—is happy at being fed.

cocked hat, knock into a   • *easily surpass or defeat*

The game of Cocked Hat was similar to ninepins except that only three pins were set up, in triangular formation. It took its name from the three-cornered hat with the brim turned up (i.e. cocked) worn in the late eighteenth and early nineteenth centuries. The expression implies a comparison between something in disarray after a defeat and the way in which pins are sent flying in a game of Cocked Hat.

cockles of one's heart, warm the   • *be very gratifying*

The *cockles of the heart* are simply the heart itself and, metaphorically, one's deepest feelings. The word *cockles* is used either as a comparison of the shape of the heart with that of a cockleshell, or because the zoological name for cockle is 'cardium'—related to the Greek for heart, as in 'cardiac'—or because the Latin name for the ventricles of the heart is 'cochleae cordis' (the first word of which means snail-shells) because of their appearance. This last explanation sounds the most likely.

cockpit   • *place from which aircraft (etc.) is controlled; arena*

Originally a pit or enclosed area for cock-fighting. Shakespeare used the word, perhaps jocularly, to mean auditorium: 'Can this cockpit hold/ The vasty fields of France?' (*Henry V*, Prologue, lines 10–11). Part of a theatre is still called the pit, though 'stalls' is the preferred term. Later the word was applied to the (possibly cramped) quarters for junior officers on board ship; in action, it was used as a hospital—Nelson died in the cockpit of his ship. Later still it was the location of the steering-wheel of a yacht or small sailing vessel and this usage came to be extended to aircraft. Perhaps the idea of smallness underlies all these different usages.

cold blood, in   • *ruthlessly, without excitement, not in a passion*

A relic of early medical theory: becoming hot with excitement or exertion was supposed to be the result of blood getting hot. The same idea persists in *make one's blood boil* (make angry). By the same token something done with deliberation, without the heat of passion, was supposed to be a product of cold blood.

cold shoulder, give or **get the**   • *display or be shown intentional coldness, indifference or rejection*

Probably from the idea of offering or being given a dish of cold shoulder of mutton left over from a previous meal, interpreted as a sign that the recipient was an unfavoured visitor.

Colonel Blimp

The name of a cartoon character, created by David Low (1891–1963) in the *London Evening Standard* between the wars, who was a retired officer and a pompous, opinionated, not very bright ultra-conservative. His name, sometimes reduced to *blimp*, is still applied to a stupid and usually elderly reactionary. The adjective *blimpish* also exists.

The word *blimp* was coined during the First World War for a small experimental non-rigid airship; Low, in adopting it, no doubt had in mind both the military connection and the fact that his colonel was a windbag. There have been several attempts to explain where the word originally came from. The most plausible is that in military jargon the test-models included an A-limp (unframed) and a B-limp, and that the latter model was adopted for manufacture.

Colossus

Strictly speaking this is a common noun, from a Greek word for a large statue, but it is usually given a capital letter because of its use in the name of the Colossus of Rhodes, a giant bronze statue of the sun god Apollo which was regarded as one of the seven wonders of the ancient world. It stood over 100 feet high beside the harbour at Rhodes (not astride the harbour mouth, as is sometimes said) and was made by Chares in the early part of the third century BC. An earthquake destroyed it in about 224 BC.

There are two modern uses of the word: a *colossus* is anything gigantic and a *Colossus* is a toweringly dominant person in his or her own field. The word has also given us the adjective *colossal*.

colours

The general name for a flag, banner or ensign of a regiment or ship, so called because the colours of these identified a particular fighting unit and were also extremely important in enabling men to keep together in some sort of organisation during the tumult of hand-to-hand battle in earlier days. Loss of colours to an enemy was a sign of disgrace if not of defeat.

This piece of military history has given rise to several popular expressions such as *with flying colours* (in triumph, with colours not captured by the enemy but still streaming in the wind) and *nail one's colours to the mast* (commit oneself firmly and openly to a course of action), as one might nail colours to a mast as a sign of defiance and to make it difficult for the enemy to seize them. A pirate ship might *sail under false colours*, a sign of deception; conversely one's *true colours* showed to which side one really belonged. The modern expression *in one's true colours* (one's true nature or character) forgets that one fought under colours, not in them.

come up and see me sometime: see *Mae West*

come up to scratch: see *scratch*

conditioned reflex: see *Pavlovian*

confusion worse confounded   ● *confusion made even worse*

A quotation from Milton's *Paradise Lost* (1667), Bk II, line 995.

cook one's goose   ● *ruin one's chances*

One of several expressions drawing a comparison between a person who is done for and food which is 'done' when it is cooked. Geese used to be much more common as food than they are now. See also **dish** and **hash**.

copper-bottomed   ● *secure, to be trusted*

Usually applied to a guarantee, assurance, etc.

Below the waterline the hulls of wooden ships used to suffer grievously from the attacks of wood-boring molluscs. After unsuccessful experiments with lead it was found that sheathing the hull with sheets of copper prevented these attacks and the build-up of weeds and barnacles. The fixing of copper bottoms began in 1761 and later became general.

copybook

In the days when schoolchildren were expected to learn mainly by mechanical practice, repetition and copying from models, a copybook contained specimens of handwriting—often in the form of proverbs and improving maxims—and other material printed with blank spaces which the pupil filled in by careful copying out. Sometimes a copybook without blank spaces was used in conjunction with an exercise book, also called a copybook because it was used for copying out. In either case to *blot* (make an ink-blot on) *one's copybook* was to commit a fault and mar one's record.

On the other hand, anything which is *copybook* (such as a procedure, tactics, etc.) is as perfect as the examples provided in a copybook. In modern terms it is straight from the textbook.

corny   • *trite, banal, boring*

Originally American slang meaning 'like corn' (i.e. commonplace) or more likely 'from the corn-belt', that part of the country where corn grows, where rustic people live and which is therefore dull and unexciting.

corridors of power   • *place(s) where governing decisions are made*

Coined by C. P. Snow in his novel *Homecomings* (1956) to describe the ministries of Whitehall, where there are a great many corridors, but better known from the title of his later *The Corridors of Power* (1963) about Westminster life. It has now passed into more general use to signify, sometimes jocularly, any location where people of authority work or meet.

counsel of perfection   • *excellent but impracticable advice*

Originally a theological term with a rather different meaning. It referred specifically to that part of scripture in which Christ gives advice to the rich young man who asked what he should do to have eternal life: 'Jesus said unto him, If thou wilt be perfect, go and sell all that thou hast, and give to the poor, and thou shalt have treasure in heaven: and come and follow me' (*Matthew*, 19: 21). Christ's counsel and definition of perfection were not impracticable but they were beyond the young man's moral capacity.

course of true love never did run smooth, the

From Shakespeare's *A Midsummer Night's Dream*, I, 1, line 134.

Coventry, send to   • *ostracise*

The Earl of Clarendon's history of the Civil War, usually known as his *History of the Rebellion* (1702–4), states that Royalists captured at Birmingham were killed or taken prisoner and sent to Coventry. This was a Parliamentary stronghold where they could expect no help or even sympathy. Even though this incident occurred in the 1640s and the popular metaphor is not recorded until over a century later, there is general agreement that either the event itself or Clarendon's reference to it is the origin of this expression.

crack of doom   • *the end of the world*

Literally the crack of thunder on Doomsday, the **Day of Judgement**; *doom* is an archaic word for judgement. The phrase was coined by Shakespeare (*Macbeth*, IV, 1, line 117). The description of the Day of Judgement in *Revelation*, chapter 20, actually makes no mention of thunder though there is much thunderous activity in the book as a whole, notably associated with the issuing of voices from heaven.

cricket, not   • *unfair*

Versions of cricket go back to the Middle Ages but the game became established in the eighteenth century when the first recognisably modern matches were played and rules were established. The game has always been synonymous—at least until recently—with gentlemanly conduct and fair play because of its leisurely nature and strong amateur tradition.

criss-cross • *mark(ed) with intersecting lines*

No other English expression contains the word *criss*. It was originally 'Christ's'; 'Christ's-cross' (sometimes 'Christ's-cross-row') was a term for the alphabet. One of the earliest teaching aids for children until the eighteenth century was the horn-book, so called because it consisted of a leaf of paper mounted on a backing of wood and protected with a sheet of translucent horn. The paper contained the alphabet, often with the Roman numerals and the Lord's Prayer. The alphabet was preceded by the sign of the cross, either to indicate that Christ was the beginning of all wisdom or as an exorcism. Children would therefore be told to study the 'Christ's-cross-row', the alphabet.

As time went by these origins were forgotten and it was assumed that *criss-cross*, as the term had become, was merely a duplication—like tip-top, zig-zag and many others—meaning no more than 'cross and cross again'. Hence the modern meaning.

crocodile tears • *hypocritical show of sorrow*

The old story that the crocodile lures passers-by by making a moaning or sobbing sound, then devours them while weeping, comes from the extensive literature, folklore and travellers' tales that grew up around the crocodile because of its notable place as a deity in the theology, myth and art of the ancient Egyptians, some of whom worshipped it. There is evidence that the crocodile has near its eyes some glands that secrete saliva or excess salt, and also that under water it emits a stream of small bubbles from its eyes as a result of air entering the tear-ducts. The first reference to these phenomena as 'tears' occurs in a learned work from tenth-century Constantinople quoting a fourth-century theologian: writing about the virtues of fasting, the author rebukes hypocrisy by alluding, as a parable, to the crocodile weeping over the remains of its prey because there is no meat on the head. The first reference to the initial luring of prey by sobbing occurs much later, in a description of Sir John Hawkins' second voyage to Hispaniola in 1565, which may imply that this part of the legend comes from West Indian sources. But it is more likely that both these references are to a much older oral tradition rooted in the fascination and veneration which the crocodile has attracted since the early days of Egyptian civilisation.

Croesus (rich as)

The fabulously wealthy king of Lydia, in Asia Minor, was reputed to be the world's richest man. He reigned from 560 to 546 BC, when he was overthrown by Cyrus of Persia.

cross we have to bear • *affliction or misfortune we have to tolerate*

An allusion to Christ's being required to carry the cross on which he was to be crucified (*John*, 19: 17), an event still commemorated or re-enacted in some modern ceremonials, though the other three Gospels say that the cross was carried by someone else.

crusade • *zealous campaign in favour of a cause*

The word was originally invented to signify a military expedition to recapture the Holy Land from the Muslims and secure the right of Christians to make pilgrimage to the Holy Sepulchre—in other words, to reverse the state of affairs that had existed since the sacking of Jerusalem by the Romans in 70 AD, an event which marked the beginning of the Jewish dispersal. Eight main crusades were undertaken by European powers between 1095 and 1272. The Christian symbol of the Cross was the badge of the crusaders, and the word *crusade* itself is derived from the Latin for 'cross'.

cry all the way to the bank • *be indifferent to criticism of one's wealth; hypocritically deny or apologise for it*

The flamboyant, sentimental, much-mocked but well-paid American entertainer Liberace (1919–87) once responded to a critic who had excoriated a performance by sending a telegram that read: 'What you said hurt me very much. I cried all the way to the bank'. This accounts for the first of the current two meanings; the second has grown out of it.

cry wolf: see *wolf*

crying in the wilderness: see *voice*

cuckold: see *cuckoo in the nest*

cuckoo in the nest   ● *misfit; person (occasionally thing) subverting or not conforming with her or his group; parasite*

The cuckoo removes and eats one egg from a number of nests built by other species, replacing it with an egg of her own. She then migrates, leaving an unsuspecting foster parent to hatch and rear her offspring. Shortly after hatching, the nestling cuckoo—which hatches earlier than the young of other birds—destroys all the other eggs in the nest by tipping them out. It then rapidly outgrows the entire nest, fed energetically by foster parents which may actually be four or five times smaller than it.

Under these circumstances it is difficult to see why the cuckoo is also synonymous with idiotic behaviour, but easy to understand the origins of *cuckold*.

cuff, off the   ● *improvised, offhand*

In the days when the cuffs of men's formal white shirts were made of celluloid they were sometimes used as improvised notepads by their wearers at dinner-tables, etc.

cup that cheers   ● *cup of tea*

Now a cliché, originally an adaptation from William Cowper's *The Task* (1785): 'the cups/That cheer but not inebriate . . . '

Cupid   ● *personification of love*

In Roman mythology Cupid was the god of love, son of Mercury and Venus, and identified with the Greek Eros. He is normally represented as a playful and cherubic winged boy armed with a bow and arrow, sometimes called darts, which aroused the passions of those they pierced.

curate's egg, like the   ● *good in parts*

An allusion to a famous cartoon in *Punch* in 1895 showing a bishop entertaining a curate to breakfast. The bishop apologises that the curate's egg is bad: the curate humbly replies that parts of it are excellent. As a bad egg is of course bad all through, the curate's reply owes more to courtesy than good sense, and the cartoon was making fun of over-dutiful (or self-serving) deference.

curfew • *rule that at a stated time, or for a stated period, people should be indoors*

Now usually an act of repression to control the population during a time of unrest, this was originally a safety measure requiring that domestic fires be extinguished at bedtime—a wise precaution in the days when houses were highly combustible and a single spark might lead to the devastation of a whole community. *Curfew* was also the name given to the ringing of a bell to remind people that the regulation was in force. The word comes from two French ones, *couvrir* (cover) and *feu* (fire), a reminder that it was after the Norman invasion that William the Conqueror introduced the *curfew* to England in 1068.

curry favour • *ingratiate oneself*

A corruption of 'curry favel', originally Favel or Fauvel. He was the horse in the *Roman de Fauvel* (1310), a French satiric poem of the kind that was a dominating literary influence in the fourteenth century. In these poems, as in Aesop, animals had human attributes: Fauvel was the counterpart of the well-known Reynard the Fox, who preyed on society and was the symbol of dishonesty and cunning. To curry a horse is to comb or dress it with a metal comb, called a curry-comb; to curry Fauvel was to minister to and serve an embodiment of duplicity.

In the course of time, as the original passed into history, 'Fauvel' became the more familiar and obvious 'favour'. In modern usage the whole phrase has lost most, though not all, of its original associations with insincere flattery and sycophancy.

curtains • *the end*

From either the dropping or closing of a curtain at the end of a scene in the theatre or the old custom of closing the curtains of a house as a sign of mourning.

cushy • *easy, comfortable*

From the Hindi *khush* (pleasant), adopted by the British Army in India, transferred by them into First World War slang and thence into mainstream English, though it remains informal.

cut and dried • *completely decided; fixed beforehand*

Now used of decisions, arrangements, opinions, etc. which are the subject of no further argument or change. Originally applied to cutting herbs in the field and then drying them, so that they could be sold cut and dried, ready for immediate use.

cut and run • *hurry off abruptly*

An old nautical expression. In an emergency it was sometimes necessary to cut the anchor cable, instead of going through the time-consuming business of winching up the anchor, in order to get away quickly ('run' before the wind, at full sail). The **Armada** was said to have done this off Calais on the approach of English fireships.

cut and thrust • *use of telling argument or point-scoring in debate, discussion, etc.*

Two strokes used in trying the win at fencing: a *cut* uses the edge of the weapon, and a *thrust* is a forward movement of the point.

cut no ice: see *break*

cynic • *person who thinks the worst of people, events, etc.*

The original Cynics, adherents of an ancient Greek school of philosophy made famous by Diogenes, held that virtue is to be cultivated by subjugating desires and they were openly contemptuous of luxury, enjoyment and ease. Their name, which comes from a Greek word for dog, may have referred to their churlish habits or to the site of their school, which was called after an incident in which a dog ran off with part of a sacrifice being made to Hercules.

The modern cynic, who sneers at or habitually doubts sincerity or goodness, is related to but by no means identical with the original.

Czar

The title of the emperor of Russia. Because of the autocracy associated with it, not to mention the vast territories ruled by

Czars and the cruelty they sometimes showed, the word has passed into journalistic use to denote an all-powerful leader in an organisation or activity (e.g. drug Czar).

The word is etymologically related to **Caesar** and Kaiser and can also be spelt as Csar or Tsar.

D

D-day   • *important day when action is due to begin*

Military jargon or shorthand for a day (d for day) which cannot be given fuller identification: for example, its date may not be known until the last minute because of weather conditions or other factors. It was made famous as the opening day of the Allied invasion of France (June 6, 1944) during the Second World War, but it had been used before (in the First World War) and it has been used since, e.g. for the introduction of decimal currency into Britain in 1971.

Damascus, (road to)   • *occasion or circumstance of changing one's allegiance, belief, point of view, policy, etc.*

An allusion to the conversion of St Paul. As Saul of Tarsus, an ardent persecutor of Christians, he was travelling to Damascus in Syria in 33 AD to find and capture some of them when God spoke to him in a blinding light. Taken to Damascus, he had his sight restored, was baptised and became the most notable advocate, missionary and preacher of the early church, his letters to which form an important part of the New Testament. He was martyred at Rome in 64. The Damascus story is in *Acts of the Apostles*, chapter 9.

   In modern use this act of divine intervention, perhaps the most dramatic and influential in the establishment of Christianity after Christ's death, is trivialised by being used in references to political U-turns or simple changes of mind.

damn with faint praise   • *express disapproval by praising inadequately*

A quotation from Alexander Pope's critical portrait of Joseph Addison in lines 201–2 of *Epistle to Doctor Arbuthnot* (1735):

Damn with faint praise, assent with civil leer,
And without sneering teach the rest to sneer.

A similar form of words had appeared earlier in one of the works of William Wycherley, who knew and was later edited (and plagiarised?) by Pope:

And with faint praises one another damn.

Damocles: see *sword*

dance attendance on   • *serve or attend obsequiously*

There may be some connection with the old custom of requiring a bride to dance with everyone who attended her wedding, however tired she might be, but the more persuasive explanation is that *dance* here is a jocular or fanciful variant of 'kick one's heels', i.e. move the feet idly while enduring the tedium of waiting, like a servant standing by to be summoned.

Daniel in the lion's den   • *person facing intimidating task or trial*

Daniel was a Jew who kept his faith in God during the Jewish captivity in **Babylon** under successive kings (see **feet of clay**). He rose to eminence and attracted the jealousy of the princes of Babylon, who conspired against him by persuading King Darius to sign a restrictive decree which they accused Daniel of breaking by continuing to pray to God. Against his will Darius had to punish Daniel by incarcerating him in a den of lions in accordance with the decree. By divine intervention the lions left Daniel unharmed, demonstrating to the king both the innocence and faith of David and the power of his God.

Darby and Joan   • *elderly man and wife, often of modest circumstances, who are very attached to each other*

Characters in a ballad by Henry Woodfall, published in 1735 and believed to refer to John Derby, to whom the writer was formerly an apprentice, and his wife. Their names became synonymous with marital affection.

dark horse   ● *person about whom little is known or who reveals little about her or himself, especially one with potential as a competitor*

To 'keep dark', meaning to keep secret, is an expression going back at least 400 years, so it is possible that the related *dark horse* (a racehorse of unknown form but thought to have a good chance) existed in racing slang before it was first recorded in print in Disraeli's novel *The Young Duke* (1831). Be that as it may, it soon became a popular metaphor for a person with unknown qualities and is now standard English.

dashboard   ● *instrument panel of car*

Originally a wooden board or leather screen at the front of a horse-drawn vehicle to protect the driver and those sitting alongside from the mud splashed up (i.e. dashed) by the horse's hooves. The name was retained for the partition between the front seat and the engine that replaced the horse when cars were invented.

David and Goliath

Used in reference to a contest or encounter in which two competitors, teams, groups, forces, etc. appear to be unequally matched.

David was a great Hebrew king to whom St Luke traced the ancestry of Christ. He was, however, only a young shepherd at the time when the Israelite army faced the Philistines (*I Samuel*, chapter 17) and he went to the battlefied to take provisions to his older brothers. Hearing a challenge to single combat issued by the **Philistine** warrior Goliath—a giant of a man ten or eleven feet tall—he volunteered himself (see **beard the lion**). Equipped only with stones and a sling against a fully armed man, he felled Goliath with a single stone, then cut off his head with the giant's own sword, causing the Philistine army to flee.

Day of Judgement

According to the prophetic book of *Revelation* in the New Testament, this is the day when God will judge humankind, pronouncing salvation for the good soul and doom for the evil, after the passing away of the world in its present form. It is also referred to as the Last Judgement and Doomsday; see **crack of doom**.

The expression is now used loosely to mean the end of the world and, without capital letters, any retribution for one's actions.

days are numbered: see *numbered*

dead as a door-nail

Door-nails were large-headed nails with which doors were studded for strength or ornamentation. There have been ingenious conjectures as to why one should be particularly 'dead', including the suggestion that a door-nail would become worn out if it was used—there is no evidence that it was—as the nail on which the door-knocker was struck.

The best explanation is from a different meaning of door-nail, that of a door-fastener, a beam of wood placed across the inside of a door, held in place by brackets, and called a *nail* because it fastened. It was rigid and therefore invited comparison with a corpse.

dead duck   • *person or thing that is useless or unsuccessful*

From the American proverb 'Never waste your powder on a dead duck'.

dead horse: see *flog*

deadline   • *time limit*

During the American Civil War, prisoners were kept inside wooden stockades. A railing placed about twenty feet inside the stockade marked the limit beyond which prisoners were told that they were not allowed to pass. This was the 'dead-line', so called because men crossing it could be assumed to be making a bid to reach the stockade to escape, and so were liable to be shot dead on sight.

First recorded in official congressional papers in 1864, the term was later applied figuratively to a limit imposed by a different constraint, that of time.

death's door, at   ● *close to death*

From Psalm 107: 18, in the Prayer Book translation.

debunk: see *bunk*

decimate   ● *destroy a large proportion of*

This is the sort of usage that infuriates purists (even though it has existed since the seventeenth century) because the derivation of the word has to do with a small proportion, not a large one. It comes from the Roman military punishment of randomly executing one in ten mutineers, cowards, deserters, etc. as an example to others. 'Ten' is indicated by the prefix of the word, as in 'decimal'.

Delilah: see *Samson*

Delphic   ● *obscure, ambiguous, enigmatic*

Situated on the lower slopes of Mount Parnassus, Delphi was the site of the most ancient and sacred sanctuary in Greece. Its celebrated **oracle** was presided over by the sun god Apollo and attracted worshippers who often came from great distances. The priestess would fall into a trance under Apollo's influence and utter mysterious words and broken phrases which were then interpreted by a sacred council and pronounced as holy truth or guidance, sometimes in enigmatic form.

Deluge

Another name for **Flood**.

denim

Originally serge *de Nîmes*, the French city where the cloth was made.

derby • *sporting contest between two teams from the same area*

The twelfth Earl of Derby gave his name to the famous horse-race he instituted at Epsom in 1780. Run annually ever since, it is the prime event in the flat-racing calendar. The name acquired its more general meaning (and its small d) because a local sporting event attracts unusual interest and attendance, as the Derby does.

derrick • *crane; framework over oil-well supporting drilling tackle*

London's first permanent gallows, big enough to accommodate multiple executions, was erected at Tyburn in 1571 with three eighteen-foot uprights connected by nine-foot cross-beams. It became known as the *derrick* during the first half of the following century from the name of the notorious public hangman, Derrick, an unsavoury character otherwise remembered as the inexpert executioner of the Earl of Essex, Queen Elizabeth's former favourite, who had previously saved Derrick's life by arranging his reprieve after a conviction for rape.

The word 'gallows' used to be applied to a number of devices for hoisting, suspending or holding things; this sense still survives in north-east England in the dialect word 'gallasses' for a pair of men's braces. After the hangman's gallows became known as a *derrick*, so did the sort of crane that resembled it in being a tall structure with ropes used for hoisting. Curiously, *derrick* did not survive as the name of the hangman's gallows, though it has done so in its transferred sense.

dervish • *person behaving in a wild, frenzied manner*

In the Muslim religion, a *dervish* is an ascetic holy man under vows of poverty and austerity, but the word is specially known from a particularly fanatical sect of dervishes who perform whirling, trance-like or ecstatic dances as a devotional exercise.

devil and the deep (blue) sea, between the • *between two equally difficult alternatives*

Here *devil* is nautical slang for a seam between planks that was difficult to caulk, i.e. make watertight by hammering oakum (fibres of rope) into the gap and then adding tar. The word was particularly used for the long seam of the first plank on the outer hull next to the keel, and for the seam along the edge of the deck where only the thickness of the hull was between this *devil* and the sea. No doubt awkward and difficult seams were given this name because they were 'the devil' to get at. The whole phrase therefore meant, literally, a physical position between two unpleasant things and, metaphorically, a dilemma.

devil to pay, the   • *trouble as the consequence of an act*

The earliest appearance of this expression has to do with paying the Devil as part of a bargain. The medieval legend of the man who sold his soul to the Devil is best known from the later Faust stories, notably the dramatised version by Marlowe (1594): his Dr Faustus enjoys 24 years during which Mephistopheles provides whatever he asks for, but he has to pay his soul to the Devil at the end of them. However, the idea of making a pact with the Devil is much older and of Jewish origin: Christ, for example, is offered such a pact in *Matthew*, 4: 1–11).

There is a later expression, *The devil to pay and no hot pitch*, which is nautical. It may be a punning extension of the earlier phrase or an entirely separate one: *devil* is a seam for caulking; *pay* is an obsolete verb meaning 'cover with pitch' (tar). The process is explained in the previous entry.

devil's advocate   • *person who presents, usually for the sake of argument, an opposing or unpopular view which he does not himself hold*

Translation of the Latin *advocatus diaboli*, a theological term used in the Roman Catholic church for the official given the duty of arguing against the proposed beatification of a dead person during the formal deliberation of the matter, in order to ensure that the case is examined from all sides.

dickens, Dickensian

The two words are not related. The first is a meaningless emphasis (What/who/why the dickens . . . ?), originally a euphemistic evasion of 'devil' dating from Shakespeare's time and perhaps invented by him (*Merry Wives of Windsor*, III, 3, line 19). The second is an adjective from the surname of the novelist Charles Dickens and is usually found qualifying words such as squalor, hardship, etc. because of his memorably vivid descriptions of appalling social conditions among the urban poor in mid-nineteenth century England. One exception to this general rule is *Dickensian Christmas*, intended to evoke Victorian good cheer and traditional observances as described in some of his stories.

die is cast   • *irrevocable decision or step has been taken*

The *die* here is the little-used singular of 'dice', which is actually a plural word though usually used as a singular. In gaming, when the die/dice is thrown or cast the players must accept the consequences.

Julius Caesar, according to the Roman historian Suetonius, his biographer, used the words *iacta alea esto* (let the die be cast) at the crossing of the **Rubicon**, which indicates the age of the metaphor. Shakespeare helped to popularise it: 'I have set my life upon a cast/And I will stand the hazard of a die' (*Richard III*, V, 4, lines 9–10).

diesel

From the name of Rudolf Diesel (1858–1913), the German mechanical engineer who patented his engine in 1892, though an engine that was effectively the prototype had been patented by a British engineer, Akroyd-Stuart, a little earlier.

digs   • *lodgings*

An abbreviation of *diggings*, one of the earliest importations from the USA (about 1838), where gold prospectors camped out near their actual diggings. This word therefore also became a name for their temporary quarters, though it had been standard English for 'mines', especially gold mines, since the early sixteenth century.

dilemma: see *horns of a dilemma*

discretion is the better part of valour   • *carefulness is the most important feature of courage*

The proverb is most famously articulated by Falstaff in *Henry IV, Part I*: 'The better part of valour is discretion'. He was commenting on an old maxim that discretion is as great a virtue as valour but that discretion and valour combined are greater still. His cynical misinterpretation, effectively a justification of cowardice, is probably more popular—and certainly more often quoted—than the original maxim.

dish one's chances　●　*ruin or spoil one's hopes, plans, etc.*

The analogy is between an animal which ends up dished (served up in a dish) and eaten and a person's chances which have come to an equally ignominious end. See **cook one's goose**.

The same idea lies behind 'pan' meaning criticise. A play that is panned (condemned by critics) is being compared to something that is chopped up and put in a pan.

divide and rule

Translation of a Latin saying.

do as you would be done by

First recorded in these precise words in a letter from the Earl of Chesterfield to his son in 1747, though less pithy versions go back at least three centuries and originate in Jesus' Sermon on the Mount: 'all things whatsoever ye would that men should do to you, do ye even so to them: for this is the law and the prophets' (*Matthew*, 7: 12). Chesterfield's formulation, which may not have been original, was given widespread currency by Charles Kingsley (1819–75), whose *Water Babies* (1863), an immensely popular moral tale for the young, has among its characters Mrs Doasyouwouldbedoneby and Mrs Bedonebyasyoudid.

dog

Used in various expressions which reflect the times when dogs held a much less privileged domestic position than they now do. Thus *a dog's life* (a wretched one) and *not a dog's chance* (no chance at all). Someone or something *going to the dogs* is heading towards ruin.

See also the following entries, **hair of the dog** and **name, give a dog a bad**.

dog in the manger   ● *selfishly depriving others of something one has no use for oneself*

From the Aesop's fable (sixth century BC, known in western Europe since the fourteenth century) of the dog which lay in a manger, unable itself to eat the barley but refusing to allow the horse, which could eat it, to come near it.

dog-days   ● *hot period of summer weather*

Sometimes used as a general metaphor for good times in the past. The phrase is a translation from Latin; in classical times the hottest period of the year, from the beginning of July to mid-August, was attributed to the rising of Sirius (the brightest star in the constellation called Greater Dog and thus known as the Dog-star) at the same time as the sun. This was believed to add to the sun's heat.

doghouse, in the   ● *in disgrace*

Doghouse is an old English word; taken to the USA by settlers it remained in use there although generally superseded by 'kennel' in British English, and finally returned to Britain in this colloquial phrase.

One commentator has said that on slave-ships the passengers were chained in the hold and the seamen slept in rough shelters on deck, known as *doghouses* because they were bare and uncomfortable. Another suggests that the expression originated with *Peter Pan* (1904) in which Mr Darling lives in the doghouse as a penance for his poor treatment of the dog, as a result of which the children run away. The first recorded date of the expression (1932) rules out the first of these explanations (the shelters may have been called doghouses but they had nothing to do with disgrace) and the American origin of the expression makes the second unlikely. There is really no need to look any further than the familiar idea of banishing a dog to its kennel in the event of misbehaviour.

dogsbody   ● *person who does menial work*

Originally *dog's body*, contemptuous naval slang for a dish of dried peas boiled in a cloth. It was later applied equally derisively

to a junior officer, who was thought to do work as unprepossess-
ing and routine as pease-pudding was on board ship, and then
came into general use as a word for any drudge.

doily   ● *small decorative mat placed under dishes or food*

Invented by Doily or Doyley, a well-known London draper of the
early eighteenth century.

dole, on the   ● *unemployed (and receiving state aid)*

This sense dates only from 1911, with the introduction of an
official scheme of financial help. Before that a dole was simply a
portion, share or distribution.

dollar

Abbreviation, and variant of the final two syllables, of
'Joachimstaler', literally 'of or from Joachimstal [Joachim's val-
ley]'. This was the place in Bohemia, now Czechoslovakia, where
silver was mined and coined in the fifteenth century and became
a standard currency.

Don Juan   ● *womaniser*

The proverbially heartless and irreligious seducer, according to a
Spanish story first dramatised by Téllez (1630), was the son of a
prominent family of Seville who killed the city's commander in a
duel after being surprised by him in the act of raping his daughter. Juan visited the commander's tomb and when the statue over
it moved he invited it to a feast. The statue went, seized Juan and
handed him over to devils. There are treatments of the story by
Molière, Byron and Mozart, among many.

donkey: see *talk the hind legs*

donkey's years   ● *a very long time*

Usually said to be an illiterate form or misunderstanding of 'as
long as a donkey's ears'. There is a simpler explanation: donkeys
are long-lived—40 years has been known or alleged—and so

donkey's years may mean no more than 'the number of years a donkey may live'.

Don Quixote: see *quixotic*

Doomsday: see *crack of doom* and *Day of Judgement*

dot the i's and cross the t's　　● *make final check to add or correct detail*

Probably originally a classroom catch-phrase, warning children to check their handwriting for missing dots over the letter i and cross-strokes in the letter t. With the exception of j, these are the only two letters requiring a separate dot or pen-stroke, which is likely to be overlooked by children.

double, at the; double-quick　　● *very quickly*

From a military command, generally given to troops required to move quickly. It originated in a more specific reference to 'double time', a number of steps per minute when marching, as compared with other marching speeds (e.g. the slow march).

double Dutch: see *Dutch*

doubting Thomas　　● *person who (habitually) will not believe something before obtaining proof of it*

An allusion to Christ's disciple, Thomas Didymus, who was not present when Christ showed himself to other disciples after the Resurrection and who said that he would not believe their story that Jesus had appeared 'Except I shall see in his hands the print of the nails, and put my finger into the print of the nails . . . ' (*John*, 20: 25). Jesus subsequently appeared before Thomas; the whole story is told in verses 19–29.

dove-cotes, flutter the　　● *cause an outburst of anxiety or excitement*

This may have been an everyday expression when pigeons were much eaten as food, dove-cotes were common and a disturbance would cause their occupants to flutter away, or it may have been invented by Shakespeare: 'like an eagle in a dove-cote I/Fluttered your Volscians' (*Coriolanus*, V, 6, lines 115–6).

down at heel: see *well-heeled*

draconian   ● *harsh; cruel*

Used of measures, laws, policies, etc. The word comes from the name of Draco, who as chief magistrate in early Athens instituted in about 620 BC a law code of which little is known beyond its severity.

Dracula

Often referred to in unflattering comparisons. He is the vampiric central figure of Bram Stoker's novel of the same name (1897) in which he is depicted as a Transylvanian count, tall and thin with a cruel face, pointed ears, a hooked nose and sharp protruding fangs. The victims of his nocturnal bloodsucking are usually young women; by day he lives in a box of earth. He is finally killed by being beheaded and stabbed through the heart, at which he turns to dust.

draw a blank: see *blank*

draw one's horns in   ● *become less active (e.g. in spending money)*

An allusion to the snail, which when disturbed draws in its tiny horns (tentacles which bear its eyes) and retreats into the safety of its shell. The idea of *coming out of one's shell* (gradually losing one's shyness) may be from the reverse process, the snail's emergence from its shell once a danger has passed. However, there is an old expression 'out of the shell' meaning, by analogy with young birds, 'newly born', 'immature' and 'inexperienced', and this may have developed a new sense having to do with loss of inhibition.

draw the line • *fix a limit (often between what one will and will not tolerate)*

From map-making, in which lines are drawn to establish boundaries, determine frontiers, etc.

drawing-board, go back to the • *start planning all over again*

From the caption to a *New Yorker* cartoon during the Second World War, showing a newly invented aircraft exploding and disintegrating while still on the ground. Its designer, apparently unmoved by such spectacular disaster, is saying: 'Ah well, back to the old drawing-board'.

dreaming spires

Literary, journalistic or ironic term for a university and especially for the happy condition of unworldly academics thought not to be burdened by hard reality. The term was coined by Matthew Arnold (1822–88), who called Oxford 'sweet city with her dreaming spires' in his poem *Thyrsis* (1866).

dressed to the nines: see *nine*

drop a brick: see *brick*

drop of a hat, at the: see *hat, at the drop of*

drum up • *obtain, summon (support, interest, etc.)*

From the military use of drums to send signals or orders, especially by recruiting parties sent into market squares and other public places; they advertised themselves by beating drums. One special use of the expression (to make a meal or a drink) may be from tramps' slang derived from the Romany 'drom' (highway), where tramps would normally take their refreshment.

duck, score a • *fail to score*

Originally a cricketing term, from the resemblance between 0 and a duck's egg, of which *duck* is an abbreviation. Also *break one's duck* (make an initial score), from the idea of breaking the 0.

ducks and drakes with, play   ● *use (especially money) recklessly*

The centuries-old game of throwing a flat stone to make it skim across water and bounce a number of times before it sinks is called *ducks and drakes* because the bobbing motion of the stone is like that of swimming ducks and drakes or the way they bob their heads in courtship ritual. From the throwing away of something and the idle amusement associated with the game comes the modern sense of irresponsible behaviour.

dunce   ● *stupid person*

(John) Duns Scotus (1266–1308) was a famous theologian whose followers, the 'Duns-men' or 'Dunses', were a predominating sect until the sixteenth century, when their beliefs fell into disrepute as a result of the new humanistic thinking and work of the reformers. From then on a *dunce* was first a pedant and then a dullard.

Dunkirk spirit   ● *courage, especially a determination to endure hardship, often by improvisation and in cooperation with others, when facing odds, disaster, etc.*

A reference to the national mood at and after the successful evacuation to England of about 350,000 Allied troops encircled at the channel port of Dunkirk during the German invasion of France in 1940. Their escape was aided by a fleet of small civilian boats from England.

The phrase implies refusal to surrender and also alludes to the years after the Dunkirk evacuation when Britain experienced bombing attacks and faced the threat of invasion.

dust, bite the   ● *come to an unsuccessful end*

This is probably no more than a jocular or blunt description of the act of falling flat on one's face, though it may be derived from 'his enemies shall lick the dust' (Psalm 72: 9), which refers to an act of humiliation or acknowledgement of defeat. The phrase is first found in Smollett's translation of *Gil Blas* (1749) but the idea of biting the ground (or the sand, in Pope's translation of the *Iliad*, 1715–20) is quite common before then.

dust off one's feet, shake the • *leave with relief or anger*

Adapted from Jesus' advice to his disciples as quoted in *Matthew* and other Gospels: 'whosoever shall not receive you, nor hear your words, when ye depart out of that house or city, shake off the dust of your feet' (10: 14). For the Jews the dust of heathen countries was unclean; to shake it from the feet indicated separation.

Dutch, Dutchman

Numerous expressions referring to the Dutch originate in Anglo-Dutch enmity during the seventeenth and early eighteenth centuries, when there were trade disputes, naval embargoes and three wars, as a result of which *Dutch* became a pejorative word. Generally it indicated a lack of genuineness: *Dutch courage* is that induced by drinking alcohol, a *Dutch uncle* gives unpalatable, heavy-handed advice (which is not to say bad advice), and *double Dutch* is gibberish or nonsense. The first of these may also allude to the Dutch fondness for gin and the second to **Calvinistic** sternness.

Later expressions are less derisive and more jocular, implying the sort of quirkiness many nations attribute to their neighbours: a *Dutch treat*, sometimes called *going Dutch*, means paying one's share of expenses (i.e. no treat at all) and *I'm a Dutchman* is a general expression of disbelief.

dyed-in-the-wool • *uncompromising and usually extreme in beliefs, opinions, attitudes, etc.*

If wool is dyed while still in its raw state (i.e. 'in the wool'), and not after it has been made up into fabric, the process is more thorough and the result more lasting.

E

ear to the ground, have one's   ● *be aware of what is going on; be alive to speculation, rumour, etc*

From the American–Indian practice—though alleged by some to be an invention of Hollywood westerns—of putting one's ear to the ground in order to detect the vibration of approaching hooves before they can actually be heard.

earmark   ● *designate for a specific purpose*

Either from the ancient and still current practice of marking the ear of a farm animal as a sign of ownership or, less likely, from scripture, where the laws for menservants say 'his master shall bore his ear through with an aul; and he shall serve him for ever' (*Exodus*, 21: 6).

eat, drink and be merry

The rich man who decided to do this, not knowing he would die that night, would have been better employed preparing his soul, according to the parable (*Luke*, 12: 16–21) which warns against attaching too much importance to physical things. The occasional addition ' . . . for tomorrow we die' is not in St Luke (though imminent death is) and is borrowed from a similar quotation in *Isaiah*: 'let us eat and drink, for tomorrow we shall die' (22: 13).

eat humble pie: see *humble pie*

eavesdrop   ● *listen to private conversation*

The Old English *eavesdrip* meant the dripping of water from the eaves (the overhanging edge of the roof, so made to keep rain away from the walls and foundations) and also the strip of ground on to which the drips dropped. The noun turned into *eavesdrop* and from this came the verb, literally meaning to stand within an eavesdrop where one could hear private conversations within a house.

Eden   ● *paradise; place of bliss, innocence, beauty, etc: see* **Adam**.

egg on   ● *incite, encourage, urge*

Nothing to do with eggs. The origin is an ancient Scandinavian word from which 'edge' is also derived. One of the meanings of 'edge' is 'sharpness' or 'urgency', which links with the meaning of this expression.

egghead   ● *intellectual*

From the jocular claim by bald-headed men that their condition has been brought on by overactivity in their exceptional brains.

eggs is eggs, as sure as   ● *absolutely certain*

Either a misunderstanding or jocular misquotation of 'x is x', an irrefutable proof in mathematics or formal logic.

eggs, teach one's grandmother to suck   ● *offer advice, instruction, etc. to an older or much more experienced person than oneself*

Raw eggs, with or without a little seasoning, used to be a popular food and regarded as healthy. Grandmothers, especially those without teeth, would have been particularly addicted to them and therefore needed no instruction about how to drink them.

One must regret the passing of a parallel expression 'teach one's grandam to grope ducks', i.e. use the fingers to measure the distance between a duck's pelvic bones; if these were close together the duck was not laying and could be consigned to the pot.

El Dorado   ● *place of vast wealth, plenty and opportunity, all easily available*

Spanish for 'the gilded man', epithet of the king of the legendary city of Manoa, believed to be on the River Amazon in South America, who was ceremonially smeared with oil and sprinkled with gold dust, thus becoming gilded. The name was later given to the city or country itself, said to be a place of fabulous riches easily obtainable. These ideas grew up from travellers' tales during the time of the Spanish conquest of South America and had such a firm hold on the imagination that two expeditions led by Sir Walter Raleigh (1552–1618) were among many that searched for the place. Even though it was shown on maps (e.g. of Brazil) it was never found. Modern scholarship places the town of the gilded chief (but not the site of legendary gold) near Lake Guatavita in Columbia.

eleventh hour, at the   ● *at the very last moment*

An allusion to the parable of the labourers in the vineyard who were hired literally 'at the eleventh hour' of a 12 hour working day (*Matthew*, 20: 1–16). This was not actually 'at the very last moment' but the point of the parable is that it was certainly later than the hour at which the other labourers were hired, and the result was a demand that those who had worked less should be paid less. The modern meaning comes from this sense of comparison between the eleventh hour and earlier ones.

Elysium; Elysian Fields   ● *place or state of ideal happiness; paradise.*

Both names are given, in classical mythology, to the abode of the dead, at first reserved for the gods' children but later opened to their favourites and to the souls of the just. Homer and Virgil describe it as a place of happiness, ease and eternal sunlight.

Emerald Isle   ● *Ireland*

Coined by William Drennan (1754–1820) in his poem *Erin*, from the country's greenness of vegetation.

éminence grise   ● *person exercising power by his or her influence (often unofficial) on person or group having titular authority*

The nickname (literally 'grey eminence') of the French monk and diplomat known as Père Joseph, who wore a grey habit. He was the secretary and confidant of Cardinal Richelieu (1585–1642), known as the *Éminence Rouge* because Eminence is a cardinal's title and red is the colour of his eccleciastical dress. As minister to King Louis XIII for eighteen years, Richelieu practically ruled France. Presumably one could gain access to the all-powerful *Éminence Rouge* only by going through the ironically named *Éminence Grise*.

The term is now usually spelt without capital letters and pronounced in the French style, though 'grey eminence' is sometimes found. The idea of shadowy influence should always be present; it is wrong to use the term merely of a senior person of influence, perhaps on the assumption that *grise* means grey-haired.

emperor's new clothes, the

The title of a fairy-story by the Danish writer Hans Andersen (1805–75) which first appeared in an English translation in 1846. In it two rogues claim to be able to make beautiful cloth which is invisible to anyone who is stupid or not fit for his or her job. The vain emperor, believing that this will enable him to identify foolish or incompetent courtiers and citizens, orders a set of clothes made from this fabric. The rogues go through the motions of weaving cloth and cutting out the garments. Courtiers who are sent to check on progress are of course unable to see any cloth but are unwilling to admit it. So is the emperor when the time comes for him to put on the imaginary clothes and go out in procession. Only a child, lacking adult dishonesty, points out that the emperor is walking about with no clothes on.

The expression is used in reference to pomposity or self-deception.

end, all good things come to an

This probably originates in scripture: 'I see that all things come to an end' is in the Prayer Book version of Psalm 119: 96. The extra word *good* somehow slipped in over the centuries during which the expression became proverbial.

ends meet, make   • *live within one's income*

This was originally 'make both ends meet', the two ends being the extremities of the year, i.e. the beginning and the end. *Meet* has its old sense of agree or tally. The whole phrase therefore means 'keep one's finances, income and expenditure, in balance throughout the year'.

England, home and beauty

A quotation from 'The Death of Nelson', an exhibition piece for tenor solo first performed as part of an opera, *The Americans* (1811), and universally known during Victorian times. The words are by S. J. Arnold. 'Beauty' appears to mean 'beautiful women-folk' in the original, though nowadays it carries its more usual abstract sense.

Englishman's home is his castle, an   • *a person has rights to property and privacy*

A proverbial popular notion, previously worded 'a man's house is his castle' from the sixteenth to the nineteenth centuries, after which it assumed its present form. It is not a legal quotation but a saying which enshrines a general principle of civil liberty. *Castle* implies impregnability.

epicurean   • *devoted to the pleasure of food and drink*

This modern meaning is a simplification and distortion of the teachings of Epicurus (341–271 BC), the Greek philosopher, physicist and logician. He did teach that pleasure was the sole good, but by pleasure he meant health of body, tranquillity of soul, calmness of thought, happiness in friendship and absence of pain. Hedonism, including food and drink, was to be cultivated but rationally selected.

error of one's ways, see the   • *(come to understand) the state of being wrong in one's course of action, beliefs, etc*

The New Testament original is slightly different: 'he which converteth the sinner from the error of his way shall save a soul from death . . . ' (*John*, 5: 20).

107

eureka!

The popular spelling of *heureka*, Greek for 'I have found [it]', said to have been the exclamation of the Syracusan philosopher and mathematician Archimedes (c.287–212 BC) on realising, while getting into a full bath, that the volume of a solid could be measured from the amount of water displaced by its immersion. The story is that he had been asked to test the purity of King Hiero's gold crown because of a suspicion that its maker had cheated by substituting cheaper metal for some of the gold provided by the king. Archimedes was able to prove that the volume of the crown exceeded the volume of the original gold, thus proving that a bulkier metal had been added. So great was his excitement that, according to Vitruvius, he ran naked from the public bath-house to his home to try the experiment, thus becoming the first mad scientist as well as the formulator of a principle of physics. His exclamation is still used to express satisfaction on finding or solving something.

Everest

The highest mountain in the world, first climbed in 1953, is named for Sir George Everest, surveyor-general of India from 1840 to 1853, though it is known by other names in Nepal and Tibet. Its name is sometimes used figuratively to denote a supreme achievement or aim in human endeavour of whatever kind.

every man jack: see *jack*

Exchequer   • *finance ministry of Britain*

The name of a department of state established in 1102 under Henry I and so called with reference to a table covered with a chequered cloth used as a counting device on which the accounts of revenue were reckoned by means of counters.

eye (and Betty Martin), all my   • *nonsense*

This was first explained by a commentator writing in 1823 as a corruption of 'O mihi, beate Martine . . . ' (O grant me, blessed Martin) from the words of a Latin prayer to St Martin. It is said to have been picked up abroad by sailors and to have come into English use in the eighteenth century by way of nautical slang.

Those who find this far-fetched prefer to think that there was a London character called Betty Martin, perhaps an actress or popular serving-wench, though this does not explain the first part of the expression. Perhaps it is a snatch of an otherwise forgotten popular song: the earliest version, in a slang dictionary of 1785, is the more intelligible 'That's my eye, Betty Martin', which could be a swain's plaintive reproach to a lady who has delivered a firm rebuff.

eye for an eye, an   ● *retaliation, especially in the same form as the offence provoking it*

The Old Testament law of punishment, 'eye for eye, tooth for tooth, hand for hand, foot for foot' (*Exodus*, 21: 24), revised in Christ's Sermon on the Mount: 'Ye have heard that it hath been said, An eye for an eye, and a tooth for a tooth: But I say unto you, That ye resist not evil . . . ' (*Matthew*, 5: 38–9).

F

FA: see *Fanny Adams*

Fabian (Society, tactics)

From Quintus Fabius Maximus, Roman consul and dictator in the third century BC, surnamed Cunctator (Latin for 'the delayer') because of his delaying tactics, notably his well-planned strategic evasion of pitched battle against Hannibal. The well-known Society, founded in 1884 by a small group of thinkers including George Bernard Shaw and Sidney and Beatrice Webb, aimed to propagate socialism and took its name from Fabius to underline its policy of careful consideration, cautious progress and avoidance of violent confrontation.

face the music: see *music*

fag-end ● *last and worst part*

A fag or fag-end was the last part of a piece of cloth, made of coarser material and hanging loose (*fag* in this sense seems to be a corruption of 'flag', meaning 'hang down'), and has long been used metaphorically of the last and poorest part of anything. For example, the stub of a cigar used to be called the *fag-end*; cheap cigarettes were called fags before the word spread to all cigarettes.

By the same derivation a *fag-end* was also the untwisted end of a rope with the strands hanging loose. It is perhaps from this sense of 'frayed' that we get *fagged-out* (exhausted), though the more likely explanation goes back to fag = flag = droop.

fagged-out: see **above**

Fagin ● *trainer of thieves; receiver of stolen goods; miser*

The evil old character in Dickens' *Oliver Twist* (1837–8), who was all of these, and especially noted for training a band of boys to be pickpockets and thieves. See also **artful dodger**.

fairy

Teutonic belief and mythology are less well-documented than those of Greek, Roman and other Mediterranean or Middle Eastern civilisations, but have a strong and older place in British folklore and superstition. In Teutonic belief the earth was peopled by superhuman creatures, prominent among whom were the souls of the dead. Other spirits intervened in people's lives. In the natural world every spot—water, woods, mountains—was inhabited by spirits; these were elves or fairies, usually thought of as smaller than people, but handsomer, living in their own regulated societies, creatures of magic, fond of singing and dancing, but avoiding people. In English poetry of the Middle Ages they are normally aerial beings full of benevolence, though some are demonic.

Modern references to a *good* or *wicked fairy* (person or influence bringing good/bad fortune) or *fairy godmother* (special protectress) are rooted in this paganism, now much sanitised through children's literature and popular pantomime.

fall

To *fall on one's feet* is to be lucky; the origin is the cat's ability to do so. A *fall guy* is a loser or victim, often one who is duped. The term comes from American wrestling matches in which an outcome was arranged in advance, the fall guy being the wrestler who agreed or was instructed to lose by allowing himself to be thrown down in a fall.

For *fall on stony ground* see **stony ground**.

Fall, fall of man, fall from grace ● *humankind's degeneracy:* see *Adam*.

fall foul of   • *come into conflict with*

From nautical jargon, in which the adjective *foul* has various meanings indicative of something wrong or difficult and the whole expression means 'collide with'.

fan   • *admirer, supporter, devotee*

From the late nineteenth-century American abbreviation of the stronger word 'fanatic'. Curiously enough, there was a British abbreviation 'phan' or 'fann' as early as the seventeenth century, but the modern word came from importation, not from the native version which had died out 150 years earlier.

Fanny Adams or **FA, sweet**   • *nothing at all*

Fanny Adams was a little girl who was murdered in Hampshire in 1867. Her body, cut into pieces, was found in a river. The adjective *sweet* was probably added in a popular poem or ballad of the sort that was often composed in the nineteenth century to memorialise drama or disaster.

With heartless humour, sailors came to apply the unfortunate child's name to the tinned mutton issued on board ship; one authority states that the joke originated in a sailor's discovery of a button in one such tin. By a natural shift, the expression transferred from mutton to monotony of diet and then to any lack of a popular or necessary item.

fascist   • *(person) opposed to democratic and liberal principles*

Fascism was an Italian political movement (1922–43) characterised by authoritarian and nationalistic attitudes. The *Fascists* took their name from their emblem, the *fasces*, a bound-up bundle of rods with the blade of an axe protuding. This was the symbol of the magistrates of ancient Rome, denoting their powers of punishment. Fascist with a small f is used of totalitarian, inhumane, ruthless and disreputable political attitudes and practices.

fast and loose: see *play fast and loose*

fat, chew the: see *chew the fat*

fat is in the fire, the • *something has been done with damaging consequences*

When cooking took place over open fires, the fat from spit-roasted meat was collected for basting or subsequent use. The loss of fat into the fire was wasteful and too much fat could cause a conflagration, as could an overheated pan containing fat. For whichever reason, too much fat in the fire was a bad thing. In its earliest use in the fourteenth century the expression had to do with failure; only later did it come to imply, as it now does, a crisis or an explosion (of anger, recrimination, etc.).

fat of the land, (live off) the • *(have) the best that is obtainable*

In modern English this is the only expression in which *fat* survives with this old meaning of 'the richest part of anything'. It is a quotation from Pharoah's words to Joseph in *Genesis*, 45: 18: 'I will give you the gold of the land of Egypt, and ye shall eat the fat of the land'.

Fates

A literal translation of the Latin word for the three inexorable goddesses of classical mythology who determined the course of human life. Clotho presided over birth, Lachesis determined the length of life and Atropos decided on death. They were cruel and unappeasable, a sense normally missing from modern uses of the word.

fatted calf, kill the • *celebrate lavishly, usually with a meal, especially as an act of welcome*

An allusion to Christ's parable of the **prodigal son** (*Luke,* 15: 11–32) who left home and wasted everything in 'riotous living' but was nevertheless welcomed back by his father. The fatted calf (verse 23) killed for the celebratory meal was presumably being kept for some such special occasion; *fatted* is the obsolete form of 'fattened' and is now found only in this context.

Faust, faustian

Used in allusions to selling one's soul or other acts of self-betrayal in return for worldly and therefore short-lived benefit, as described under **devil to pay**.

feather in one's cap   • *achievement one can take pride in*

A reference to the plumes worn in the helmets of knights as a sign of their distinction. The frequent attribution of the expression to American Indian custom is suspect: the Prince of Wales' three white ostrich feathers, for instance, have been known since the Battle of Crécy (1346), when the Black Prince is said to have won the right to display them after the death there of the king of Bohemia (whose crest they previously were). The expression has been metaphorical in English since the sixteenth century, which makes an American origin unlikely.

feather one's nest   • *enrich oneself*

A figurative application to people of something that birds do literally, though birds line their nests with feathers for a different purpose: to ensure safety for their eggs and warmth for their young. The expression is now normally used of people in a disapproving way, implying self-enrichment while in someone else's employment or trust.

feather, (show the) white   • *(show) cowardice*

A white feather in the tail of a fighting-cock was held to be a sign of inferior breeding and therefore became a metaphor for lack of fighting spirit. Hence the practice of handing white feathers to civilians assumed to be afraid of joining the army during the first part of the First World War before conscription was introduced.

feet of clay   • *fundamental weakness (of a person)*

Also *idol with feet of clay*: person (occasionally thing) much admired but fatally flawed.

The reference is to a biblical event during the reign of Nebuchadnezzar, a great king of Babylon (604–561 BC) during the Jewish captivity there. He had a dream of a great image: 'This image's head was of fine gold, his breast and his arms of silver, his belly and his thighs of brass, his legs of iron, his feet part of iron and part of clay' (*Daniel*, 2: 32–3). Called in to explain this dream-image, **Daniel** interpreted it as a vision of the declining kingdom: 'And as the toes of the feet were part of iron, and part of clay, so the kingdom shall be partly strong, and partly broken' (verse 42).

fell swoop: see *swoop*

ferret (out)   • *search persistently (and find)*

A ferret is a variety of polecat able to enter confined spaces. It was formerly much used for destroying rats and driving rabbits from their burrows so that they could be snared. This practice is not much found these days, but the verb continues in use with its figurative sense.

few and far between

A **hackneyed** expression. The original, lines 376–7 of Thomas Campbell's *Pleasures of Hope*, part 2 (1799), deserves better:

What though my wingèd hours of bliss have been,
Like angel-visits, few and far between.

In view of Robert Blair's 'Its visits, like those of angels, short and far between' (*The Grave*, 1743) and J. Norris's 'Like Angels' visits, short and bright' (*Miscellanies*, 1687) it could be that Campbell merely gave final form to an existing idiom.

fiddle, fit as a: see *fit*

fiddle while Rome burns   • *occupy oneself with something unimportant while a crisis remains unattended to*

The great fire of Rome (64 AD) gave the Emperor Nero (37–68 AD) and his city-planners an unparalleled opportunity to rebuild. Included in the plans were a fabulous villa and pleasure park for Nero, the Golden House (64–68 AD), which gave rise to rumours that Nero had started the fire himself in order to clear the site and had moreover celebrated it with music. It is true that he had artistic pretentions and was certainly capable both of initiating the catastrophe and of being insensitive to the suffering it caused, but if the story is true—some historians have argued that he was not in Rome at the time—he would have played a lyre (forerunner of the modern violin and used as an accompaniment to song), not a fiddle.

field-day • *period of excitement, success and freedom from restraint*

This is now not quite what the original was—a day on which troops, after much training and practice, were drawn up for review and exercise in field (i.e. battlefield) tactics and manoeuvres, watched by high-ranking officers and other visitors, in what was intended to be a brilliant and noisy display with plenty of dashing movement.

fifth column • *traitors; people within a country, organisation, etc. who secretly work against it*

Popularised by Ernest Hemingway's play *The Fifth Column* (1938), the expression was first used two years previously in a radio broadcast by the **fascist** General Mola during the Spanish Civil War. While besieging Madrid with an army of four columns of troops he claimed that he also had a 'fifth column' in the shape of the citizens of the city who were ready to rise up in his support.

fig-leaf • *(absurd, inadequate) concealment of reality, especially when shameful*

For the story of the disobedience of Adam and Eve see **Adam**. Following it, 'the eyes of both of them were opened, and they knew that they were naked; and they sewed fig-leaves together, and made themselves aprons' (*Genesis*, 3: 7). The metaphorical meaning of *fig-leaf* comes from this symbolism of the consciousness of shame and from its common use in painting and sculpture to cover the sexual organs.

figurehead • *nominal head or prominent person in an organisation, but actually having no authority*

Literally the carved and often painted ornament, usually a female bust or figure, often related to the name of a ship, placed at a ship's bows and having a decorative but no practical function.

filthy lucre • *money*

Now a jocular term, it is from the Bible (*Titus*, 1: 11) where it is a translation of the Greek for 'dishonourable gain'. *Lucre* is obsolete, though *lucrative* (providing gain) is still common.

final straw: see *straw*

fine kettle of fish: see *kettle of fish*

fingers crossed, keep one's • *hope for the best*

From the religious act of making the sign of the cross as one crosses oneself to sanctify or protect oneself.

fire and brimstone, breathe or **preach**

Brimstone is the obsolete name for sulphur, a noxious substance. In *Genesis* God rains down 'brimstone and fire' to punish (19: 24). The more familiar pairing of *fire and brimstone* occurs as a means of torture in *Revelation*, 14: 10. The idea of breathing it probably originates in the same book, where 'fire and smoke and brimstone' issue threateningly from the mouths of warriors' horses (9: 17).

A person who breathes fire and brimstone is therefore expressing an angry determination to do something furious, but a person who preaches it does so to threaten damnation in hell for his or her hearers' sins: 'the lake which burneth with fire and brimstone' is hell in *Revelation*, 21: 8.

fire, baptism of: see *baptism*

first-rate • *of the best quality*

Warships used to be classified according to six divisions called 'rates', in the sense of kinds or sorts, depending on the number of guns they carried. A ship 'of the first rate' belonged to the highest of these divisions and was therefore among the most powerful. This phrase became shorter as it passed from naval into general use.

fit as a fiddle   ● *in very good health*

Fit has has this sense of 'in good condition' only since the nineteenth century. Before that it meant only 'convenient, becoming, right and proper' (i.e. fitting), which explains why the earliest recorded form of this expression (1595) is 'as right as a fiddle'. One can only guess why a fiddle was thought to be particularly fit in this sense: perhaps because it was a piece of skilled craftsmanship and therefore to be admired, or because its playing required dexterity. People used to say that a person who was liked had a face 'made of a fiddle': they meant that it was always wreathed in smiles, as a fiddle has a much-curled shape. The origins of the modern expression probably lie somewhere among these associations, assisted—as is often the case with popular expressions—by alliteration.

flak   ● *criticism; opposition*

A German abbreviation of a longer German word meaning anti-aircraft gun or gunfire. It became well-known in the Second World War in RAF usage and now signifies attack or hostility of a different kind.

flash in the pan   ● *thing or person enjoying only short-lived success*

In old-fashioned firearms the *pan* was the part of the mechanism that held the priming gunpowder. On occasions the spark, made by the action of the trigger on the flint, caused the priming to flare up (i.e. to *flash in the pan*) without then exploding the main charge which was intended to discharge the shot. In other words a *flash in the pan* was a happening that did not lead to anything important.

flea in one's ear, (get) a   ● *(receive) a verbal rebuke*

From the discomfort experienced by animals, especially dogs and cats scratching themselves to relieve the irritation of fleas biting or moving inside their ears. There is an obvious metaphorical link between the unpleasantness of such a nuisance and that of a word of rebuke in a person's ear.

A *flea-bite* (trifling matter), on the other hand, is of little consequence compared with the bites of other creatures.

flea-bite: see *flea in one's ear*

fleshpots, the • *bodily pleasures or places where they are gratified*

Literally, pots in which flesh (meat) was boiled to eat. The origin is biblical: when the Israelites were in the wilderness they complained 'Would to God we had died by the hand of the Lord in the land of Egypt, when we sat by the flesh pots and when we did eat bread to the full' (*Exodus*, 16: 3). In later use the word meant sinful or enviable luxury. Its current use is facetious.

flog a dead horse • *act to no good effect, often on something that is already settled, worn-out, etc*

Because a dead horse was useless and could no longer be worked for profit, seamen used to describe as 'dead-horse time' the period of usually a month for which they were paid in advance when signing on. Perhaps having spent all the money before setting sail, they felt they were then working for nothing. Be that as it may, they certainly celebrated the end of the dead-horse month and the beginning of a new pay period by parading an effigy of a horse round the ship or hauling one up a mast.

Flogging a dead horse was therefore working (expending energy, as one does in flogging) for nothing, so to speak. Or perhaps officers, who had the power to punish seamen by flogging, used the term to describe their exasperation: getting good or extra work out of a crew that was still working off its dead-horse time was *flogging the dead horse*.

Flood, before the • *a very long time ago*

The rains with which God destroyed all living things except for Noah, his family and his livestock are known as the Flood or Deluge. See also **ark**.

flutter the dove-cotes: see *dove-cotes*

fly a kite: see *kite*

fly in the ointment   • *small disadvantage in otherwise happy circumstances*

An Old Testament allusion from about the fourth century BC: 'Dead flies cause the ointment of the apothecary to send forth a stinking savour: so doth a little folly him that is in reputation for wisdom and honour' (*Ecclesiastes*, 10: 1).

fly off the handle   • *lose one's temper*

Either from the loss of control, and possible danger, when the head of an axe works loose and flies off the handle as the axe is swung, or from the user's exasperation when this happens—as was likely when axe-handles were home-made in American pioneering days. It is one of several expressions reflecting that country's comparatively recent history of forest clearance as a prerequisite of settlement and farming.

fly-by-night   • *unreliable or untrustworthy person*

The term goes back to the idea of witches flying on their broomsticks by night and has had a number of meanings over the centuries (e.g. a wheeled sedan chair in Regency times). The current meaning has to do with fleeing overnight, the sort of thing a swindler might do. Indeed the term is sometimes used of a defaulting debtor.

flying colours: see *colours*

fool's gold   • *false prospect of wealth; swindle*

The name originally given to iron pyrite(s) because of its yellow colour. It may have been coined after Frobisher's three expeditions in search of the North-West Passage in the 1570s, when cargoes of ore containing the substance were brought back in the mistaken belief that they contained gold, but it is not recorded in writing until much later and may therefore have been a subsequent coinage.

fool's paradise   • *state of illusory happiness*

Medieval Christian (Roman Catholic) theologians considered the problem of the souls of the mentally deficient, who could not be held responsible for their own actions during their lives. It was decided that after death they could not be punished in **purgatory**, yet they were not fitted for heaven, so they were destined for a special **limbo** or Paradise of Fools. The term has been metaphorical since the fifteenth century and has long since lost whatever theological sense it had.

fools rush in where angels fear to tread

From Alexander Pope's *Essay on Criticism* (1711), line 625.

foot in it, put one's   • *blunder; get into trouble*

In 1528 William Tyndale, translator of the Bible, wrote that if porridge was burnt or meat over-roasted people would say 'The bishop hath put his foot in the pot' because 'the bishops burn whom they lust and whoever displeases them'. Seven years later he himself was strangled and burnt at the stake.

   The idea of blaming a bishop for putting his foot in something (especially milk that had boiled over) lasted many centuries and is likely to have been the origin of the modern expression.

foot the bill   • *pay the bill*

Footing was the act of adding up figures in a list and placing a total at the foot of the column. It was polite to ask a customer to *foot the bill* (check the arithmetic) as a euphemism for 'pay the bill'. In time the euphemistic sense dropped away.

forbidden fruit   • *anything tempting but prohibited*

Explained under **Adam**.

foregone conclusion   • *something bound to happen; a result that might have been foreseen*

A Shakespearean coinage (*Othello*, III, 3, line 434), except that Shakespeare was referring to something that had already actually happened ('gone' or occurred before).

fork out or up   • *pay, contribute (money)*

In slang, from the late seventeenth century, the 'forks' were the forefinger and middle finger and the verb 'to fork' was to pickpocket, especially by inserting the two 'forks' into a victim's pocket. In standard English a fork is, among other things, a bifurcation, v-shape or division into two branches, and it is easy to see why this came to be applied to the first two fingers of the hand. To *fork out* (now colloquial rather than slang) developed naturally from the basic idea of fingering money and bringing it out of a pocket.

forlorn hope   • *faint hope*

On the face of it this is a curious expression because 'forlorn' does not normally mean 'faint'; it means 'miserable, lonely, forsaken or sad'. The explanation is that a *forlorn hope* was originally a body of troops chosen to spearhead an attack. The rather odd name was an adaptation of the Dutch 'verloren hoop' (literally, 'lost troop'), a term which implied that the soldiers selected for this troop had faint hope of success. The English version meant the same, which is why a term which originally had nothing to do with forlornness or hope now means what it does.

fort, hold the   • *look after things or keep them running in the absence of the person normally responsible*

Popularly believed to be the words semaphored by General Sherman to General Corse from the top of Kennesaw Mountain, near Atlanta, Georgia, during the Battle of Allatoona (1864) in the American Civil War, though historians have given at least two other versions. This matters little, because the expression owes its currency—at least in Britain—to the use made of this famous historical incident in a poem or hymn by Philip Bliss (1838–76) about spiritual assistance in a time of difficulty:

'Hold the fort, for I am coming',
Jesus signals still.

This poem or hymn was introduced to the British public by the well-known American evangelists Moody and Sankey during their campaign in 1873. Their popular hymn-book, *Sacred Songs and Solos*, remained in widespread use in Protestant churches and chapels in Britain until the middle of the twentieth century, with the result that *hold the fort*, jocularly secularised, entered everyday vocabulary.

forty winks   ● *a short nap*

Forty used to be not only a precise number but also an indefinite term for a large number. There are frequent biblical references to 'forty days' which mean no more than 'for a long time', and because of this frequency the number 40 came to have an almost sacrosanct quality. It is probably this sense, jocularly applied, that lies behind 'forty winks', a wink itself being a short spell of sleep.

Fourth Estate, the   ● *journalists*

In rather dated terminology the three estates of the realm are the three bodies of people who constitute Parliament: the Lords Spiritual (archbishops and bishops) and Lords Temporal (hereditary and life peers) who form the House of Lords, and the Third Estate—elected representatives—who form the House of Commons. The Fourth Estate, now often spelt without capital letters, is the name for the press said to have been coined by Edmund Burke (1729–97), the philosopher and parliamentarian, when remarking that the Press Gallery in the House of Commons was more important than the other three estates.

Frankenstein

Not, as is usually thought, the name of a monster but of its creator, an idealistic student in Mary Shelley's horror story *Frankenstein, or the Modern Prometheus* (1818). Discovering the secret of giving life to inanimate things, he collects some bones together and **galvanizes** a huge, strong and ugly creature which, loathed by all, becomes dejected and solitary. It finally leads its creator to his death before destroying itself. A *Frankenstein's monster* is therefore something horrific, beyond control and likely to destroy those who made it, though in the original story it is something essentially good made degenerate by ill-use.

Fred Karno's Army   ● *(comically) shambolic organisation*

Fred Karno was the stage name of Fred Westcott, a British acrobat turned impresario who during the late nineteenth and early twentieth centuries formed famous troupes of comedians to perform on the circuit of music-hall theatres which stretched

123

across Britain and was the most important source of popular entertainment in the days before cinema and television. His companies specialised in sketches of a broad, **slapstick**, often mimetic kind in a style preserved in the silent films of Chaplin (who was, with Stan Laurel, a leading member of the troupe before entering films). Karno was therefore well known, his name synonymous with uproarious disorganisation, at the time of the First World War. *Fred Karno's Army* was the good-natured, slightly cynical nickname adopted—and celebrated in marching song—by the huge volunteer army which rushed to join up during the early months of the war in response to public appeal, were trained in often makeshift circumstances, and retained a cheerful irreverence. Their name is still used, though no longer confined to military contexts.

freelance • *self-employed (person)*

Coined, originally as two words, by Walter Scott in his novel *Ivanhoe* (1819) to describe a mercenary soldier of the Middle Ages: *lance* meant the same as lancer and *free* meant free to fight for any person who would pay him. In general use the term has never had any military connotations.

French leave, take • *leave or be absent without permission*

Originally a term describing a custom, prevalent in France in the eighteenth century but regarded in England as impolite, of leaving a social function without saying farewell to one's host or hostess. It is now used of any unauthorised absence or departure, e.g. from one's place of work.

fresh as a daisy • *not tired*

This comes from the fanciful assumption that the daisy is never tired because it 'sleeps' regularly, closing at sunset and opening in the morning. The name of the daisy in fact comes from the Old English for 'day's eye', from its opening with the sun as the human eye opens in the morning. Perhaps its petals, which close over its bright centre at the end of the day, were also thought to resemble human eyelashes.

fresh fields   • *new opportunities*

John Milton actually wrote 'Tomorrow to fresh woods and pastures new' as the final line of *Lycidas*, but the misquotation is firmly established.

Freudian slip

Sigmund Freud (1856–1939), Professor of Neurology at Vienna University from 1902–28 and one of the first great exponents of psychology, devised pyschoanalysis as a system for treating neurosis. Much of his teaching was devoted to the relationship between the conscious mind and the unconscious, which he defined as a reservoir of sometimes primitive or anti-social instincts, thoughts, desires and emotions, some of which may be consciously repressed or unconsciously suppressed in a way that may lead to neurotic symptoms.

A *Freudian slip* is an inadvertent remark, often a mispronunciation of a single word, which is thought (usually jocularly) to reveal what one really thinks, feels or is, as distinct from how one would like to appear. It gives a glimpse into the unconscious mind, revealing more than one intended.

The expression is a popular rather than a scientific one, though it accurately reflects Freud's view of the unconscious as the true source of mental energy.

Friday the thirteenth

Doubly unlucky in bringing together Friday, the day of the Crucifixion, and thirteen, the number of people who sat down to the Last Supper of Christ and his disciples before that event. Superstition about the number thirteen, however, is much older than Christ, and too ancient to have any explanation.

frogmarch   • *make (one) walk or march as if one were a prisoner*

This sense is milder than the original, which has to do with the resemblance between a frog and a refractory or drunken prisoner being carried bodily, face downwards, by four captors, two holding him up by the arms and two by the legs.

full blast, (at) • *at maximum speed, capacity or volume*

Among the meanings of *blast* is that of a strong current of air, artificially produced, especially for iron-smelting. A forge or blast furnace is said to be at *full blast* when it is fully at work. The term has come to be applied to other sorts of operations, especially noisy ones.

fur fly, make the • *cause a disturbance (often a serious quarrel)*

American slang, from fighting between cats (or other furred animals).

Furies, the

From the Latin word for the infernal deities sent from the hell of Roman and Greek mythology to avenge crime or punish wrong, especially violations of kinship. They are normally represented as three fierce women encircled by serpents and armed with whips who appeared at the threshold when a crime was committed within a family and who remained implacable and merciless.

G

Gadarene • *mindlessly headlong (usually in the company of others)*

The first three Gospels (see for example *Mark*, 5: 1–13) have the story of a miracle performed by Jesus in the country of the Gadarenes. He encountered a man possessed by demons and cast them out, whereupon they entered the bodies of about 2,000 swine feeding close by. The swine ran into the sea and were drowned.

In modern use the adjective is usually coupled with such nouns as stampede, rush and panic, and is now sometimes spelt with a small g.

gaff, blow the • *let out a secret*

Gaff was originally 'gab', a colloquial word (from 'gabble') for too much talking or glib prattling of the kind which may be indiscreet at times. If, as is likely, gab is related to 'gob', slang for 'mouth', we get an idea of 'blowing' the mouth (as one blows an instrument) as a term for letting out too much air, i.e. talking too much or too loudly.

There is no connection with the French *gaffe* (blunder), which came into English much later.

From this meaning of gab we get *gift of the gab*, the ability to talk fluently or persuasively. This has lost the pejorative overtones of the original 'gab'; usually, though not always, it is thought of as quite a useful gift.

gaffer   • *owner or boss (in factory, etc.); elderly man*

A contraction of *grandfather* and formerly a term of respect pre-fixed to a man's surname or trade. Its modern use is colloquial and affectionate.

Galahad, Sir   • *chivalrous and good man who comes to one's aid*

In legends of King Arthur, Galahad is the purest of the Knights of the **Round Table** and dies in ecstasy after achieving a vision of the **Holy Grail**. The modern use of his name owes more to general romantic notions of a **knight in shining armour** than to his precise role as a model of chastity in Malory's *Morte D'Arthur* (1485).

galvanize   • *stimulate to action as if by electric shock*

Luigi Galvani (1737–98) of Bologna in Italy discovered that electricity could be produced by chemical action. As a professor of anatomy he conducted experiments in animal electricity and it is this aspect of his work that is memorialised in the verb derived from his name.

game (for)   • *willing; ready (for)*

A dilution of the older and still current meaning: full of fight. This in turn was derived from 'game-cock', i.e. a cock bred for the *game* or sport of cock-fighting.

game is up, the   • *success is no longer possible*

Originally a hunting term with a quite different meaning: 'the game (i.e. quarry) is leaving its cover and the sport can begin'. Presumably the expression changed from one about a beginning to one about an end because non-hunters assumed that *game* meant activity and *up* meant over.

game not worth the candle: see *candle*

Garden of Eden: see *Adam*

garden path, lead up the   • *entice, lead on, deceive*

A cynical reinterpretation—for reasons which can only be guessed at—of a romantic original or poetic cliché, a garden being traditionally thought of as a suitable place for courtship, as in Tennyson's 'Come into the garden, Maud'.

gargantuan   • *enormous*

Gargantua is, in medieval legend, a giant with an enormous appetite: his name comes from the Spanish word for gullet. The adjective entered English, however, by way of two famous satirical novels by the French scholar and humanist Rabelais, *Gargantua* (1534) and *Pantagruel* (1532–3), in which the hero Gargantua is a gigantic, adventurous, exuberant and popular prince of extraordinary strength and appetite.

See also **Rabelaisian**.

gatepost, between you, me and the   • *between ourselves, in confidence*

Formerly ' . . . and the bedpost', which made better sense in implying intimacies as of people in bed together. Perhaps as the expression passed round among people who knew nothing of four-poster beds they substituted a sort of post that was more familiar to them. But 'post' had long been metaphorical for anything deaf, lifeless or ignorant; what matters is not the type of post but the fact that any post can be relied on not to reveal a confidence.

gauntlet

To *throw down the gauntlet* is to issue a challenge. The expression comes from the medieval custom of throwing down a glove or gauntlet when offering to fight; to *take up the gauntlet* was literally to pick it up, as a sign of accepting that challenge.

To *run the gauntlet* has nothing to do with this. Here *gauntlet* comes, by confused etymology, from the earlier and now obsolete *gantlope*, which in turn came from the Swedish 'gata' (lane) and 'lopp' (running course), a seventeenth-century military punishment in which a culprit was stripped to the waist and made to run between two rows of men who aimed blows at him with sticks or knotted ropes. The expression now means to be attacked, criticised or exposed to danger from two or more sides.

geese are swans, believe that all one's   • *have too optimistic a view of one's possessions, attributes, prospects, etc.*

This expression dates from the time when geese were commonplace and much used for food, whereas swans were rarer, regarded as more beautiful, and often used in literature as an image of faultlessness.

gen   • *information*

RAF slang from the 1920s, made popular by the Second World War and the subsequent spate of popular war films. It is an abbreviation of the word 'general' in the standard phrase 'for the general information of all ranks' routinely used as a heading for bulletins of information and instruction circulated round RAF stations. Such a bulletin was known as a or the *gen*.

ghost, give up the   • *die, stop working*

In this sense, *ghost* is the obsolete word for 'soul' or 'spirit' and the fact that it is given up implies that it has an existence separate from and outliving the human body. The phrase is found frequently in the Bible to mean 'die', though in modern use it is jocularly applied to a piece of equipment, occasionally to a person, that ceases to function.

gift of the gab: see *gaff, blow the*

gift-horse in the mouth, don't look a   • *do not find fault with a gift or chance benefit*

Even as early as the late fourth or early fifth century St Jerome quotes this expression (in Latin) as being proverbial. In English, early versions of it refer to a 'given horse' and the now familiar version emerged in the seventeenth century. There are similar expressions in several other European languages.

A young horse is a more desirable gift than an old one. A horse's teeth reveal its age, just as old people without dental care suffer from receding gums and become *long in the tooth*. The sense of the expression, therefore, is that if you receive a horse as a gift it is bad manners to look in its mouth to establish its value.

If something is *straight from the horse's mouth* it is from a reliable source. This again has to do with looking at teeth to establish age and therefore value; this information is likely to be more accurate than any other, such as that provided by a dishonest horse-trader.

Gilbertian   ● *ludicrous in a whimsical or paradoxical way*

Namely, in the characteristic style of W. S., later Sir William Gilbert (1836–1911), who wrote the libretti for the well-known operettas with music by Sir Arthur Sullivan, and specialised in topsy-turvy plots.

gild the lily   ● *add unnecessary ornamentation to something already beautiful in itself*

An established misquotation from Shakespeare's *King John*, IV, 2, lines 11 and 16:

To gild refinèd gold, to paint the lily . . .
Is wasteful and ridiculous excess.

gilt off the gingerbread, take the   ● *deprive something of (some of) its attractive qualities*

Gingerbread, a cake spiced with ginger, was often sold in toy shapes, especially as a flat human figure, covered or ornamented with either real or more usually imitation gilt. It was a metaphor for anything showy but insubstantial as early as Elizabethan days. The idea of taking off the gilt to reveal something less valuable developed in the nineteenth century, perhaps as a result of the popularity of gingerbread stalls at country fairs.

gilt-edged   ● *of the highest quality and reliability*

Now usually coupled with such nouns as guarantee, security, promise, etc., this term was introduced towards the end of the nineteenth century to describe especially safe government securities. They were so called because the splendid certificates issued to holders of the stock were ornamented with gilt edges. The term is still a stock-exchange one as well as being in more general metaphorical use.

gird up one's loins   ● *prepare oneself for strenuous activity*

A biblical expression (e.g. *I Kings*, 18: 46) for the action of tucking the end of a long robe into one's girdle or belt so as to be able to move the legs more freely when running, working, etc. To *gird* is to fasten by means of a girdle; the *loins* are that part of the body between waist and hips.

give a dog a bad name: see *name*

glitters, all that: see *gold*

gnashing of teeth   ● *expression of frustration or anger*

Found frequently in the Bible, especially the New Testament (e.g. *Matthew*, 8: 12), as an expression of despair or mourning.

go for broke

To *go for* in this sense is to make a choice with an element of risk. *Broke* is the familiar word for 'bankrupt'. The whole term therefore means to risk everything, including the possibility of total loss, in the hope of winning. The expression is from gambling.

goat, get one's   ● *annoy one*

A twentieth-century Americanism said to have originated in the practice of stabling a goat as a soothing mascot with a highly-strung thoroughbred racehorse. The horse could be made fractious and prevented from winning if its goat was taken away unscrupulously.

gobbledegook   ● *official jargon; pretentious verbiage, especially that used by people in authority*

The invention of the word has been confidently attributed to Maury Maverick, a distinguished American lawyer and politician, in reference to the US civil service. It is a whimsical reproduction of the sound made by a turkey and is a nonsense word, like much of what it signifies.

gold, all that glitters is not

This is the normal modern version of a Latin proverb, though 'glitters' has been common only since the seventeenth century. Earlier the verb was 'glisters' (in, for example, *The Merchant of Venice*, II, 7, line 65) and before that it was 'shines', as in Chaucer's *Canterbury Tales* of about 1387 ('The Canon's Yeoman's Tale', lines 962–3).

golden age   ● *most flourishing period*

A direct translation of a Latin phrase used by classical poets to define the first age of human history, a period said to have been one of ideal harmony, innocence, prosperity and happiness, free from all strife. The modern meaning is narrower and largely to do with success.

golden calf   ● *false ideal; money as an object of worship*

Chapter 22 of *Exodus* tells how the Israelites, after leaving Egypt and during Moses' protracted communion with God on Mount Sinai, made a golden calf to worship. On his return Moses, angered by their idolatry, broke the stone tablets on which the finger of God had inscribed the Law, and God plagued the Israelites for their apostasy. In modern use the *golden calf* has become a metaphor for any object of improper veneration, especially material wealth.

Goliath: see *David*

gone to pot: see *pot*

good books, in one's   ● *enjoying one's favour*

Explained at **black books, in one's**.

good riddance to bad rubbish

Catch-phrase expressing satisfaction at being rid of something or someone unpleasant. Coined by Dickens in *Dombey and Son* (1847–8), chapter 44.

good Samaritan: see *Samaritan, good*

good wine needs no bush: see *bush*

goose that lays the golden egg, kill the • *destroy, usually by greed or folly, one's source of profit*

The metaphor is from Aesop's fable of a man who, having been given a goose that laid golden eggs, could not bear to wait for wealth to come gradually in small quantities. Hoping to get all the eggs at once he killed the goose to get at them and thus cut off the supply.

See also **cook one's goose** and **geese are swans**.

Gordian knot

Gordius, a peasant, became king of Phrygia (now in Turkey) in obedience to an **oracle** which decreed that the first person to drive to the temple of Zeus in a wagon should be crowned. He dedicated his wagon to Zeus and yoked it to a beam in the temple with a knot of great complexity. Alexander the Great, in the course of his **crusade** to the east in the fourth century BC, learnt of an oracle that whoever loosed the knot would become master of Asia. He cut it with a stroke of his sword, then went on to conquer the whole of the Persian Empire. The story is usually thought to be legend, though some scholars believe it could be true.

The Gordian knot (sometimes with a small g) remains a popular metaphor for a complicated difficulty. To *cut the Gordian knot* is to resolve that difficulty with a decisive act that ignores the subtleties it seems to invite.

Gordon Bennett

This mild oath is usually traced back to James Gordon Bennett (1841–1918), the editor of the *New York Herald* who commissioned the journalist/explorer Henry Stanley to search for the British explorer David Livingstone in central Africa. Bennett spent much of his life in Paris, where there is an avenue named after him, and was a colourful character of whom many picturesque anecdotes are told. He was associated with polo and horse-racing, gave trophies for motor races and spent money freely: he is reputed to have got through a fortune of tens of millions of dollars and to have bought a restaurant and a cable company on the spur of the moment for his personal convenience.

Why an American in Paris should have given his name to an English expletive has never been explained. There is an alternative, though duller, possibility: 'Gordon' may well be no more than an evasion of 'Gawd!', with 'Bennett' as a purely arbitrary addition, the whole expression being unrelated to a specific person.

Gorgon   • *fierce and intimidating woman*

In Greek legend the Gorgons were three monstrous and ugly sisters who lived at the earth's extremity. They had tusks, serpents in their hair, brazen claws and golden wings; their looks could turn people to stone. The most famous story about them is that of Medusa, the only one of the three who was mortal, being slain by Perseus, who successfully avoided her fatal gaze by looking at her reflection in his shield. He cut off her head and presented it to the goddess Athene.

gospel

From the Old English *godspel* (glad tidings). It is a general word for the teachings of Christ and a particular one for any of the first four books of the New Testament, which describe his life. It has come to mean, less specifically, any guiding principle or anything unquestionably authoritative.

It is common to use a capital G in Christian contexts and a small g otherwise ('preach the Gospel,' 'the gospel truth').

grace, fall from: see *Adam*

grace of God (go I), there but for the

A comment on someone's ill fortune, meaning that it could easily have happened to oneself (or to anyone at all). It is based on a remark reputed to have been made by the much admired clergyman John Bradford on seeing some criminals going to execution. He himself was charged with heresy during the reign of Mary I and burned at the stake in Smithfield in 1555 as part of the official persecution of Protestants.

grade, make the ● *reach the required standard*

An Americanism, still slightly informal, from the vocabulary of railroad construction, in which *grade* meant gradient. The huge task of linking the east and west coasts in the nineteenth century involved numerous calculations to ensure that railway engines could *make* or surmount the gradients being planned.

Grail: see *Holy Grail*

Grand Guignol

The name of a small theatre in Montmartre, Paris, which specialised in short, gruesome and melodramatic plays in a style which therefore became known as (Grand) Guignol. Anything now described as Grand Guignol is akin to a horror story, often involving violent death. Guignol was originally the name of the main character in an eighteenth-century French puppet show similar to Punch and Judy.

grapevine, on the ● *by unofficial circulation of information (or rumour) from person to person, usually in a large organisation*

Short for 'grapevine telegraph', a cynical American Civil War term for the route by which information, much of it inaccurate (e.g. news of victories not in fact won), was received. It is thought to have originated in 1859 with the construction of an actual telegraph line slung from tree to tree; the swaying of the trees stretched the line until it sagged, reminding some soldiers of the trailing Californian grapevine after which they duly named it.

grass roots, the • *ordinary voters*

In American mining terminology this denoted the level of soil beneath the earth's surface. It was then adopted as a political metaphor to signify rural voters with old-fashioned virtues in contrast to city folk cut off from them. In Britain it has no rural connotations and merely distinguishes ordinary voters from professional politicians or commentators.

grass widow • *woman whose husband is temporarily away from her*

The expression goes back to the sixteenth century, when it was applied to an unmarried woman (i.e. one like a widow in having no husband) who was sexually promiscuous or had a child. *Grass* may have implied furtive sexual activity in a field or hay-loft.

great guns: see *guns*

great I am, the • *a conspicuously self-important person; (jocularly) the boss*

God's definition of himself as self-existent: 'And God said unto Moses, I AM THAT I AM: and he said, Thou shalt say unto the children of Israel, I AM hath sent me unto you' (*Exodus*, 3: 14).

great Scott: see *Scott!, great*

great unwashed: see *unwashed*

Greek(s)

It's all Greek to me is a way of saying 'I don't understand it at all'. The expression is well known from Shakespeare's *Julius Caesar*: in discussion among the conspirators Casca is asked if Cicero has said anything and replies, 'Ay . . . but for mine own part it was Greek to me' (II, 2, lines 277–84). Casca is a blunt character and his remark is probably no more than a sardonic dismissal of Cicero's scholarship and legal subtlety, though the more discerning members of Shakespeare's audience would know of Cicero's devotion to Greek philosophy and of his nickname 'the Grecian', according to Plutarch, who was Shakespeare's source.

Although Shakespeare is responsible for the popularity of the phrase, it may have existed earlier. ''Tis Greek to me' is found in Robert Greene's play *James IV* of 1598, probably—but only probably—the year before *Julius Caesar*. Shakespeare might have found it there, or both writers might have taken it from contemporary idiom.

Beware Greeks bearing gifts is a less familiar catch-phrase, used to counsel caution when someone previously unsympathetic appears to offer a favour. It is a rough version of a line in Virgil's *Aeneid* (Bk II, line 49) where Laocoon warns the Trojans not to accept from the Greeks the wooden horse that was to prove their undoing. See **Trojan**.

green with envy　　● *very envious*

Before Shakespeare, a green complexion (i.e. pale and sickly) was associated with other things besides envy: these included fear, ill-humour and illness. In a famous passage Iago warns Othello to 'beware, my lord, of jealousy;/It is the green-eyed monster which doth mock/The meat it feeds on' (III, 3, lines 169–71), a metaphor from the green-eyed cat family which is prone to play with (mock) its victims as a cat plays with a mouse. Though green has continued to have other associations, notably immaturity and gullibility, it is envy that now predominates.

green-eyed monster: see above

gremlin　　● *imaginary imp humorously said to be responsible for breakdowns in machinery*

Now standard English, originally RAF slang from the First World War or the 1920s and popularised by the Second World War. It may be a modification of the Irish Gaelic *gruaimin* (ill-humoured little fellow) though more colourful guesswork has identified it as a goblin living in a Fremlin beer bottle.

grey eminence: see *éminence grise*

grim death, like or **for**　　● *very firmly*

Shakespeare coined *grim death* in *The Taming of the Shrew* (Induction, 1, line 33), where *grim* means fierce, cruel and ugly. The idea of *hanging on (etc.) like grim death* came much later, as an intensive form of *hanging on grimly*, i.e. as if with one's face twisted in fierce effort.

grind the faces of the poor　　● *ill-treat the poor, especially by keeping them in poverty*

Still sometimes heard as an evocative political phrase, though not as often as it was in days gone by when it was thought to epitomise the attitude of employers and landowners. It is an ancient Hebrew expression which passed into English by way of *Isaiah*, 3: 15: 'What mean ye that ye beat my people to pieces, and grind the faces of the poor? saith the Lord God of hosts'.

grist to the mill: see *mill*

groggy　　● *weak, faint, dazed or staggering*

Few people who complain of feeling groggy realise that they are referring to Admiral Edward Vernon (1684–1757), nicknamed Old Grog because of his cloak of grogram (a coarse fabric of silk, or wool and mohair, or silk mixed with these). In 1740 he ordered that his sailors' rum ration be diluted with water. The resultant mixture became known—no doubt unaffectionately—as *grog* and its effects were known as making one *groggy*: even diluted it was powerful. *Grog* is now used of alcoholic drink more generally, and *groggy* too has widened its meaning.

grotty　　● *unpleasant, dirty, ugly*

Slang abbreviation of 'grotesque', which actually means 'twisted, bizarre, absurd'. Perhaps the abbreviation, which seems to have originated in Liverpool, was intended to poke fun at a rather upper-middle-class word.

ground: see *break*

Grub Street • *having the nature of literary hack-work*

According to Dr Johnson's *Dictionary* (1755) this was originally the name of a London street 'much inhabited by writers of small histories, dictionaries, and temporary poems, whence any mean production is called grubstreet'. It was renamed Milton Street in the nineteenth century and is near the Barbican Centre.

Grundy, Mrs • *person of rigid, conventional and usually censorious propriety*

First heard of in Thomas Morton's successful comedy *Speed the Plough* (1798) in which there are several fearful references to what she may say or think. She never actually appears, which makes her even more memorable, and she has remained a symbol of forbidding and tedious rectitude ever since.

gubbins • *anything of little value; gadget*

A variant of the obsolete 'gobbon' (which is related to 'gobbet'), meaning 'portion' or 'slice'. It came to mean 'fragments', especially of fish, and then 'trash' more generally. This meaning was applied in First World War slang to stores, personal belongings, general untidiness or anything one was too lazy or preoccupied to name. From this developed the habit of using the same word for a tool, piece of equipment, thingummy, anything of which the name was unknown or temporarily forgotten.

guillotine

The physician Joseph Guillotin (1738–1814) did not invent the execution apparatus named after him: versions of it had existed for centuries. What he did do was to propose to the French National Assembly that all members of French society should have the privilege, previously restricted to high-ranking ones, of being humanely beheaded. The new name for the machine entered English in 1793 and is now also used of a paper-cutter and of a British parliamentary procedure to curtail debate. It is also a verb.

guinea-pig • *person (or thing) used in an experiment*

From the use of this animal in scientific research, especially that using vivisection.

gum-tree, up a • *in a predicament*

Thought to be from the hunting of the opossum, which took refuge in trees and, in addition to being cornered there, would have difficulties of movement if they were of the gum-exuding variety. The phrase, however, could equally have come from the obvious human problems of climbing gum-trees, which are common in the USA where the phrase originated.

gun, jump the • *act before the agreed or permitted time*

From athletics: the *gun* is the starting-gun and *jump* is used in the sense of 'act to gain an advantage over', as in queue-jumping.

gung-ho • *excessively enthusiastic or zealous*

From the Chinese for 'work together'. During the Second World War the term was adopted as a motto by a US marine division whose colonel knew it from his period of attachment to the Chinese army as an observer. He may not have known that the words are short for an expression meaning Chinese Industrial Cooperatives Society.

The term became more generally known as the title of a later film about the marines. Thus *gung-ho* became associated with tough adventurism. In general use it now implies a dangerous insensitivity, especially when applied to political attitudes or military mood.

guns

The military term for cannon or any ordnance mounted for firing was 'great guns', as distinct from small guns that were handheld. Figuratively, a wind that *blows great guns* is violent and noisy, like cannon, and anything that is *going great guns* is enjoying a roaring success, carrying all before it.

To *stick to one's guns*, originally another military term, meaning to keep firing and not abandon the guns, now means to adhere to one's position (principles, beliefs, opinions, etc.) under attack.

guru

Strictly, a Hindu or Sikh personal religious teacher and spiritual guide. Loosely, the chief theoretician or proponent of an idea or cult, such as a political or economic philosophy. The word, originally Sanskrit, came to prominence in the 1960s when Indian philosophies were embraced by popular singers. It is now a jocular, slightly derogatory word for any thinker who has a following, especially when both are thought to be cranky.

H

hack: see *hackneyed*

hackles rise, make one's   • *make one angry or resentful*

The hackle of a cock, peacock, pigeon, etc. is the long shining feathers on the neck which are puffed out when the bird is angry. The word was later used in the plural for the hairs on the back of a dog's neck, which also rise when it prepares to fight, and metaphorically for angry feelings in people.

hackneyed   • *trite, dull, commonplace as a result of over-use*

In Old English a hackney was an ordinary horse (i.e. not a thoroughbred) suitable for general use, especially for riding by ladies; the name may have come from Hackney in London, where horses used to be raised. Shortened to *hack*, the word is still in use for a horse of this kind. By the sixteenth century a hackney had also become a horse available for hire: this enabled the word to become a metaphor for a person hired to do low-grade work. This contemptuous sense is found, again abbreviated to *hack*, in such terms as *hack-work* (drudgery) and *hack-writer*, as well as in *hack* in the sense of 'low-grade journalist'. The modern meanings of *hackneyed* can readily be traced back to the idea of a hired horse worn out by overwork.

Hades   • *hell*

Originally the name of the god ruling over the world of the dead in Greek mythology, but better known from its later mythological use as the name of the abode of the dead, a place of melancholy but not necessarily of torment. The word is used in the Revised Version of the Bible but the Authorised Version prefers 'hell'; both correspond to the Hebrew *sheol*.

hail from • *come from, live*

In its sense of 'call from a distance to attract attention', *hail* was originally nautical and remained chiefly so until the mid-eighteenth century. It was natural for sailing ships passing at sea to hail each other, and a ship which announced that it was from a certain port was said in nautical jargon to 'hail from' it. The term gradually came to be transferred to people and their home towns.

hail-fellow-well-met • *breezily and heartily friendly and informal from the first moment of meeting (sometimes excessively so)*

This is made up of two now obsolete greetings, 'Hail, fellow' and 'Well met'. In the first, *hail* meant (good) health and *fellow* was, roughly, comrade; *hail(-)fellow* used also to be an adjective or adverb expressing close friendship. The second greeting meant no more than the modern 'Good to see you' and came to be tacked on to the adjectival *hail-fellow* as reinforcement.

hair of the dog • *(small) alcoholic drink taken as an antidote to a hangover*

An allusion to an old belief that the (burnt) hair of a dog would act as an antidote to the bite of a mad dog if it was placed on the wound. This belief was in accordance with an older Roman one that 'like is cured by like'.

hair stand on end, make one's • *terrify one*

A reference to the effect of extreme terror on the hair of the arms, head, etc. as noted for example in *Job*: 'Fear came upon me, and trembling . . . the hair of my flesh stood up' (4: 14–5). Hence *hair-raising* and its slang abbreviation *hairy* (dangerous, risky).

hairy: see above

halcyon days • *calm, peaceful, happy time*

Halcyon is the Greek, and in English literature a poetic word, for a *kingfisher*. In Greek mythology this bird was fabled to breed at the time of the winter solstice (December 21), the shortest day of the year, in a nest floating on the sea, which it was able to charm into calmness so that its eggs could be safely hatched. A period of calm usually lasting about a fortnight before and after the winter solstice was therefore known as the *halcyon days*, though the expression has come to have a wider application.

half-seas-over • *drunk*

A nautical term denoting the condition of a ship stranded on a reef, rock, etc., partly ('half') submerged and with seas breaking over it. The ship's helplessness is compared to that of a drunken person equally unable to steer a course.

hallmark • *distinguishing characteristic*

Literally, the mark stamped on gold and silver to guarantee their purity. The *hall* is Goldsmith's Hall, London, where grading and stamping used to take place.

ham • *person (especially actor) who overacts*

An abbreviation of the American 'hamfatter', an ineffective actor (1887). The idea may have been that hamfat was a poor substitute for good lean ham, so a hamfatter was by definition second-rate. An alternative explanation is that nineteenth-century black-face comedians, generally among the least distinguished of theatrical performers, used hamfat on their faces as a base for their burnt-cork make-up and as a removal cream, and that this gave them their derogatory name.

A *radio-ham*, on the other hand, seems to have become so called from being an *am*ateur.

Ham is also used adjectivally (*a ham actor*) and as a verb (often *ham it up*, meaning overact) from the senses already quoted.

Hamlet without the prince • *event from which the principal performer or star attraction is absent*

The reference is to the play *Hamlet* in which the central character is the prince (of Denmark), namely Hamlet himself. It was

145

Wordsworth who first noted, in a letter of 1793, the story of a company of strolling players who advertised a performance of *Hamlet* and announced, at the beginning of the performance, that they hoped the audience would forgive the omission of the character of the prince.

hammer and tongs   ● *with great force or violence*

From the effort and energy needed by a blacksmith holding a piece of hot iron in place with tongs while hammering it on the anvil. The smith has to act quickly to *strike while the iron is hot*, for cold iron cannot readily be shaped. He may also have *other irons in the fire*, material being prepared for working on.

hand over fist   ● *rapidly*

Normally used of making money or overhauling someone. This was originally 'hand over hand', a nautical expression applied to the speedy hauling in or descent of a rope by using alternate hands, rather than by the slower method of using both hands together.

hand that feeds one, bite the   ● *show ingratitude to someone who deserves thanks*

First used in this sense by Edmund Burke (1729–97), the writer, orator, statesman and thinker: 'And having looked to government for bread, on the very first scarcity they will turn and bite the hand that fed them' (*Thoughts and Details on Scarcity*). Previously it meant to commit a blunder: 'He is wonderfully unlucky, insomuch that he will bite the hand that feeds him' (John Addison in *The Spectator*, 1711).

handicap   ● *disability, disadvantage*

A contraction of 'hand in cap', the name of a very old betting game (described in *Piers Plowman* (1367–86), for instance) in which players put forfeit-money in a cap or bag and then drew from it. A version of this process was later applied to arrangements for a race between two horses, the superior of which carried an extra weight. Racing authorities took over the term when formulating modern rules to give a weight advantage to some horses in order to equalise chances in a race. Handicap is now more generally used of anything that hampers or hinders.

hands down, win   ● *win with little or no effort*

In horse-racing a jockey who is winning comfortably rides with hands held loosely down, there being no need to use them to bring pressure on the horse.

hang by a thread: see *thread, hang by a*

hang fire   ● *delay; hold back, hesitate*

A gunnery term, used of a gun that was slow to discharge because its spark took longer than usual to reach the gunpowder-charge through its vent.

hang out   ● *live*

From the old custom of hanging out a sign or some other indication of one's trade outside one's premises. See **bush, good wine needs no**.

hangdog   ● *looking shamefaced, furtive or downcast*

Literally, like a dog deserving or about to be hanged. Perhaps from 'give a dog a bad name'. See **name, give a dog a bad**.

hanged, drawn and quartered

People sentenced to be executed used to be drawn to the site behind a horse or cart. At first they were dragged along the ground, but so many failed to survive that the custom grew up of drawing them on a hurdle or hide or in a cart. After being hanged, but while still alive, they were lowered to the ground and castrated; disembowelment and the burning of viscera were performed before their eyes. They were then decapitated and quartered, the resultant pieces being preserved for exhibition by being boiled and perhaps coated in pitch.

   Hanged, drawn and quartered was not a legal formula but a common expression summarising a much longer and more detailed sentence delivered by a judge. It is not clear whether *drawn* refers to the conveyance to execution or to the removal of viscera ('draw' is an old word for disembowel)—probably the latter, judging from its position in the expression.

hanged for a sheep as a lamb, as well be   ● *if the outcome (punishment, risk, etc.) is going to be the same, one might as well do something drastic rather than trivial*

Sheep-stealers used to risk capital punishment. A sheep, having a fleece and more meat, was a more saleable commodity than a lamb.

happy as a sandboy   ● *very happy*

Not a boy playing in the sand but one peddling it, often from panniers slung from a donkey, to the owners of shops and taverns where a fresh layer was spread on the floor every day to absorb the mud from customers' boots. Why a sandboy should be proverbially jolly is not clear. In Dickens' *Old Curiosity Shop* (1840) there is an inn called The Jolly Sandboys 'with a sign representing three sandboys increasing their jollity'. This indicates that 'jolly as a sandboy' was familiar enough to have an inn named from it, but if sandboys' jollity was really inspired by their proverbial intake of alcohol it is hard to believe that an inn-sign would celebrate the fact, unless the sandboys were actually men. Probably they were just happy because what they sold for money cost them very little or nothing; it has been estimated that they could make over £5 a morning, and if they were also given the job of clearing out the old sand before laying the new their happiness might well have been enhanced by the possibility of finding dropped valuables in it.

hard and fast   ● *inflexible*

From a nautical term applied to a ship grounded on the shore, *hard* meaning firmly and *fast* meaning fixed.

hard lines   ● *bad luck; hardship*

Lines used to mean one's lot in life, which is why *hard lines* were bad fortune. The origin appears to be Psalm 16.6: 'The lines are fallen unto me in pleasant places; yea, I have a goodly heritage', apparently referring to lines marking out the boundaries of one's land and home. Attempts to explain *hard lines* as a nautical term for inflexible or frozen ropes are weakened by lack of evidence that seamen used 'lines' in this sense.

hard up   • *short of money (etc.)*

Originally a nautical command for the tiller to be put as far as possible to windward, i.e. so as to turn the bows away from the wind. This was done under the stress of weather, which gave the term its metaphorical sense of stress of a different kind.

hard-boiled   • *toughly practical, sometimes even callous*

An Americanism from the boiling of cloth, especially the material for men's hats, to make it stiff and hard. The process became a popular metaphor for similar characteristics in human behaviour or attitudes.

hark back (to)   • *return to an earlier subject; recall*

'Hark', an old-fashioned word for 'listen', was used in hunting cries to call attention to something or to give encouragement. *Hark back* was one such cry, given to the hounds to return along their course to find a lost scent.

harpy   • *mean-tempered, scolding or grasping woman*

In Greek mythology the Harpies were tempest-goddesses. They were monsters with the face of an old hag, bears' ears and the body of a bird with hooked claws. They snatched food from tables, spread excrement and caused famine. It is for the first of these activities that they were specially noted, which is why *harpy* used to mean a rapacious person, though it is now a more general term of abuse.

hash

A *hash* is a dish of meat and vegetables cut into small pieces. As it is a mixture it is colloquially used for 'mess', so to *make a hash* of something is to muddle it.

However, in *settle one's hash* (silence, subdue or defeat one) the *hash* is a dish of food and *settle* means to reduce to order. The whole phrase is similar to **cook one's goose** and other phrases in which a person who is to be dealt with is compared with a dish of food that has to be attended to in different ways.

hat

To *take one's hat off to* someone is to feel respect for her or him. Men normally remove their hats as a sign of respect, for example when entering a house; this custom may date back to the warrior's removal of his helmet to demonstrate (e.g. in surrender) that he was undefended and thus meant no harm.

To *throw one's hat into the ring* (announce one's intention to be a contestant) seems to have originated in sporting circles: throwing one's hat into the (boxing) ring, in the days when men generally wore hats, was perhaps a sign of a spectator's willingness to respond to a prize-fighter's challenge, perhaps as an updated version of throwing down the gauntlet.

For *pass the hat round* see **hat trick**. See also below.

hat, at the drop of a   • *immediately*

Said to be from the American frontier practice of asking someone to drop a hat as a signal for a fight to begin, in the days when few other rules seem to have existed. It is also possible that informal races were begun with a sharp lowering, rather than an actual dropping, of a hat previously held high as a 'get ready' signal.

hat trick   • *three successes by a person or team, usually in a sporting contest*

Specifically, in cricket, the dismissal of three batsmen with three successive balls from the same bowler, a rare feat formerly rewarded either by the gift of a hat from the bowler's club or by passing a hat round among spectators for a collection of money. The term passed from cricket to other sports and also into non-sporting vocabulary but retained its sense of triple success.

Although a trick is usually a prank or crafty device it can mean, as here, a clever expedient or piece of skill.

hatchet

The original *hatchet man*, now a person employed to carry out an unpleasant assignment requiring ruthlessness, was a pioneer serving with an American military unit. He was so called because he used a hatchet in his work, which was to march at or near the front of a body of troops to clear the way for them and afterwards to dig trenches, etc. The term was later applied to a hired **assassin**, often Chinese, in the lawless early history of California; from this emerged its present milder, though related, sense. A *hatchet job* (ruthless attack on a person's reputation, reform of an organisation, etc.) is from the same source.

hatchet, bury the ● *end a quarrel*

An American Indian custom was to bury a tomahawk or other weapons on the conclusion of a peace. The expression is found in writing as early as the eighteenth century and came into general use by being popularised in such works as Longfellow's much-read *Song of Hiawatha* (1858).

haul over the coals: see *coals*

hay while the sun shines, make ● *take advantage of a favourable opportunity*

To make hay is to cut grass and spread it out to dry, for later use as fodder. The proverb is very ancient, and very English in its reference to variable weather.

haywire, go ● *(begin to) function erratically (applied to things); become seriously upset or crazy (applied to persons)*

Haywire (originally an American word) is used for binding bales of hay. If bound tightly round a bale, the wire may whip back sharply and dangerously when it is cut to release the hay for use. It may also become entangled in the baling-machine during the actual process of baling. This unpredictability explains its appearance in the familiar expression.

There is a less satisfactory explanation in terms of an earlier American slang use of *haywire* to mean 'makeshift', from the idea of making a temporary repair with a piece of wire. There may be some link between such a *haywire repair* and something which needs repair being said to have *gone haywire*, i.e. to have become in need of haywire.

head in the sand: see *ostrich-like*

head on a platter or plate, one's   ● *revenge on one; one's punishment*

An allusion to the death of John the Baptist, who was beheaded on the orders of Herod. The daughter of Herodias, whose marriage John had criticised, danced before Herod to such pleasing effect that he offered her whatever she asked for; prompted by her mother she asked for John's head, which was duly delivered to her on a dish. The story is in *Matthew*, 14: 1–12.

head over heels   ● *completely (often, in love)*

Also used of a headlong fall; literally, 'in a somersault'. It is a curious expression as *head over heels* is of course the normal posture of the body. It is a corruption of the earlier and more intelligible 'heels over head' (upside down), perhaps as a result of confusion with the proverbial 'over head and ears' (completely immersed) which is now usually expressed as 'up to the ears'.

heap coals of fire: see *coals*

heart of hearts, in one's   ● *in one's innermost feelings*

An anatomically curious but firmly established variant of the older and more sensible 'heart of heart' (i.e. very centre of the heart) coined by Shakespeare in *Hamlet* (III, 3, lines 69–71):

> Give me that man
>
> That is not passion's slave, and I will wear him
> In my heart's core, ay, in my heart of heart . . .

152

heart on one's sleeve, wear one's   ● *be very open in showing one's feelings*

From the old custom in which a young man tied to his *sleeve* a favour—perhaps a ribbon or handkerchief—given to him by a lady as a sign of her affection (i.e. of her *heart*). The expression is now used of one's own heart (i.e. feelings) on one's own sleeve.

Heath Robinson

The artist William Heath Robinson (1872–1944) is chiefly remembered for cartoons depicting bizarre, ingenious and comic pieces of mechanical engineering, sometimes intended to perform simple tasks that could be readily performed by hand, to satirise twentieth-century preoccupations with technological gadgetry. His name is still applied to any unfamiliar contraption of homemade appearance.

hector   ● *bully; verbally intimidate or domineer*

Hector was the **Trojan** hero celebrated in Homer's *Iliad* as the son of King Priam and the commander of the Trojan Army. He was a dominant and magnanimous warrior who was killed by **Achilles** in single combat outside the walls of Troy. He hardly deserves to have entered the language, as he did in the mid-seventeenth century, as a synonym for unpleasant blustering or browbeating; this transformation may have had its origins in the debunking of the great Greek and Trojan heroes by Shakespeare in *Troilus and Cressida*.

heel, bring to   ● *bring (usually a person) under control*

Originally a hunting term from the training of hounds to come to a position close behind the hunter where they were under control.

hell broke loose, all   ● *there was terrific uproar, confusion, violence, etc*

A colloquial expression coming unexpectedly and not at all colloquially from John Milton's majestic epic *Paradise Lost* (1667). Before expelling Satan from the Garden of Eden the chief of the angelic guards, Gabriel, asks him why he has come alone: 'Wherefore with thee/Came not all hell broke loose?' i.e. all the denizens of hell, having broken loose (Bk IV, lines 917–8).

Similar expressions occur in literature up to a century earlier, but Milton was the first to provide the exact words quoted and the great popularity of his work accounts for their survival.

hell for leather   • *very quickly*

From horse-riding, probably an obscure mixture of 'like hell' (very vigorously) and 'leather' as a verb meaning to thrash.

hell hath no fury like a woman scorned

A misquotation from William Congreve's tragedy *The Mourning Bride* (1697), III, 8:

Heaven has no rage like love to hatred turned,
Nor Hell a fury like a woman scorned.

henchman   • *faithful attendant or assistant*

Now slightly derogatory or even menacing; originally it meant no more than a groom or servant, the first syllable deriving from an Old English word for horse.

Herculean   • *requiring great strength*

Hercules, son of Zeus, was one of the greatest heroes of Greek mythology, the personification of physical strength but also famed as a friend and counsellor. He showed his might in infancy by strangling two serpents which attacked him in his cradle, and as a youth by killing a lion. After success as a warrior he became mad, killing his wife and children. He consulted the **oracle** at Delphi and was commanded to carry out twelve gigantic labours to remove the stain of his crime; see **Augean stables**. On his death after many other successful adventures he was admitted to Olympus to live with the gods.

The adjective *Herculean* (increasingly spelt with a small h and common enough to deserve this familiarity) is usually found with nouns such as task, efforts, strength, etc.

Herod: see *out-Herod*

hewers of wood (and drawers of water) ● *people doing dull, menial work*

Literary and jocular, originally biblical: 'Now therefore ye are cursed, and there shall none of you be freed from being bond-men, and hewers of wood and drawers of water for the house of my God' were the words of Joshua cursing the Gibeonites during his conquest of Canaan (*Joshua*, 9: 23).

hide one's light under a bushel: see *bushel*

hidebound ● *bigoted, inflexible, restricted by (petty) rules, conventions or attitudes, usually conservative*

Literally, in the condition of an underfed animal, especially a cow, with skin (*hide*) closely attached (*bound*) to bones, i.e. without fat. Applied to people it suggests the idea that their skin is so tight that they cannot move (act, think) freely.

high and dry ● *stranded; without resources or support*

A nautical metaphor: a ship that is beached or on the rocks is left *high* by the receding tide and *dry* by being out of the water.

high horse, be on one's ● *stand on one's dignity; behave in an overbearing manner*

A *high horse* used to be a strong warhorse or charger ridden by a person of rank.

high jump, be for the ● *be required to face punishment or reprimand*

A development, probably via military slang, from an earlier meaning which simply had to do with facing a difficulty. The origin is in steeplechasing, in which a *high jump* is a major obstacle.

highbrow • *(person) of intellectual interests or refined taste in cultural matters*

Originally standard English 'high-browed' (having a high forehead), then US colloquial 'highbrow' with the modern meaning, based on the jocular assumption that a person with lofty interests needs a high brow to contain her or his mental capacities. *Lowbrow* and *middlebrow* are later derivatives with obvious meanings.

hijack • *forcibly and improperly take control*

Originally a person—a High Jack, a travelling hold-up man, especially one bootlegger robbing another, in American railroad or hobo slang. He got his name from his habit of saying 'High, Jack' as a command to his victim, familiarly addressed, to put his hands up. It sounds unlikely, but it is the best explanation on record.

hit and run

Applied to a driver who fails to stop after an accident or to a criminal who acts swiftly and flees. The term is from baseball, describing a manoeuvre when a base-runner starts to run as the pitcher throws and the batter attempts a hit.

hit or knock for six: see *six*

hitch one's wagon to a star: see *star*

hoax: see *hocus-pocus*

hobby • *abbreviation of* **hobbyhorse**

hobbyhorse, (on or **riding one's)** • *(talking about one's) favourite topic*

A hobbyhorse (in which *hobby* is an obsolete word for a small light horse) was a covered wickerwork frame in the shape of a horse that was fastened round the waist of a comic performer in a morris-dance or on the stage so that the performer appeared to be riding it. It was also the name of a child's toy in the form of a stick with an imitation horse's head which children could pretend to ride. From this it came to mean a favourite pursuit or pastime, by jocular reference to a child's fondness for toys. This sense of jocularity (or sometimes impatience) persists in the modern use of the term, though it is quite absent from the abbreviation *hobby*, now the normal word for a spare-time activity.

Horseplay, meaning rough or boisterous play, may well have originated in the knockabout comedy of the *hobbyhorse* in the first meaning given.

hobnob ● *associate familiarly*

From an earlier form 'to hob and nob' (literally, to give and take), meaning to drink to each other in turn. This was from an even earlier form 'hab (or) nab', a phrase related to Old English forms of the verb 'have' and meaning 'have or have not'—obviously related to the later 'give and take'. The modern phrase, which is slightly derogatory in tone, derives its meaning from the drinking associations of 'hob and nob' and from the implications of friendliness in 'give and take'.

Hobson's choice ● *no choice at all*

Thomas or Tobias Hobson (1544–1631) was a Cambridge carrier who hired out horses but compelled customers either to take the horse next in line or to go without. Because he insisted on this strict rotation everyone was treated alike and no horse was overworked. He is referred to in literature as early as about 1599; after his death John Milton wrote two affectionate epitaphs on him, describing him as 'the University carrier' who had fallen ill at a time when he was prevented from making his weekly journeys (he also carried the mail) between Cambridge and London because of the plague. No doubt he was known to generations of Cambridge undergraduates and their slang was responsible for broadcasting his name and scrupulousness.

hocus-pocus ● *gibberish; pointless activity; trickery*

A meaningless Latin-sounding formula which used to be spoken with other **mumbo-jumbo** by conjurers or jugglers to give an air of mystery or magic to their performance. It may have originated with a specific early seventeenth-century conjurer who not only used the formula but also adopted it as his stage-name; it certainly became popular as a name or nickname of conjurers. There have been conjectures that the expression is a parody of the Latin 'Hoc est corpus meum' ('This is my body', the words of consecration in the Mass) but this is impossible to prove.

Hoax is almost certainly a contraction of *hocus*.

hog, go the whole • *do something in a thoroughgoing way*

In his poem *The Love of the World* (1778) William Cowper describes the difficulties which Muslim holy men had in deciding which parts of the hog had really been prohibited as food by Mohammed, whose vagueness on the subject left them free to indulge their personal tastes:

> Thus, conscience freed from every clog,
> Mahometans eat up the hog.

However, the popular expression appears to have originated in the USA, where *hog* has always been commoner than 'pig', and is therefore more likely to be related to the slang use of *hog* as a word for a dime, the same word having been used earlier in England as slang for a shilling. The name came from the depiction of a hog on one side of the coin. If this is so, the expression would have originally meant to spend the whole of a coin at once, a boldness echoed in the modern meaning.

Alternatively, there is evidence from American butchers' slang that customers were invited to 'go' the whole hog, i.e. buy the whole pig, which was cheaper than buying piecemeal. This provides the most convincing explanation of the term.

hoist by one's own petard • *made a victim of one's own (malicious) intentions or actions*

Properly 'with', not 'by', if one is to be true to the original in *Hamlet* (III, 4, lines 206–7):

> For 'tis the sport to have the enginer
> Hoist with his own petard.

A *petard* is a bomb, *hoist* means 'blown up' and an 'enginer' is a person who makes engines of war.

hold a candle: see *candle*

hold the fort: see *fort*

holds barred, no   ● *without any rules or constraints, especially those of fair play*

From all-in wrestling of the most primitive kind, in which no hold or grip or indeed any method of dealing with an opponent was forbidden.

holier-than-thou   ● *offensively self-righteous*

A quotation from the words of the prophet Isaiah about people who say 'Stand by thyself, come not near to me; for I am holier than thou. These are a smoke in my nose . . . ' (65: 5).

Holocaust, the   ● *the mass murder of Jews by German Nazis during the Second World War*

This old but previously unfamiliar word has been adopted and given this new and specific meaning by recent writers and historians, notably Donat in *The Holocaust Kingdom* (1965), presumably because better known words seemed inadequate to define the unique horror of what happened. From the Greek for 'wholly burnt', the word originally meant a sacrifice wholly consumed by fire, then came to mean complete destruction by fire, especially involving many people, and finally any great massacre, whence the modern application.

Holy Grail   ● *uniquely prized object of search or quest; high ideal*

According to Arthurian legend, the *Holy Grail* was Christ's cup (or plate) at the Last Supper. It was then used by Joseph of Arimathea to catch some of Christ's blood at the Crucifixion and was brought by Joseph to North Wales, where it disappeared. Manifesting itself from time to time to a chosen few, the Grail became the object of sacred quest by the Knights of the **Round Table**, the three purest of whom—including **Galahad**—finally received it from Christ's hands at the castle of Corbenic, from where they carried it to Sarras. *Grail*, an old word for bowl, cup or platter, now exists only in this context.

The story, principally told in Malory's *Morte D'Arthur* (1485) and popularised in Tennyson's *Idylls of the King* (1891), though also existing in other languages and versions, is part of a great body of literature which mixes Christian legend, pagan fertility ritual and Celtic mythology. In popular modern metaphor the *Grail* has become debased ('Energy from fusion is the Holy Grail of energy research'), though some sense of awe remains.

holy of holies, the   • *a room of which the privacy is jealousy guarded or whose occupant is regarded with awe*

A literal translation, found in early versions of the Bible (e.g. Wyclif's: see *Exodus*, 26: 34) but not in the Authorised Version, of a Hebrew term for the innermost apartment of the Jewish Temple where the **Ark** of the Covenant was kept, only to be opened by the High Priest on one day a year, the Day of Atonement (Yom Kippur).

home sweet home

The title of an immensely popular song taken from the melodrama *Clari, or the Maid of Milan* (1823) written by the American John Howard Payne (1791–1852)—who never had a home in his life—with six musical numbers composed by Sir Henry Bishop (1786–1855), a noted home-wrecker. The words do not actually occur in the body of the song, though 'home, sweet sweet home' does. Although the poet insisted that the verses came to him 'as spontaneously as a sigh', it has been noted that a translation of the old Latin song *Dulce Domum* (literally, 'sweet home') appeared in the *Gentleman's Magazine* in 1796 with the line 'Home, sweet home! an ample treasure', which should be regarded as the true if not the popular origin. See the next entry for evidence of other plagiarism in the song.

The English musicologist Percy Scholes notes that an Oklahoma attorney sang *Home sweet home* in court in 1935 to beg mercy for his client, a bank robber. The jury brought in a sentence of life imprisonment.

home, there's no place like

From the opening lines of the hugely popular Victorian song *Home Sweet Home* (see previous entry) of 1823.

'Mid pleasures and palaces, though we may roam,
Be it ever so humble there's no place like home!

These bear a suspicious resemblance to lines by the American J. K. Paulding in his poem *The Backwoodsman* (1818):

Whate'er may happen, wheresoe'er we roam,
However homely, still there's naught like home.

(Here 'homely' means 'simple'.)

honeymoon   ● *holiday after marriage; period of goodwill*

Originally the first month (i.e. *moon*) after marriage. *Honey* is thought to be a reference to an old Germanic custom according to which a newly wed couple drank mead, a fermented mixture of honey and water, for a month after their wedding. There are similar expressions in French and Italian, though not in German.

hooch   ● *alcoholic drink*

American slang took this from Hoochino, the name of a tribe of Alaskan Indians and of the liquor they made. The abbreviation was first used for any inferior alcoholic drink, especially whisky, in Alaska and the Canadian north-west.

hoodwink: see *pull the wool*

hook, line and sinker, (swallow)   ● *(believe, accept, etc.) completely*

From angling: the *hook*, which carries the bait, is attached to the fishing *line*, and the *sinker* is the weight which keeps the hook beneath the surface. A fish that swallows all three shows unusual, even improbable, greed.

hook or by crook, by   ● *by any means possible; by fair means or foul*

The modern meaning is different from the original one, which was that only two means were allowed—the *hook* or bill-hook, a chopper with a hooked end, used for pruning, and the shepherd's *crook*, a long staff with a bigger hook at the end for catching

161

the back leg of a sheep. The reference is to medieval laws or rights which restricted the gathering of firewood to prevent depradations: one was allowed to cut off, with the *hook*, only those branches that could be pulled down with the *crook*.

hooligan   ● *ruffian*

An English approximation to an Irish surname often rendered as Houlihan. The word stems from the rough behaviour associated with a number of Houlihans, probably immigrant labourers in the eighteenth century. Its earliest appearance is as the name of Larry Hoolagan, a drunken and rascally Irish servant in T. G. Rodwell's farce *More Blunders Than One* (1824), written at a time when it was still conventional to name dramatic characters with words that indicated types of behaviour or temperament. This suggests that *hooligan* or some such word was already in existence as slang (though not recorded in print) before the date of this play and with something of the meaning it still has.

hoop, go or put through the   ● *undergo or make to undergo a test*
(often ordeal or punishment)

From the use of hoops in the circus ring, where animals or acrobats show their prowess by jumping through them.

hoover   ● *(clean with) vacuum-cleaner*

W. H. Hoover (1849–1932) did not invent the vacuum-cleaner but he was a businessman shrewd enough to buy the rights to an invention of a caretaker working in an Ohio store and subsequently to mass-produce it. Despite rival products it was Hoover's that became best known and (with a small h) passed into the language, usually as a verb indicating the use of any make of vacuum-cleaner.

hope springs eternal (in the human breast)

Catch-phrase taken from Pope's *Essay on Man* (1732–4), Epistle I, line 95.

horns in, draw one's: see *draw one's horns in*

horns of a dilemma, on the ● *having to choose between two things, courses of action, etc., each of which is equally unfavourable*

Dilemma is a technical term of logic and means a form of argument forcing one's adversary into a choice between equally unacceptable alternatives. The Romans called this *argumentum cornutum*, an argument with horns: the image illustrated the argument's capacity to impale an opponent. Translated from the Latin, the image has remained in popular use, though often incorrectly weakened to mean no more than a mere difficulty.

horse: see *flog a dead horse, gift-horse, cart.* For **horseplay** see *hobbyhorse.* For **straight from the horse's mouth** see *gift-horse*

horses in midstream, change or **swap** ● *change (allegiance, method, etc.) at a difficult moment*

In a speech in 1863 referring to the risk of replacing a candidate for political office, the US President Abraham Lincoln (1809–65) quoted a Dutch farmer's remark that is was best not to swap horses when crossing a stream. The metaphor, drawn from the American experience of pioneering journeys, acquired the terser 'in midstream' nearly a century later and passed from political into more general use.

hot and cold, blow ● *alternate between being favourable and unfavourable; vacillate*

An allusion to a fable by Aesop in which a satyr meets a traveller blowing on his fingers to warm them. Invited home by the satyr, the traveller blows on his soup to cool it. The satyr turns him out, wishing to have nothing to do with someone who can blow hot and cold from the same mouth.

hotbed ● *environment that encourages the development of something, usually bad*

From gardening, where a *hotbed* is a bed of earth heated by fermenting manure and used to force growth.

163

Houdini ● *(characteristic of) person who surprisingly manages to escape from trouble, blame, difficulty, etc*

The stage-name of Erik Weiz (1874–1926), the celebrated escapologist and illusionist. His family emigrated from Hungary to the USA, where he began his stage career in 1890, appearing in London in 1900 and becoming famous for the imaginative variety of circumstances from which he contrived to escape.

house on fire, like a ● *very well*

Originally, very quickly or vigorously; the simile made better sense in the old days when houses were of wooden construction and had thatched roofs, etc.

how the other half lives ● *how other people live*

In its full form the proverb is 'One half of the world does not know how the other half lives'. Its earliest appearance in English is dated to 1607 but it is found in French in Rabelais' *Pantagruel* in 1532. More recently it gained currency as the title of a book (1890) by Jacob Riis. It is now most commonly used as a jocular or envious comment on the lifestyle of the wealthy, though originally the *other half* was the poor.

hubris ● *pride, arrogance, usually overweening and leading to fall*

A Greek word used in the technical language of literary criticism. It was used by the Greek thinker Aristotle (fourth century BC) in his influential treatise *The Poetics* to signify over-confidence, pride or ambition, one of the tragic flaws or errors of judgement leading to the downfall and death of the classical tragic hero. The word has been common in the vocabulary of English scholars since *The Poetics* came to prominence in the middle of the sixteenth century and has since passed into more general use.

hue and cry ● *public outcry of alarm, protest, etc*

This was originally a legal formula to be used when calling for assistance in the pursuit of a criminal; failure to respond was an offence. The term is Anglo-Norman: *hue* is from an Old French word meaning 'shout' and is found nowhere else in modern English in this sense.

humble pie, eat   ● *apologise, behave humbly*

'Umbles' (occasionally 'humbles') were the edible offal of deer and other animals; 'umble' pie was therefore eaten many centuries ago, but only in the early nineteenth did it acquire its current metaphorical meaning. This started life as a punning joke: there is no connection between 'humble' and 'umbles/ humbles' in derivation or meaning, only in sound. Some commentators disagree, suggesting a different sort of connection in that servants would eat umble pie while lordly folk had the better cuts of meat, but actually umble pie was a perfectly respectable dish in the seventeenth century and its consumption was not confined to the humble.

Huns: see *Attila*

hydra-headed   ● *variously and persistently troublesome or evil*

The *hydra* was an enormous nine-headed serpent in Greek mythology. It lived in a marsh in the Peloponnese, ravaging herds and crops and killing people with the poison of its breath. One of the **Herculean** labours was to destroy it; when Hercules attempted to do so he found that if he cut off one head two grew in its place, but he finally succeeded with the help of red-hot brands. In modern imagery the *hydra* is used of any multi-faceted problem or wickedness which presents fresh difficulties as soon as one is solved.

I

ice: see *break*

iconoclast   • *peson who attacks cherished beliefs or institutions, or breaks venerated conventions*

The historical *iconoclasts* (from the Greek, literally 'image-breakers') were members of a movement in the eighth and ninth centuries which aimed to stop the use of icons in the Eastern or Orthodox Christian church; icons were pictures, low-relief sculptures and mosaics of Jesus, the Virgin and the Saints, used as objects of veneration. The movement was begun by the Byzantine Emperor Leo III in 726 and ended in 843 after opposition by various religious bodies and successive popes.

idol: see *feet of clay*

ignoramus   • *fool; ignorant person*

A term of abuse originating, oddly, in a legal formula of quite different significance. It is Latin for 'we do not know' and was used in early English legal proceedings by Grand Juries as an official endorsement (signifying 'we take no notice of this') on a bill or indictment when they considered the evidence insufficient to justify prosecution. The shift of the word into the public domain was brought about—or, if not, much assisted—by its being used as the title of a famous university farce by George Ruggle (1575–1622) produced before James I in 1615. The title part was a burlesque of the then Recorder of Cambridge, who suffers various humiliations in the play and is depicted as an *ignoramus* in the now familiar sense.

ignorance is bliss

The original is a wistful contemplation of the innocence of youth by the poet Thomas Gray in his *Ode on a Distant Prospect of Eton College* (1747), lines 98–100:

> Thought would destroy their paradise!
> No more; where ignorance is bliss
> 'Tis folly to be wise.

Ignorance here does not carry, as it now often does, a sense of impoliteness; it simply means 'lack of [adult] knowledge'.

ill wind, it's an   • *Someone profits from every loss*

Said comfortingly of misfortunes that may bring some benefits. The full saying is 'It's an ill wind that blows nobody good', the emphasis being 'it is indeed a harsh wind if it damages everybody'. It was already proverbial when recorded by Thomas Tusser in *Five Hundred Points of Good Husbandry* (1580) as 'It is an ill wind turns none to good' (. . . if it makes nobody turn to doing something worthwhile), a version that makes better sense in implying that misfortune brings out the best in people.

ill-starred   • *ill-fated*

An allusion to the astrological belief that one's fate or fortunes are influenced by the motions and positions of the planets.

Indian summer   • *period of summery weather in autumn*

It was in the northern USA that the phenomenon of mild and pleasant weather in late autumn was first observed and frequently commented on in early American writings. At the time, the part of the country in question was still occupied by American Indians.

innings, have a good   ●   *die in ripe old age; leave a post after a long or successful period*

In cricket, the time that a batsman spends in play is called an innings; if he plays well or scores highly, he has a good innings. Often, though not necessarily, a good innings is also a long one, either because many runs are scored or because it keeps one side in play, so enabling others to score, preventing the other side from coming into play, or forcing a draw in preference to a defeat.

insult to injury, add

First found in a play by Edward Moore, *The Foundling* (1748), V, 2, though it may owe something to a fable by Aesop in which a bald-headed man suffers the indignity of hitting himself on the head in a vain attempt to swat the fly which has just bitten him.

iota: see *jot*

iron curtain

The invention of this graphic expression, which used to be applied to the boundary between western European countries and communist eastern Europe, is usually credited to the Russian philosopher Vasily Rozanov, who in 1918 wrote that 'an iron curtain is descending on Russian history' following the 1917 revolution. In 1920, in a book describing her visit to Russia, Ethel Snowden described the country as being behind an 'iron curtain'. The British wartime Prime Minister, Winston Churchill, used the term in a telegram to President Truman of the USA in 1945, shortly after the end of the war in Europe, to illustrate his anxieties about the demarcation line between the Russian forces and those of the western Allies. It may or may not be significant that *The Times* had printed the expression only nine days earlier in a report translating part of a broadcast by the German Foreign Minister, who in turn may have known that Goebbels had used the same phrase three months earlier.

There can be no doubt that what gave the phrase its widest publicity was Churchill's speech at Westminster College, Fulton, Missouri, in 1946, when he defined what had happened in Europe and was to dominate world politics until the late 1980s: 'From Stettin in the Baltic to Trieste in the Adriatic, an iron curtain has descended across the Continent'. Churchill must be credited with the everyday currency of the expression from then on, but not with its invention: the earliest quoted sighting is actually in the Earl of Munster's journal of 1817.

irons in the fire: see *hammer and tongs*

ivory tower   • *lifestyle or place of retreat detached from that of ordinary people*

First used in English in about 1911, this is a direct translation of the French *tour d'ivoire* coined by the poet and critic Sainte-Beuve in his poem *Pensées d'Août* (1837) . He used it to describe his fellow poet Alfred de Vigny's seclusion in a turret room and de Vigny's preoccupation with inspiration unconnected with practical matters.

J

jack, Jack

Jack is a familiar, affectionate or diminutive version of John, perhaps the commonest British name, and occurs in numerous expressions to mean an ordinary man, fellow, chap, etc. Thus *jack of all trades* (person who does a variety of work), *every man jack* (everyone without exception), *jack-in-the-box* and **cheap jack** (originally Cheap Jack, man who travels about offering bargains for sale). The word is also used for a labouring man (*steeplejack*) and to express masculinity: a *jackass* (fool) is originally a male ass. It is a nickname or familiar term of address in *Jack Frost*, *I'm all right Jack*, and *Jack Tar*, a rather old-fashioned term for a sailor in which *Tar* is short for *tarpaulin* (canvas covered with tar) in reference to the extensive use of tar by sailors in times past. A jack is also something taking the place of a man to save labour, as in *car-jack*, etc. See also **Union Jack**.

jackanapes • *conceited, impudent; mischievous child*

Perhaps from 'Jack of the ape', nickname of William de la Pole (1396–1450), first Duke of Suffolk, whose badge included an ape's ball and chain. 'Jack' would have been familiar: see above.

jackass: see *jack*

jam today • *immediate gratification*

Said of something that cannot be; also *jam tomorrow*, a meaningless promise of better things to come. From Lewis Carroll's

Through the Looking-Glass (1872): 'The rule is, jam tomorrow and jam yesterday—but never jam today'. The words parody what is said to children when denying them jam as a treat: 'You can't have jam today, you had it yesterday' or 'you can have it tomorrow'. The nonsensical point is that tomorrow always becomes today so that the 'rule' or promise is meaningless. In the original the 'rule' is one of the conditions offered to Alice by the White Queen when discussing her employment as a ladies' maid.

January: see *Janus-like*

Janus-like ● *two-faced*

Janus was a Roman god of great antiquity; his cult may have been established by Romulus himself. Among his many functions he was the god of doorways and communication. He was represented as having two faces, one on the front and one on the back of his head, allowing him to see the interior as well as the exterior of buildings and all comings and goings. *January* derives from his name because he also presided over the entrance into a new year.

jeans

The thick cotton cloth called fustian was known as *jean* in Britain and *jeans* in America centuries before its name was given to the distinctive trousers made from it. *Jean* was short for the earlier *jene fustian*, in which *jene* was an adjectival version of the old name for Genoa, where the cloth was made. It is still discernible in the modern French name of the Italian city, Gênes.

jeep

Primarily from 'GP', abbreviation of 'general purposes', the vehicle's official designation in the code-book jargon of the US Army in the Second World War, but undoubtedly influenced by the name of the cartoon character Eugene the Jeep in the comic strip *Popeye*, created in 1936. Eugene was a creature who made a 'jeep, jeep' sound and, like the later vehicle, was amazingly versatile.

171

Jekyll and Hyde • *showing contradictory character traits, as if having a split personality*

In *The Strange Case of Dr Jekyll and Mr Hyde* (1886) R. L. Stevenson tells the story of a doctor who discovers a drug which enables him to create for himself a separate personality expressing all his own evil instincts. This is Mr Hyde, repulsive and purely wicked, whose personality Dr Jekyll assumes from time to time so as to be able to enjoy his baser impulses. However, Hyde becomes more powerful, the drug loses its capacity to restore Jekyll entirely to his original form, he finds himself changing involuntarily, and he finally takes his own life.

Jeremiah, jeremiad

Jeremiah was a Hebrew prophet of the sixth and seventh centuries BC who lived at the time of the Jewish captivity by the Babylonians. He is regarded as author or part-author of two Old Testament books, *The Book of the Prophet Jeremiah* and *The Lamentations of Jeremiah*, both of which are characterised by a sense of pain, desolation and sadness. A person who is gloomy by temperament and pessimistic about the future is still sometimes called a *Jeremiah*. From this is derived *jeremiad*, a more recent word (1780) for a lengthy, mournful complaint.

jerry-built • *unsubstantially constructed, using bad materials, etc*

Despite the likelihood that this comes from someone's name, no actual Jerry has ever been identified, and claims that there was a nineteenth-century building firm of this name on Merseyside have not been verified. Various nautical expressions include an unexplained use of 'jury' to mean 'temporary': a jury-mast, for instance, was a temporary replacement for a mast lost in a storm. As a result of this, 'jury' passed into general use as a synonym for 'makeshift'. Perhaps this became mispronounced as *jerry*. There remains the ingenious but not implausible suggestion that *jerry* was builders' slang, from 'Jericho', the walls of which came tumbling down. (For the full story of how God caused this with the sound of trumpets and shouting see *Joshua*, 6: 1–21.)

Jerusalem, the new • *paradise on earth, especially the establishment of social justice, equality and freedom from strife*

A rather literary phrase sometimes used in the vocabulary of socialist idealism, sometimes sneeringly by opponents of this. The origin is St John's vision of the Christian paradise: 'I John saw the holy city, new Jerusalem, coming down from God out of heaven, prepared as a bride adorned for her husband' (*Revelation*, 21: 2). The 'old' Jerusalem had probably by this time been destroyed by the Romans (70 AD); it was of course a place of unique importance to Jews and Christians alike. For the modern use compare William Blake's *Jerusalem* (1804–8):

> I will not cease from mental fight,
> Nor shall my sword sleep in my hand,
> Till we have built Jerusalem
> In England's green and pleasant land.

Jezebel • *shameless, immoral, scheming woman*

Jezebel was the wife of Ahab, king of Israel, whom she introduced to the worship of Baal, the god of the Phoenicians, while persecuting the prophets of the Hebrew god, Jehova, and drawing down upon herself the denunciation of Elijah. In *II Kings*, 9, she is referred to in connection with 'whoredoms' and 'witchcrafts', and her use of cosmetics (verse 30) has given rise to the expression *a painted Jezebel* for a woman who flaunts herself provocatively.

jingo, jingoism

Like **hocus-pocus** and **abracadabra**, jingo was originally a word from conjurers' gibberish when calling for something to appear. It passed into more general use in several emphatic expressions underlining the firmness of a speaker's declaration; *by jingo* is still sometimes heard as a mild asseveration in this way. It was probably slightly stronger when it was used in a popular British music-hall song during the Baltic crisis of 1877–8:

> We don't want to fight but, by jingo, if we do
> We've got the ships, we've got the men, and got the money too . . .
> The Russians shall not have Constantinople.

From this, those who supported the sending of the British fleet into Turkish waters to halt the Russian advance in 1878 were nicknamed *jingoes*. *Jingoism* was coined at the same time to denote belligerent patriotism or warmongering, as it still does.

Job

His story, told in the Old Testament *Book of Job*, is that of a God-fearing man who is suddenly prostrated by a succession of calamities which strip him of goods, children and health. He remains steadfast throughout and these disasters are then revealed to have been God's tests of his faith. Because of his endurance, Job is blessed by God and his prosperity is made greater than before. The *patience of Job* thus became proverbial and is referred to as early as the New Testament (James, 5: 11).

Job also had friends who wrongly attributed his misfortune to his sinfulness. He rejected their interpretation: 'miserable comforters are ye all' (*Job*, 16: 2). A *Job's comforter* is now a person who, in trying to offer help or advice, says something that merely adds to distress.

John Bull   • *personification of the English nation*

John Arbuthnot's *History of John Bull* (1712), a collection of pamphlets advocating an end to the war with France, introduced the allegorical characters of John Bull (representing England), Nicholas Frog (the Dutch), Lewis Baboon (the Bourbon King Louis XIV of France) and others. John Bull then became better known as a cartoon character, originally as a rather stupid figure weighed down by taxation but later as a portly and prosperous one. In the middle and late nineteenth century the *Punch* cartoonists John Leech and Sir John Tenniel developed the now familiar image of a jovial but determined man wearing a **union-jack** waistcoat and accompanied by a **bulldog**, the latter no doubt chosen because of its master's surname and its own qualities of stubborn fearlessness.

Both *John* and *Bull* are common English names, and Arbuthnot originally chose the latter because his satiric purposes required the name of an appropriate animal, but it is interesting to note that there was an actual and famous John Bull (1562–1628) who is sometimes said to be the composer of the British national anthem.

Jonah • *person bringing bad luck*

Ordered by God to go to Nineveh, capital of Assyria, to preach to non-Jews there, Jonah instead took ship for Spain. A furious storm arose and Jonah confessed to the mariners that he was a Hebrew fleeing from God's presence. He asked to be thrown overboard so that God would calm the waters. After having been swallowed by a whale and then spending three days cast up on the shore, he went on to Nineveh and brought the people to repentance. The modern use of his name is based on the incident with the mariners, described in the Old Testament *Jonah*, 1.

Joneses, keeping up with the • *competing with one's neighbours, often to keep up appearances*

Although often used as a disparaging description of social aspiration, this expression had a more jocular origin as the title of a cartoon strip in the New York *Globe* and other newspapers; it first appeared in 1913 and ran for many years. As one of the commonest of surnames, Jones was chosen by the artist, Arthur Momand, in order to indicate the common nature of social rivalry.

jot and tittle, every • *every tiny detail*

From Jesus' Sermon on the Mount: 'Think not that I am come to destroy the law, or the prophets . . . Till heaven and earth pass, one jot or one tittle shall in no wise pass from the law.' (*Matthew*, 5: 17–18). *Jot* is from the Latin *iota*, meaning the Greek letter i, the smallest in the alphabet. A *jot* is therefore a little bit, as is an iota. *Tittle* is a rare word meaning a small mark used in printing or writing; in *jot or tittle* it means the dot on the letter i and therefore merely reinforces the smallness implicit in *jot*.

Tittle also survives in *to a t* (short for tittle), meaning 'with minute exactness'. *Tittle-tattle* is gossip; *tattle* is an old word for chatter and *tittle* was added either to underline the insignificance of small talk or merely to reinforce the onomatopoeia.

journey's end

'Journeys' is a plural noun in 'Journeys end in lovers meeting', a line from the song 'O mistress mine' in *Twelfth Night* (II, 3, line 42). *Journey's End* was the bitter adaptation of the quotation as the title of R. C. Sherriff's lastingly popular play (1928) about young men under stress in the trenches of the First World War; it ends with an explosion in mid-battle.

jovial   • *jolly*

From Jove, an older name for Jupiter, the supreme god of Roman mythology. Astrology held that those born under the planet Jupiter were joyful by temperament.

Judas   • *traitor*

Judas Iscariot, one of the original twelve disciples of Christ, agreed to betray him in return for a bribe (see **silver**). When armed men came to arrest Jesus to take him off for trial, Judas identified him for them by kissing him (*Matthew*, 26: 48–50). He later threw away his bribe and hanged himself. See also **kiss of death**.

judgement: see **Day of Judgement** and **Solomon**

juggernaut   • *overpowering force or object crushing anything in its path; institution or notion requiring complete self-sacrifice; large heavy lorry*

From a Hindi word meaning 'Lord of the World', a title of Krishna, the god of fire, lightning, storms, the heavens and the sun. He was the eighth avatar (incarnation) of Vishnu, the second member of the Hindu trinity, though worshipped by many Hindus as the supreme deity. Krishna's temple is at Puri in Orissa and his idol is annually dragged in procession in an enormous cart; devotees are said to have thrown themselves under its wheels to earn immediate entry to heaven. Hence the modern use of the word to mean an inexorable force, such as a war entailing sacrifice.

jumbo

Originally a noun for a big and clumsy fellow by jocular reference to the imagined size and primitive shape of the **mumbo-jumbo**, a grotesque African idol. The word was thus used as the name of an African elephant acquired by London Zoo in 1865. Jumbo was an enormously popular attraction until he became too dangerous to be ridden by children. His sale in 1882 to the American impressario Phineas T. Barnum caused a public outcry. He was killed by a railway engine in 1885.

Thus the word entered popular vocabulary to signify anything very big, though it has shed its original overtones of comic clumsiness.

jump the gun: see *gun, jump the*

K

kamikase • *potentially self-destructive*

From the Japanese for 'divine wind', the name given in Japanese lore to the wind that destroyed the Mongols' invading navy in 1281. The term became known during the Second World War when some Japanese airmen saw themselves as having a similar role, to the extent of deliberately crashing their planes, sometimes loaded with explosives, into such targets as ships. The adjective is now used figuratively of any thoroughly reckless behaviour, not necessarily military.

kangaroo court • *irregular court, especially one held by striking workers to punish breaches of their rules*

Kangaroo courts originated in American prisons in the nineteenth century as secret, though sometimes condoned, gatherings of inmates to regulate the sharing of tobacco or money or to deal with breaches of the prisoners' code of behaviour. The explanation that *kangaroo* was used in allusion to Australia's history as a prison colony is rather far-fetched. The more likely origin is a comparison between the kangaroo's unconventional method of movement and prisoners who 'jumped over' the rules.

keeping up with the Joneses: see *Joneses*

kettle of fish, pretty or **fine** • *awkward or muddled state of affairs*

A kettle of fish used to be a Scottish term for a picnic by a river, where a kettle of fish, often freshly caught salmon cooked in boiling water, would be served. Whereas a kettle is now thought of as a vessel for heating water and nothing else, it used to be a more general name for a cooking-pot and still has that sense in *fish-kettle*. Why such an outing should have become proverbially associated with muddle is not known, unless it has something to do with Scottish weather.

kibosh or **put the kibosh on**   ●   *put a stop or end to*

The etymology is dubious; it may be from Yiddish, but the most persuasive explanation derives *kibosh* from the Irish *cie bais*, pronounced kye-bosh and meaning 'cap of death', as formerly put on by a judge passing a sentence of death. This clearly relates to the modern meaning and could have been brought over by Irish immigrants as an existing colloquial or slang metaphor.

kick one's heels: see *dance attendance*

kick over the traces: see *traces*

kick the bucket: see *bucket*

kick up a shindy: see *shindy*

kidnap

Simply *kid* (slang for 'child') + *nap* (obsolete slang for 'snatch' or 'seize'). *Nap* was a variant of 'nab', which still exists as a colloquial word with that sense. *Kidnap* was therefore originally a slang term, though it no longer is, and was coined in the seventeenth century to denote the stealing and carrying off of children (and others) to work on the American plantations.

kill the fatted calf: see *fatted calf*

kingdom come   ●   *the next world; life after death*

A rather loose, originally (eighteenth-century) slangy use of a quotation from the Lord's Prayer (*Matthew*, 6: 9–13), where the sentence 'Thy kingdom come' (may thy kingdom come) refers to a present longing, not a future expectation.

kiss of death   • *act or association entailing failure or ruin*

An allusion to the kiss given to Christ by **Judas** which led to Christ's arrest, trial and execution.

kite, fly a   • *express an opinion or proposal to test opinion and gauge opposition or support.*

Kite used to be stock exchange and commercial slang for an accommodation bill, a bill of exchange not representing an actual commercial transaction but drawn up for the purpose of raising money on credit with no capital as security. A person who raised funds in this way was therefore said to be *flying a kite*. The modern meaning, however, does not appear to relate to this but to be a separate metaphor from the idea of 'seeing how the wind blows' (which is what one does in flying a real kite), i.e. finding out in what direction things are tending.

kith and kin   • *blood relatives; members of one's own nation or race*

Originally, and strictly speaking, kith are the people one knows and kin are those to whom one is related, but this distinction is not generally recognised. *Kith* is obsolete except in this expression, and *kin* is not much used except here and in 'next of kin', an official term for one's nearest blood relatives.

knickers

Short for knickerbockers. Either because Knickerbocker was a common surname among Dutch settlers in the USA, or more specifically (and probably) because Diedrich Knickerbocker was the fictitious author of Washington Irving's highly popular burlesque *A History of New York from the Beginning of the World to the End of the Dutch Dynasty* (1809), knickerbockers became the name of the loosely fitting knee-breeches that were favoured by Dutch men and also depicted in George Cruickshank's illustrations to Irving's book. The later abbreviation, *knickers*, was applied to garments that resembled these, such as the baggy golfing trousers that were formerly fashionable and also the women's undergarment of similar appearance in the days before the modern shorter and lighter garment was developed.

knight in shining armour   • *person showing chivalry, especially to women, or coming to the rescue*

Despite its medieval feel this is a twentieth century phrase, first recorded in print in Victor Channing's *Whip Hand* (1965). It originates in the general romantic conception, found in old tales, fairy-stories and Victorian poetry, of the noble knight wandering on horseback in search of good deeds such as rescuing damsels in distress.

See also **Galahad**, **round table** and **Holy Grail**.

knobs on, with   • *with embellishments*

Although primarily a practical object a knob is often decorated, or may be merely an adornment, but in this expression *knobs* is scornful and implies vulgar or spurious adornment. This sense comes from the slang retort 'Same to you, with knobs on', meaning 'I wish the same to you, and much more', said in response to an insult and perhaps drawing some of its force from one of the slang meanings of *knob*, i.e. penis.

knock for six: see *six*

knock spots off: see *spots*

know the ropes: see *ropes*

knuckle

Although the word now generally signifies the finger-joint, it used to be applied to other joints such as the knee. To *knuckle under* (yield) therefore meant to bend the knee in respect or submission.

To *knuckle down* (apply oneself diligently) is, however, a reference to the knuckle of the hand. The term is from marbles, where the knuckle has to be placed down on the ground when playing. It is an important rule of the game that the knuckle must be placed exactly at the spot where one's previous marble ended up. From this sense of strict observance of a rule comes the modern sense of earnest application.

Near the knuckle (almost indecent) is more difficult. It may come from an old proverb expressing approval—'The nearer the bone the sweeter the flesh [meat]'—or from the old school punishment of *rapping the knuckles* of a child with a ruler. The most likely explanation is that when carving a joint of meat one may get 'near the knuckle [bone]' and be unable to cut any further; thus a remark that is *near the knuckle* is close to the limit (of propriety). There is in fact an expression 'near the bone' that means the same.

kowtow   ● *show obsequious deference*

An approximation to a Chinese word for the custom of touching the ground with the forehead as a sign of worship, respect and submission. Variously spelt, it entered English through early nineteenth-century travel literature, acquiring not only a non-literal meaning but also a derogatory sense because the custom was thought to demonstrate unEnglish servility.

L

la-di-da • *affectedly refined, especially in speech*

Originally slang, either an imitation of affected speech or from 'Lard' or 'Lardy', eighteenth-century foppish pronunciation of 'Lord' as a mild oath. The word gained more general currency through a popular and mocking music-hall song of 1880, 'He wears a penny flower in his coat, la-di-da!'. It is now informal rather than slang, and applied to behaviour as well as speech.

labours of Hercules: see *Herculean*

lackadaisical • *listless; lazy, especially in a casual or dreamy way*

Alack is an old exclamation of regret and *alack-a-day* an obsolete one meaning 'what a sad day it is'. From the implied sense of helplessness, or of self-pity as a substitute for self-help, comes the meaning of the familiar modern adjective, itself derived from *alack-a-day*.

laconic • *terse*

From the Greek for 'Laconian', i.e. **Spartan**, an allusion to the reputation of the folk of Sparta for being people of few words.

Lady Bountiful

A wealthy and good-natured lady in *The Beaux' Strategem* (1707), the comedy by George Farquhar (1678–1707). She has somehow passed undeservedly into popular metaphor as the personification of disagreeably patronising or ostentatious charity.

Lady Godiva: see *Tom*

laissez(-)faire • *non-intervention by government in economic (or other) matters*

Laissez faire et laissez passer (roughly, let people do as they think best and let things move as seems necessary) was the maxim of a school of French economists of the eighteenth century, notably Gournay. The philosophy was advocated in England by Adam Smith, the exponent of free trade, and Jeremy Bentham, advocate of individualism. The shortened form of the French slogan, sometimes with an r in place of the z to indicate an infinitive rather than an imperative, is still used in political language.

lamb to the slaughter • *helpless, innocent or naive victim of sacrifice or catastrophe*

The phrase is originally scriptural (*Isaiah*, 53: 7), from a passage normally interpreted as a prophecy of the humiliation and suffering of Christ. The sacrifice of lambs was a feature of Jewish ritual, and references to Christ as 'the Lamb of God' point to his own sacrificial death. These religious senses are absent from modern uses of the expression.

lame duck • *person or thing (often commercial operation) unable to succeed because of irremediable handicap*

Originally stock exchange slang from the mid-eighteenth century for someone unable to meet his or her financial obligations. In nautical slang a damaged ship was known as a *lame duck* because neither can make good progress in the water. Perhaps stock exchange language absorbed the terminology from marine insurers at nearby Lloyds.

land of Nod, in the • *asleep*

A jocular reference to the land to which **Cain** was exiled after his fratricide: 'And Cain went out from the presence of the Lord, and dwelt in the land of Nod, on the east of Eden' (*Genesis*, 4: 16). Jonathan Swift first made the pun on the familiar verb *nod* (show drowsiness) in his *Complete Collection of Polite and Ingenious Conversation* (1738).

landlubber   • *person unfamiliar with the sea and sailing*

Lubber is an obsolete word for a clumsy, slow-witted person. Sailors added the prefix to form what used to be a term of contempt.

lark (about)   • *(enjoy) piece of fun or mischief*

Almost certainly not from the bird, which is not a specially frolicsome one, but from a dialect word *lake* (play) still found in Yorkshire, originally from Scandinavia.

Skylarking, a more recent variant of *larking about*, may have had the same derivation. However, as it seems to have originated in nautical slang for horseplay by seamen up in the rigging, there could additionally be a punning reference to the bird, known for its soaring.

Last Judgement: see *Day of Judgement*

last straw: see *straw*

laugh

The *last laugh* is final success, usually at someone's expense, after previous or apparent defeat. It is a reference to a proverb variously expressed since the fifteenth century but currently *He who laughs last laughs longest*.

To *laugh up one's sleeve* is to laugh secretly, often in mockery or self-satisfaction, usually nastily. It may allude to the time when sleeves were wide enough to hide the face if required (the phrase is first recorded in 1546), or it may merely be a fanciful description of the action of covering a smile with the hand as if actually laughing up one's sleeve.

laureate: see *laurels*

laurels

In the ancient Pythian games held at Delphi in Greece and regarded as second in importance only to the Olympics, the winner was crowned with a wreath of laurels, which has remained a symbol of victory or distinction to the present day. The adjective *laureate* means 'as if crowned with a laurel-wreath as a sign of special honour'. To *rest on one's laurels* is (ill-advisedly) to live off one's reputation or refrain from further effort because of satisfaction with what one has already achieved. To *look to one's laurels* is to take care that no one betters that achievement.

law is an ass, the   • *the law is silly*

Mr Bumble actually said 'If the law supposes that, . . . the law is a ass, a idiot' (Dickens, *Oliver Twist*, 1837–8), but it would be pedantic to insist on accurate quotation of the wording, which was intended to prick the speaker's pomposity. There is a line in *Revenge for Honour* by George Chapman (1559–1634), 'I am ashamed the law is such an ass', but it is Dickens' use that accounts for the currency of the expression.

law of the jungle   • *rules for surviving or succeeding in competition by fighting for oneself*

As law exists to define and safeguard people's rights, the use of *law* in this expression is inexact in that the spirit of 'everyone for himself' is incompatible with fairness or regard for others. There is no such sense in the original coinage by Rudyard Kipling in *The Jungle Book* (1894), which sentimentally portrays the jungle, where the boy Mowgli is educated by animals, as having a rather more caring ethos. Like many expressions, this one has changed its meaning since it was first formulated.

law unto oneself   • *person who follows her or his own rules, not normal conventions*

Biblical, from *Romans*, 2: 14.

lay it on with a trowel: see *trowel*

lead by the nose: see *nose, pay through the*

Lead on, Macduff

A catch-phrase used as a jocular invitation to someone to go first. It is an inveterate misquotation of Macbeth's 'Lay on, Macduff', i.e. 'Come on, attack me', in a sword-fight (V, 8, line 33).

lead up the garden path: see *garden path*

leading question   ● *question that suggests a desired answer*

A legal term for the sort of question not permitted in a court of law in certain circumstances because it puts an answer into the mouth of a witness, i.e. it 'leads' him or her to a particular answer. The term is, however, widely and wrongly used as if it meant 'difficult question'.

leaf from/out of someone's book, take a   ● *follow someone's example*

From the idea of borrowing, stealing or copying a page of someone else's work or, more likely, emulating her or his record (literally, written account) of achievement.

leaf, turn over a new   ● *improve one's conduct*

This does not refer to the leaf of a tree, but of a book. The comparison is between a new page and a new beginning. The earlier form of the expression, simply 'turn the leaf', was rather clearer.

leap in the dark   ● *something done without knowledge of the consequences*

The dying words of the philosopher Thomas Hobbes (1588–1679) are usually quoted as 'I am going to take a great leap into obscurity', though some authorities quote him as saying ' . . . a fearful leap in the dark'. The phrase became better known through Sir John Vanbrugh's comedy *The Provok'd Wife* (1697): 'Now I am in for Hobbes' voyage, a great leap in the dark'.

leave in the lurch: see *lurch*

leave no stone unturned: see *stone unturned, leave no*

left hand does not know what the right hand is doing
● *confusion reigns (e.g. in a large organisation)*

The original is in fact an injunction to be discreet in doing good: 'But when thou doest alms, let not thy left hand know what thy right hand doeth: That thine alms may be secret: and thy Father which seeth in secret himself shall reward thee openly' (from Jesus' Sermon on the Mount, *Matthew*, 6: 3–4).

Legion, their name is; they are legion　　● *they are numerous*

Variants of 'My name is Legion, for we are many' (*Mark*, 5: 9), the words of an 'unclean spirit' when asked by Jesus to name itself. The spirit or devil had been tormenting a man; once it had identified itself as a body of demons, Jesus cast them out into a herd of swine: see **Gadarene**. The *legion* referred to was a body of Roman troops, about 3,000–6,000 strong excluding cavalry.

lemmings

The popular superstition that these small Arctic rodents (they look like six-inch-long fieldmice with short tails) periodically take part in mass migrations to the sea only to plunge in and deliberately drown themselves is without foundation. They do migrate, and some do drown, but suicide is no part of their purpose.

Some expressions compare people with lemmings. These comparisons are valid if they imply mindless rushing along with the herd, but not if they imply inevitable self-destruction.

Leninism: see *Marxist-Leninism*

leopard cannot change its spots, the　　● *a person's character cannot be changed*

An allusion to the Old Testament book of *Jeremiah*: 'Can the Ethiopian change his skin, or the leopard his spots' (13: 23).

leotard • *skin-tight garment worn by dancers, gymnasts, etc*

Invented by the popular and successful French trapeze-artist Jules Leotard (1842–70), said to be the original 'daring young man on the flying trapeze' in the popular song of 1860. He wrote: 'Do you want to be adored by the ladies? A trapeze is not required, but . . . put on more natural garb, which does not hide your best features'.

lesbian • *homosexual female*

Derived from the name of Sappho of Lesbos, a Greek poetess of about 600 BC whose verses are about love between women. Lesbos is an island in the Greek archipelago.

let the cat out of the bag: see *cat out of the bag*

letter, the • *the strict or literal meaning, often as opposed to the spirit in which something (e.g. the law) is intended*

The distinction between *letter* and spirit originates in scripture, where Christians are described as 'ministers of the new testament; not of the letter but of the spirit: for the letter killeth but the spirit giveth life' (*II Corinthians*, 3: 6).

leviathan • *something huge and powerful*

This is from a Hebrew word for a sea-monster, real or imaginary, frequently mentioned in Hebrew poetry and familiar in English from the Old Testament, where it seems to mean a whale (*Job*, 41: 1; Psalm 74: 14, etc.) or sea-serpent (*Isaiah*, 27: 1). In modern use the word does not necessarily imply any connection with the sea.

liberty hall or **Liberty Hall** • *place where one may do as one pleases*

A coinage by Oliver Goldsmith in *She Stoops to Conquer* (1773): 'This is Liberty-hall, gentlemen. You may do just as you please here'.

189

lick and a promise • *something done hurriedly, especially a quick wash*

Probably a fanciful reference to the way in which a cat licks its paw and passes it over the face as if promising to have a more thorough wash later.

lick into shape • *put into proper form or condition*

The widespread old belief that bear-cubs are born shapeless and have to be literally licked into their familiar shape by their parents is first recorded in English in *The Pilgrimage of Souls* (1413): 'Bears be brought forth all foul and transformed and after that by licking of the father and the mother they be brought into their kindly [natural] shape'. The same idea occurs in writings as various as those of the fourth-century Roman grammarian Donatus and the eleventh-century Arab physician Avicenna.

life: see *Riley, live the life of*

Lilliputian • *very small (person)*

The inhabitants of the island of Lilliput in Jonathan Swift's satire *Gulliver's Travels* (1726) were only six inches high, with the result that their civil disturbances, their war with their neighbours and the pomp of their emperor look ridiculous, in accordance with the author's intention of mocking aspects of human behaviour. In modern use *Lilliputian* often implies puny moral stature.

limb, out on a • *in an exposed and precarious position*

Limb has long been standard English for a main branch of a tree, though it is little used in that sense. American English has retained the use of the word, however, and has recently (about 1945, perhaps from infiltration by American servicemen's vocabulary) exported the idea of someone being *out on a limb*, i.e. at the end of a branch, unable to go any further or at risk of having his position collapse under him.

limbo, in • *in a state of being lost, forgotten, deserted or unwanted; not knowing what to do because of lack of information, etc*

Originally a technical term in medieval Christian (Roman Catholic) theology. It is a form of the Latin *limbus* (border, edge), as found specially in *limbus infantum* (the abode of children who died before baptism) and *limbus patrum* (the abode of the just who died before Christ, thus lacking redemption but not through their own fault). These notions were much discussed and were referred to in imaginative literature such as Dante's. From meaning a region on the border of hell, not in hell but not in heaven either, *limbo* came to acquire its modern meaning.

limelight • *centre or position of public attention*

In the days before electric lighting, theatre stages were illuminated by the intense white light produced by heating lime in an oxyhydrogen flame. This was called limelight, as was the mechanism that produced it. A person who is said to be in or enjoy the limelight is therefore being compared to an actor on stage.

lion, beard the: see *beard the lion*

lion's den: see *Daniel in the lion's den*

lion's share • *largest portion*

Aesop tells the story of a hunt by a lion and an ass at the end of which the lion divides the spoils into three. He claims the first as king of the animals and the second as equal partner with the ass. As for the third, he advises the ass that it will get him into trouble unless he makes himself scarce.

lips are sealed: see *seal*

little bird told me: see *bird told me, little*

live the life of Riley: see *Riley*

live to fight another day • *survive an ordeal*

'He that fights and runs away may live to fight another day' is an old saying known in various forms in English since 1250 but found also in Greek, perhaps originating with the orator Demosthenes in the fourth century BC.

191

lock, stock and barrel   • *completely*

The three principal components that make up an entire firearm: the *lock* is the firing mechanism, the *stock* is the handle or wooden shoulder-piece to which it is attached, and the *barrel* is the tube down which the bullet is fired.

loggerheads, at   • *in a state of dispute*

This expression has been much discussed, with reference to several meanings of *loggerhead*: a heavy wooden block fastened to the leg of a grazing animal to prevent straying (liable to entanglements, as a quarrel is?); an implement for melting tar on board ship (used as a weapon?); a wooden post on a whale-boat for wrapping a rope round (therefore associated with friction?).

All these are suspect in various ways and as usual the simplest explanation is the best. *Logger* is dialect for 'log' in the first of the above senses. The primary meaning of *loggerhead* is therefore 'blockhead' (wooden head) or 'fool'. As two people locked in dispute are usually equally pig-headed it seems obvious to say that they are both (at) *loggerheads*.

long chalk(s): see *chalk up*

long in the tooth: see *gift-horse*

long shot: see *shot*

long time no see

Catch-phrase used on meeting someone after a long time. It apparently comes from the USA, but far from being a jocular or Hollywood parody of the limited English of the American Indians, as has been suggested, it is a direct translation of the Chinese equivalent and obviously originated among Chinese immigrant communities learning to speak English in the United States.

loophole   • *anything providing a means of taking advantage*

A vertical slit or opening in the wall of a fortification such as a castle, allowing a defender to look out or shoot while remaining protected, was called a *loophole* from a Dutch word meaning 'to peer'. Metaphorically, therefore, the word means a gap (e.g. omission, error, ambiguity) that one can exploit.

loose end(s)

To be *at a loose end* is to be unoccupied. The phrase was originally 'at loose ends', a nautical term for the condition of a rope when unattached and therefore neglected or not doing its job. When one *ties up the loose ends* one settles the final details of a matter as a sailor makes the loose ends of ropes shipshape.

lose one's rag: see *chew the rag*

Lothario, (gay)　　● *(cheerful) womaniser*

The original was actually a heartless seducer in Nicholas Rowe's tragedy *The Fair Penitent* (1703). The name, but not the character, is found in other and earlier works.

lotus-eater　　● *person living in dreamy indolence, detached from reality*

Travelling homeward from Troy, Odysseus and his followers came to the North African land of the Lotophagi or lotus-eaters, a people who lived on the fruit of the lotus, which induced dreamy forgetfulness. When Odysseus sent out a search party its members tasted the lotus, became oblivious to friends and homes, lost all desire to leave the country and had to be forcibly brought back to the ship (Homer, *Odyssey*, IX, line 90ff). This legend, later popularised by Tennyson's poem *The Lotos-Eaters* (1833), is the origin of the phrase, which now sometimes has overtones of luxurious ease.

love lost, no　　● *dislike, hatred*

A curious phrase which originally meant what it looks as if it ought still to mean, i.e. that no love is lost and that affection is mutual. This sense dates from the sixteenth century and was still found in the nineteenth. However, an opposite meaning—that no love exists—inexplicably started to appear in the seventeenth century and has outlived the first.

lowbrow: see *highbrow*

lucre: see *filthy lucre*

Luddite   ● *opponent of change in working practices, especially automation or innovation in industry or technology*

At the beginning of the Industrial Revolution a group of Nottinghamshire textile workers, fearing unemployment as a result of the introduction of new labour-saving machines, smashed them in order to protect the traditional exercise of their own skills. They called themselves *Luddites*. Their movement spread throughout the Midlands and northern England; riots, beginning in 1811, lasted some five years and brought imprisonments and executions in their wake.

No one is sure where the name *Luddite* came from. The most common explanation is that the machine-breakers took it from Ned Lud(d), a labourer of the nearby county of Leicestershire, who is said to have broken up knitting machines belonging to a stocking-maker towards the end of the previous century. It is not known whether he did this because of his opposition to mechanisation, or because, being reputedly half-witted, he went **berserk**, or indeed whether he ever existed.

The word is sometimes used in contexts unconnected with industrial practices but it is always derogatory, implying stubborn wrong-headedness, short-sightedness or violent obstructiveness.

lumber, lumbered

The Lombards, natives of Lombardy, a region of what is now northern Italy, were successful as bankers, money-lenders and pawnbrokers; 'lombard' entered the English language to denote a person engaged in any of these activities. A lombard, of which a variant was *lumber*, was additionally a pawnbroking establishment, and the modern expression *to be in lumber* (in trouble) stems from this association with debt.

Another meaning of *lumber* is disused furniture, useless odds and ends and other things that take up space (as in *lumber-room*). It is possible that this sense comes from one of the meanings of lombard—a pawnshop does contain a miscellany of goods—but it is impossible to be sure. What can be said is that *lumbered* (left with something unwanted or unpleasant) comes from this general sense of clutter.

lunacy: see *midsummer madness*

lurch, leave in the   • *leave (person) in adverse circumstances; abandon in a vulnerable position*

Lurch was an old game resembling backgammon. The word also came to be used, in a number of games, to denote a score in which the winner was far ahead of the opponent; in cribbage, for example, one was said to be *in the lurch* if the winner scored the full 61 before one had turned the corner of the board by scoring 31. From this idea of disadvantage the now-familiar meaning of the term emerged over 400 years ago.

It is impossible to explain the connection between *lurch* as the name of a game and the use of the word to mean a decisive defeat. Both usages are lost in the mists of time. *Lurch* itself, like several terms in sports and games, is from the French. No doubt the expression survived because of its neat alliteration, a feature of many popular terms.

lynch   • *execute illegally by mob action*

Believed to be derived from the name of one of two men called Lynch, both operating in Virginia, USA, in the late eighteenth century. One of them was Charles (1736–96), a magistrate who presided over extra-legal trials of Tories during the war of independence. The more popular candidate is a Captain or Colonel William Lynch (1742–1820), known to have formed squads of vigilantes who took the law into their own hands. He first organised illegal judicial tribunals in 1780 and is believed to have originated the so-called *Lynch law*, i.e. law as defined by an unconstitutional court, though the term now usually means rule by the mob.

Some have objected that neither man was famous for hanging people, an important part of the modern definition of lynching. That is immaterial: in its original definition a lynching was a summary punishment by a self-constituted body without legal authority; it was not necessarily a hanging—whipping and tarring and feathering were also used. Historically, *Lynch law* came first, then the verb *lynch*, then the association with hanging.

M

macadam: see *tarmac*

machiavellian   ● *cunning, deceitful, unprincipled and opportunist*

Niccolò Machiavelli (1469–1527), the Florentine statesman and political theorist, is best known for his influential *The Prince* (1513) which taught that the acquisition and use of political power may require unethical methods. He was scholarly, subtle and realistic, and much of what he wrote was inspired by current turbulence in Italy and directed to the achievement of peaceful and prosperous government. However, it is his advocacy of unscrupulous and brutal tactics that is mainly remembered and is commemorated in the opprobrious adjective his name has given to the language.

mack or **mac**   ● *raincoat*

Short for 'mackintosh', occasionally more correctly spelt 'macintosh', after Charles Macintosh (1766–1843), the industrial chemist who discovered a method of waterproofing cloth by cementing layers of it with india rubber. A surgeon called James Syme is said to have invented the method but Macintosh perfected and patented it (1823) and set up a company under his name to sell the first ready-to-wear garments in 1830. He also gave his name to the material and to the clothes made from it (originally known by their full names as Macintosh coats, cloaks, etc.). The word is still used for a raincoat, even though the heavy, bulky material Macintosh developed has long since been superseded by modern and lighter products.

mad as a hatter or March hare

Although the Mad Hatter and March Hare are best known as eccentric characters in *Alice's Adventures in Wonderland* (1865), they were proverbial before then.

The expression *mad as a hatter* may be related to the use of a mercury compound in the treatment of felt in hat-making; its vapour was said to cause twitching in the limbs and affect the brain. Another explanation is that *hatter* is a development from the obsolete 'atter' (meaning venom, especially that of reptiles), so that the expression originally had to do with the imagined effects of poisoning. But in view of the existence of many other expressions such as 'mad as a hornet/buck/wet hen/meat-axe', it is likely that *hatter* is equally fanciful.

There is similar uncertainty about the March hare. Some say that *March* was originally 'marsh', a place where various factors (damp, lack of cover, difficulty of burrowing) caused unpredictable behaviour. A better explanation is that the hare is prone to skittish behaviour in March because it is the mating season.

maddening crowd • *people, or society in general, behaving in a way that makes one angry*

A common misquotation, and consequent misinterpretation, of a phrase from Thomas Gray's *Elegy Written in a Country Churchyard* (1751):

Far from the madding crowd's ignoble strife,
Their sober wishes never learned to stray . . .

from which Thomas Hardy took the title of his novel *Far from the Madding Crowd* (1874). 'Madding' means 'acting madly', which is not the same as *maddening* (intolerable).

Mae West • *inflatable life-jacket for airmen*

This Second World War nickname derives from the supposed resemblance of the shape of the wearer of this jacket, when inflated, to that of the popular film actress (1892–1980) who had a buxom figure. She is also held responsible for the suggestive catch-phrase 'Come up and see me sometime' which does not in fact occur in any of her films, though she does say, 'Come up some time and see me' in *She Done Him Wrong* (1933).

maelstrom   • *exceptionally turbulent state of affairs, especially one with destructive power*

A metaphorical use of the name of a famous whirlpool near the Lofoten Islands off the north-east coast of Norway, formerly reputed to be able to suck in and sink ships within a wide radius. Legend has it that the original maelstrom was created when a ship carrying two magic millstones sank there and that the millstones continue to revolve at the bottom of the sea. The first syllable of the word is from a Dutch verb meaning 'grind'.

mafia   • *clique exercising powerful influence and control*

A jocular but uncomplimentary allusion to the criminal organisation founded in Sicily and taking its name (with a capital M) from a Sicilian dialect word for 'boldness' or 'bragging', probably derived from an Arabic word meaning 'boasting'.

magazine   • *periodical publication with articles by various writers*

Originally this word meant 'storehouse' (from an Arabic word of the same meaning), a sense now retained only in military terminology. The modern meaning is entirely due to the publication in 1731 of *The Gentleman's Magazine*, the first issue of which explained its choice of title in terms of its intention 'to promote a monthly collection to treasure [store] up, as in a magazine, the most remarkable pieces . . . '

Mahomet   • *Old name for* **Mohammed**

make assurance doubly sure: see *assurance*

make do and mend   • *manage with whatever is available*

An adaptation of the earlier 'make and mend', a nautical term for a period—usually an afternoon—set aside for mending clothes.

make ends meet: see *ends meet*

make no bones about: see *bones*

malapropism • *misuse of a word by unintentionally substituting it for the correct one, with ludicrous effect*

An example of a malapropism is 'sociable worker' instead of 'social worker'. The word had its origin in Mrs Malaprop, a comic character in Sheridan's comedy *The Rivals* (1775) who was prone to making such errors. Sheridan derived her name from the existing 'malapropos' (from the French *mal à propos*, inopportune), meaning 'inappropriate'.

mammon • *wealth seen as a cause of corruption or as a false god*

The word, ultimately from the Aramaic for 'riches', came into English by way of the Bible: 'Ye cannot serve God and mammon' (*Matthew*, 6: 24). Because of this juxtaposition with God it is often written as *Mammon*, a personification of riches and greed regarded as an idol.

man of straw: see *straws, clutch at*

mandarin • *high-ranking bureaucrat, especially civil servant*

Anglicisation of the Portuguese name for a senior official under the Chinese Empire who belonged to any of the nine ranks of officialdom. Perhaps these oriental associations were thought apt for inscrutable British civil servants, members of a race apart with a language all their own.

manna from heaven • *unexpected gift or source of benefit*

When the Israelites complained of hunger on their way from Egypt to the **Promised Land**, God assured Moses that he would 'rain bread from heaven' (*Exodus*, 16:4). They subsequently found one morning 'a small round thing, as small as the hoar frost on the ground' (verse 14) and called it *manna*. 'And Moses said unto them, This is the bread which the Lord hath given you to eat' (verse 15). It is described as being sweet like honey and the Israelites lived off it for 40 years. In the New Testament *manna* is referred to as a symbol of God's blessing (*Revelation*, 2: 17) and the modern meaning is a debased form of this.

manner born, to the   • *naturally suited to a particular position or activity as if accustomed to it by birth and breeding in society*

The full Shakespearean quotation from which this comes is given at **more honoured in the breach**. When Hamlet used the expression of himself he meant 'destined by birth to be subject to a particular custom'.

man's inhumanity to man

A quotation from Robert Burns' poem *Man was made to Mourn* (line 55):

Man's inhumanity to man
Makes countless thousand mourn!

marathon   • *long-distance race; any very lengthy proceeding*

In 490 BC the outnumbered Greeks won a decisive victory over the Persians at Marathon, north-east of Athens, killing over 6,000 Persians and suffering losses of only 200. Legend has it that news of the victory was brought to Athens by a runner who promptly collapsed and died after his arrival there. When the first modern Olympic Games took place at Athens in 1896, a race called the *marathon* was instituted to commemorate this event and was run over 26 miles; the current distance, which adds 385 yards to that, was standardised in 1924 when the finishing line was repositioned in front of the royal box.

It is alleged that the original story is a mis-reporting of an even greater feat of stamina, a 150-mile run in two days from Athens to Sparta by Pheidippides to call soldiers to the Battle of Marathon. Perhaps both runs took place; in any event it is the courier from Marathon who is normally thought of as having founded the race.

The word is usually spelt with a capital letter in the name of a particular race (*the Berlin Marathon*) and with a small one in more general contexts (*a marathon court-case*). Both usages date on from 1896 as a direct result of the establishment of the modern Olympics.

mare's nest   • *supposedly important but actually valueless or illusory discovery; hoax*

An old country joke: horses, of course, do not nest.

marines, tell that to the   ● *that is nonsense*

Or, more accurately, the marines may believe that but no one else will.

Before marines achieved their modern reputation as commandos they were soldiers raised for sea-service (originally in the seventeenth century) and trained for maritime warfare. As such they were looked down on by sailors, who saw themselves as skilled members of a senior service; in fact soldiers at that time were not highly regarded by anyone. The expression originated in naval circles with the implication that marines were ignorant enough to believe anything.

mark, up to the   ● *up to standard*

The starting-line for a race used to be called the *mark*, perhaps a line scratched on the ground, which is why a starter still orders runners to 'take your marks'. A person who comes *up to the mark* is therefore fit and ready. *Mark* is also, however, a word for criterion or sign of quality (as in **hallmark**) and the expression is probably literal rather than figurative.

martinet   ● *strict disciplinarian*

An eponym derived from the name of the Marquis de Martinet, a seventeenth-century French colonel or general who served under Louis XIV and devised a system of training, including drill and punishment, of exceptional fierceness. The noun is no longer restricted to military discipline.

Marxist-Leninism   ● *the political and economic principles of Marx as put into practice by Lenin*

Karl Marx (1818–83), the German philosopher, was the principal theoretician of communism who devised the maxim 'from each according to his abilities, to each according to his needs', defined economic value in terms of human labour and wrote of a class struggle leading to a classless society and the end of capitalism. Lenin (1870–1924) led the Russian Revolution and established in 1917 a government on communist lines, a 'dictatorship of the proletariat' soon to be overtaken by **Stalinism**.

masochism • *(apparent) enjoyment of abuse, pain, domination or cruelty inflicted on oneself by another person*

Initially a scientific term coined by the German neurologist and psychiatrist Krafft-Ebing from the name of Leopold von Sacher-Masoch (1836–95), an Austrian novelist who wrote of the sexual pleasure gained from pain and humiliation inflicted on him by women. The word was therefore an academic identification of a specific form of sexual perversion. It retains this meaning, but is now also more generally used of submissiveness not associated with sexual gratification.

See also **sadism/sado-masochism**.

masterpiece • *most outstanding piece of work*

Originally a craftsman's piece of work done as a test-piece to gain the recognised rank of 'master' from a guild, the medieval con-fraternity responsible for standards (etc.) within a particular craft.

Mata Hari • *alluring, mysterious woman whose attraction brings men into danger, betrayal, compromise, etc*

This was the stage name of a striptease-dancer who became a famous First World War spy. She was of Dutch nationality and was persuaded by the Germans to spy on Allied officers by seducing them and passing back secrets. When discovered, she was tried and sentenced to death by the French in 1917, and embellished her reputation by allegedly opening her dress to reveal her naked body in a last-minute but unsuccessful attempt to unnerve the firing squad.

matinée idol • *handsome man of the kind supposed to be attractive to women attending matinée (i.e. afternoon) theatre performances*

That is to say, conventionally clean-cut, correct, romantic and rather shallow. Matinée audiences used to be rather looked down on, the assumption being that they were composed of bored middle-aged women who went to the theatre as much for the tea as the cultural experience, and whose interests focused on the actors' appearance more than on their ability.

maudlin • *mawkishly or tearfully sentimental, especially when drunk*

The vernacular form of 'Magdalen(e)' (which is why the names of Magdalen College, Oxford, and Magdalene College, Cambridge, are pronounced 'maudlin'). Mary Magdalene (i.e. Mary from Magdala in Israel) was a follower of Jesus (*Luke*, 8: 2) who has been identified, perhaps incorrectly, as the prostitute forgiven by him in the previous chapter (verses 36–50). In Christian art St Mary Magdalene—as she later became—is often depicted washing the feet of Jesus with her tears (verse 44) or weeping at his crucifixion. This accounts for the lachrymose associations of *maudlin*.

mausoleum • *stately tomb, especially in the form of a building*

After the death in 353 BC of Mausolus, king of Caria in Asia Minor, his widow constructed at Halicarnassus a magnificent tomb 140 feet high, decorated with colossal statues and beautiful friezes carved by leading Greek sculptors, which became one of the seven wonders of the world. This tomb was known as the Mausoleum; it was later destroyed, though parts survive in the British Museum. The word has passed into English as a common noun now chiefly found in comparisons designed to bring out the deathly silence, cheerlessness or gloom of particular places.

maverick • *independent, unorthodox or nonconformist person*

Samuel Maverick (1803–70) was a Texan ranch-owner who in 1845 accepted 400 cattle as payment for a debt but neglected to brand them; they ran wild and were caught, branded and claimed by others. Although this was legal (ownership being determined by branding), it was not regarded as honest, and as a result of Maverick's objections unbranded cattle found wandering became known as *Maverick's* or *mavericks*. The word spread to politics—Maverick himself was involved in the struggle for Texan independence and served in the Texan legislature—as a name for unattached politicians, those giving no allegiance to a political party or leadership, but it no longer has this exclusively political connotation.

McCarthyism • *use of crude, unsubstantiated accusation, espe-cially that of disloyalty or subversion, to discredit an individual*

Joseph McCarthy (1909–57) was a US Senator who in 1950 was appointed chairman of a sub-committee on investigations whose proceedings came to be nationally known through television. The committee concerned itself with alleged communist infiltra-tion of national life, notably in the State Department and the film industry. Many individuals were ruthlessly cross-examined and effectively discredited in an atmosphere of fanatical witch-hunting, even though actual proof was usually lacking. McCar-thy's activities came to an end in 1954 when his excesses were censured by the Senate.

McCoy, the real • *the genuine person or thing*

Boxers, like wrestlers, actors and circus performers, have some-times preferred more glamorous names than the ones they got from their parents. Either for this reason or simply because he felt his name lacked punch, the successful American boxer Norman Selby (1873–1940) adopted the professional name Kid McCoy, a neatly near-alliterative combination of slangy youthfulness and exotic Irishness. There is no agreement about where the 'real' came from. One story has it that Selby/McCoy, challenged by a man in a bar to prove his identity, knocked him out and was then pronounced 'the real McCoy', a term which McCoy liked so much that he retained it. Another story is that he had to start billing himself as 'the real McCoy' to distingish himself from another boxer of that name, or from prize-fighters who styled themselves 'Kid McCoy' at fairgrounds and elsewhere to gull the public; the sport was not much regulated at the time.

In transferring itself to Britain the expression may have modi-fied an existing one, 'the real Mackay', used to promote a brand of whisky in a running dispute over leadership of the clan.

mealy-mouthed • *unwilling or afraid to speak plainly*

Although this now implies insincerity or even hypocrisy, it originally meant no more than 'soft-spoken'. *Mealy* is the adjec-tive from 'meal' in its sense of powdered grain, as in wholemeal. *Mealy-mouthed* therefore expressed a comparison between a soft voice (of diminished strength) and soft grain (reduced to powder from its original size).

meat is another man's poison, one man's

Described as an 'old moth-eaten proverb' as long ago as 1604, this was first expressed in *De Rerum Natura* by Lucretius, the first-century BC Roman poet, as 'What is food for some is black poison to others'.

mecca   • *outstanding place attracting many devotees because of its unique importance as a centre of excellence in a particular activity*

For example, Wimbledon as the *mecca* (or *Mecca*) of tennis. The real Mecca, in Saudi Arabia, is the birthplace of **Mohammed** and therefore the holiest city of Islam. The faithful turn towards it whenever they pray and it is a major centre of pilgrimage.

melting pot: see *pot*

mentor   • *guide or wise counsellor*

From the name of Mentor, friend and adviser of Odysseus and tutor of his son Telemachus in Homer's *Odyssey*. The goddess Athene assumed Mentor's shape when she guided Telemachus in his search for his father after the fall of Troy.

Mephistophelean   • *devilish*

Mephistopheles is the German name for the devil-figure to whom **Faust** sold his soul in German legend. It first appears in the *Faustbuch* of 1587 and was used by Marlowe and Goethe in their versions of the story.

mercurial   • *volatile; subject to rapid, unpredictable fluctuations*

An allusion to one of the properties of mercury, sometimes called quicksilver, which is very responsive and can form itself into globules that move rapidly on a surface of the slightest uneven-ness. The metal is named after the Roman god Mercury, who acted as the swift messenger of the gods and is normally repres-ented as having a winged helmet and sandals. Quickness is therefore common to the adjective, the chemical and the god.

merry England

Not mirthful (or tipsy) but pleasant and delightful, the original but now obsolete meaning of *merry*.

mesmerise   • *hold in a trance-like state*

Friedrich Mesmer (1734–1815), a German doctor, developed a theory of 'animal magnetism' by means of which he claimed to be able to effect cures, especially of nervous disorders. His methods were discredited, but after his death a Scottish surgeon, James Braid, helped to mend his reputation by identifying as 'hypnosis' the method Mesmer had used; it continues to have a place in medical practice. *Mesmerism* has now lost this technical sense and the verb which is derived from it means no more than to spellbind or fascinate.

mess of pottage, sell one's birthright for: see *pottage*

method in one's madness   • *an element of good sense in otherwise senseless behaviour*

An adaptation of Polonius' comment on Hamlet's madness in which there are moments of sanity: 'Though this be madness, yet there is method in't' (II, 2, line 211). *Method* here means 'orderliness of thought'.

Methuselah, as old as   • *extremely old*

Methuselah was an Old Testament patriarch known only as grandfather of Noah and the oldest man in the Bible: according to *Genesis*, 5: 27, he lived for 969 years.

Micawber(-ish)

Mr Micawber, a character in Dickens' *David Copperfield* (1849–50), is impecunious but incurably optimistic, always expecting something to 'turn up'. He is portrayed as mercurial but essentially good-natured and ends as a respected magistrate, albeit in Australia.

mickey mouse • *inferior, cheap, shoddy*

The name of the popular film-cartoon character invented by Walt Disney acquired this modern slang meaning in the USA, and later in Britain, after the 1940s as a result of one of the earliest examples of linking the sale of a commercial product with the name of a 'sponsoring' celebrity. Children's 'Mickey Mouse watches' were both cheap and unreliable, which is how the name (usually without capital letters) came to be applied to anything, including organisations, thought to be third-rate.

mickey, take the • *make fun of*

Mike Bliss, sometimes shortened to Mike, is Cockney rhyming slang for 'piss'; it is not known who he was or even if he ever existed. To *take the mickey* (Mickey being a variant of Mike, short for Michael) is a euphemism for 'take the piss' (jeer at, deride, deflate—perhaps from the idea of deflating the bladder). The meaning is kinder too.

Midas touch • *special knack of making money*

Midas succeeded his father Gordius (see **Gordian knot**) as king of Phrygia. According to Greek legend, he earned the gratitude of Dionysus by showing kindness to one of the god's followers and so was granted a wish. Midas asked that everything he touched should be turned to gold, but soon came to regret this when his food was made inedible whenever he touched it. Fortunately Dionysus took pity on him and revoked the gift.

middlebrow: see *highbrow*

midnight oil: see *burn the midnight oil*

midsummer madness • *the height of folly*

Intermittent insanity used to be attributed to the changes of the moon, which is why the word 'lunacy' is derived from the Latin for moon, *luna*. The height of madness was supposed to coincide with the height of summer (i.e. midsummer, the period of the summer solstice, about June 21) and with the lunar month during which it falls.

207

milk

The *milk of human kindness* is ordinary everyday kindness. The phrase was first coined by Shakespeare in *Macbeth*, I, 5, lines 13–14:

Yet I do fear thy nature
It is too full o' th' milk of human kindness . . .

As the speaker, Lady Macbeth, regarded this as a weakness (milk being baby-food), the image did not mean quite what it now does.

The phrase *milk and honey* is sometimes used to mean abundance and ease. It first occurred in 'a land flowing with milk and honey', an image of the divine blessings available in the **Promised Land** (*Exodus*, 3: 8).

milksop   • *ineffectual person*

Originally, a milksop was a piece of bread soaked in milk. As such it was suitable food for a baby, invalid or old person without teeth. From these associations developed the modern meaning. See also **sop**.

mill

'Grist' is corn that is to be ground; *grist to the mill* thus used to mean business providing profit, but it now more usually means work that has to be done. To be put *through the mill* is to suffer an ordeal, as if being crushed by a **millstone**, like grain.

Anything *run of the mill* is routine, ordinary and to be expected. The expression was originally a technical or jargon term in manufacturing. A 'run' is, among other things, a spell of allowing machines to operate or a period of manufacturing a product. The 'run of the mill' was the material produced (in a mill) before its inspection for quality: in a cotton or woollen mill, for example, it might include both good and inferior cloth, which then had to be sorted or trimmed. Thus anything *run of the mill* was average or undistinguished.

The *mills of God* are the workings of God's purposes. The expression is best known from Longfellow's poem 'Retribution':

Though the mills of God grind slowly, yet they grind exceeding small;

Though with patience He stands waiting, with exactness grinds He all.

The same image, however, with 'gods' rather than 'God', is found in the Greek of Sextus Empiricus (second century AD) and variants occur in some later writers before Longfellow.

millennium   ● *period of bliss and benign government in the distant future*

A secular and often cynical adaptation of the Christian millennium, which is the period of 1,000 years during which Christ will reign in person on earth, according to the prophecy of *Revelation*, 20: 1–5. A millennium is, literally, 1,000 years or a thousandth anniversary.

millstone round one's neck   ● *thing or person acting as an encumbrance*

'Whoso shall offend one of these little ones [children] which believe in me, it were better for him that a millstone were hanged about his neck, and that he were drowned in the depth of the sea' (*Matthew*, 18: 6). A millstone was a large, heavy, flat circular stone with a central hole; turned by the action of a water-wheel, sails, etc. at a mill, it was used to grind or crush grains.

mince matters or **one's words, not to**   ● *speak bluntly*

An image from the mincing of meat to make it easier to swallow or more digestible.

mind one's p's and q's: see *p's*

miss is as good as a mile, a

A comforting catch-phrase used of a lucky escape. It would make better sense as 'a near-miss . . . ', for that is what it means. It is a modern version of a much older and more explicit expression 'An inch in a miss is as good as an ell'; an ell was originally 18 inches and later 45.

miss the bus   ● *lose an opportunity*

This expression is said to originate in an Oxford story of the 1840s about John Henry Newman, fellow of Oriel College, vicar of the University Church and one of the foremost theologians of his time. Newman's decision to join the Roman Catholic Church—in which he later became a Cardinal—was an event of great importance in its day. One of his Oxford adherents, Mark Pattison, set off to talk to him at the time this fateful decision was being made, but missed the bus and therefore also missed a conversation that may have taken him too to Rome. Unkind commentators suggested that Pattison's mishap was in fact a serious failure of nerve, and this gossip gave jocular notoriety to his excuse that he had merely missed the bus.

moaning Minnie or **minnie**   ● *person who complains a lot*

This is not First World War slang, despite what some commentators have said. 'Minnie' was: it was the name given to the devastating German trench-mortar (*Minenwerfer*). It was never called 'moaning', however, for it did not make a moaning sound in flight; small ones arrived silently and larger ones made a woofing sound as they turned in the air.

The full expression made its first appearance in Second World War civilian slang. Air-raid sirens were given several nicknames: the warning siren was variously called Wailing Winnie, Mona (existing London slang for a complaining female, a pun on 'moaner') and Moaning Minnie, a mixture of the previous two. There is evidence that after the **blitz** the phrase *moaning Minnie* was adopted by the army to designate the multi-barrelled German field-mortar and its shell, thus uniting trench slang of the First World War and civilian slang of the Second.

After the war the expression continued in use, though 'moaning' now means 'grumbling', as it has done informally for a long time, and Minnie can be a person of either sex.

mogul   ● *wealthy and prominent businessperson, usually male*

Originally a mispronunciation of 'Mongol', an inhabitant of Mongolia. It was also used as the name (often Great or Grand Mogul) of any of the emperors of the great Muslim-Tartar empire in India (1526–1857), centred on Delhi and at one time covering most of Hindustan. Something of the autocracy and grandeur of empire has passed over into the modern metaphorical use of the word.

Mohammed • *(properly Muhammad)*

The founder (570–632 AD) of Islam, the Muslim religion. *If the mountain will not come to Mohammed, Mohammed must go to the mountain* advises swallowing one's pride in order to take the initiative in something. The story behind the saying is that when people asked Mohammed to give miraculous proof of his teaching he ordered a mountain to move towards him; when it did not do so he used the incident as a lesson that God had spared them from destruction by the mountain, and he went to it to offer thanks for God's mercy. The story first appeared in English in Francis Bacon's *Essays* ('On Boldness', 1625) to illustrate boldness in an orator or leader, not with the interpretation now placed on it.

mollycoddle • *treat with too much attention or indulgence*

A 'Molly' or 'Miss Molly' was a colloquial expression, dating from about the middle of the eighteenth century, for an effeminate man or **milksop**. To *coddle* is to treat like an invalid. The two words merged into *mollycoddle*, which is also used occasionally as a noun meaning 'weakling'.

Moloch • *implacable thing demanding sacrifice*

In the Old Testament Moloch was a Canaanite god or idol to which parents sacrificed their children as burnt offerings. See for example *Leviticus*, 18: 21.

molotov cocktail • *crude home-made petrol bomb*

Molotov (1890–1986) was the Soviet foreign minister when Finland was invaded by the USSR in 1939. Petrol bombs were thrown at Soviet tanks by the Finns, who invented them. They were called *cocktails* because they were in bottles, and given Molotov's name because, as foreign minister, he was seen as personifying the aggression.

moment of truth ● *time when person or thing is put to the test*

A literal translation of a Spanish expression for the moment in a bull-fight when the bull is killed.

monarch of all I survey

A quotation from the opening line of *Verses Supposed to be Written by Alexander Selkirk* by the eighteenth-century poet William Cowper. Selkirk spent five years on an uninhabited Pacific island, having been put ashore in 1704 at his own request following a quarrel with the captain of his ship. Defoe used the story in his *Robinson Crusoe*.

money is the root of all evil

This may be so, but what the Bible actually says is 'the love of money is the root of all evil' (*I Timothy*, 6: 10).

-monger: see *warmonger*

moonshine ● *nonsense*

More particularly, the word means foolish or visionary talk, ideas or plans. The popular expression for this used to be 'moonshine in the water' (i.e. appearance without substance), but it was shortened in the sixteenth century. Perhaps there is an allusion to the old belief that madness was linked to the moon: see **midsummer madness**.

Moonshine is also illegally distilled liquor, originally called 'moonlight' because it was smuggled, and sometimes made, at night.

more honoured in the breach than the observance

Popularly used of a desirable practice, convention, rule, belief, etc. that is more often ignored (breached) than observed. The original meant something quite different. Hamlet comments (I, 4, lines 14–16) on the king's custom of holding drunken revels:

But to my mind—though I am native here,
And to the manner born—it is a custom
More honoured in the breach than the observance.

He means that it would be more honourable to put a stop to the custom than to go along with it.

more sinned against than sinning

Coined by Shakespeare as the king's description of himself in *King Lear*, III, 2, line 59.

mountain out of a molehill, make a   ● *exaggerate something trivial out of all proportion*

First recorded in Nicholas Udall's *Paraphrase of Erasmus* (1548–9) as 'The Sophists of Greece could through their copiousness make an elephant of a fly and a mountain of a molehill'. The elephant/fly expression goes back at least as far as the Greek satirist Lucian (second century AD) and became proverbial in French, but the mountain/molehill improvement has the air of being original.

mountain will not come to Mohammed: see *Mohammed*

movable feast   ● *event whose date or time can be changed*

An ecclesiastical term for a day of religious observance which does not always fall on the same date, in the way that immovable feasts such as Christmas do. Movable feasts depend on Easter, the date of which is fixed by reference to the calendar moon and therefore differs from year to year.

Mrs Grundy: see *Grundy*

much of a muchness   ● *very much alike*

The old word *muchness* (size) survives only in this quotation from the opening scene of *The Provok'd Husband* (1728), a comedy by Sir John Vanbrugh (1664–1726) finished by Colley Cibber.

mud, one's name is   ● *one is unpopular, discredited, blamed, etc*

It is interesting that the doctor who in 1865 treated the assassin of Abraham Lincoln for the fractured leg he sustained in making his escape, and who was later given life imprisonment for conspiracy (even though he had reported his patient to the authorities on hearing of the murder), was named Samuel Mudd. It is also irrelevant, despite what some commentators have said, because this expression had already been in use for several decades before the event. *Mud* had long been a term for anything worthless; 'one's name is . . . ' introduced an obvious pun on the surname Mudd long before the unfortunate doctor gave it a different notoriety.

mufti • *civilian clothes as opposed to military uniform*

A Mufti—the word is originally Arabic—was a Muslim priest or expounder of the law. The word would have been known to British troops serving abroad during the period of empire. Their officers favoured, and are depicted in contemporary plays as wearing, an off-duty dress of flowered dressing-gown and smoking cap and this gave rise to facetious comparisons with the appearance of Muftis. Hence the modern use of the word, now used without its capital letter.

mug • *rob with violence in the street*

As a noun for a person who is easily taken in, *mug* has been slang for about 150 years and is probably based on a comparison between a person who will believe anything and a drinking-mug into which one can pour anything. The verb originally meant to rob or swindle someone by treating him as a *mug* in first getting him filled up with drink to facilitate the theft.

muggins

This came into use at the same time as **mug**, as a variant with the same meaning of 'simpleton'. It exists as a surname and in its slang use it is often a substitute for a person's name or for oneself. 'I suppose muggins will have to do it' is a grumble that I, fool that I am, am being put upon, as usual.

multitude of sins, hide a • *conceal blemishes*

Of biblical origin, though with a slightly different meaning: 'he which converteth the sinner from the error of his way shall save a soul from death, and shall hide a multitude of sins' (*James*, 5: 20).

The variant *cover a multitude of sins* is also biblical (*I Peter*, 4: 8), but is now often used to mean 'include or mean all manner of things'.

mum's the word • *say nothing*

Mum in this sense of 'silence' is a word fabricated from the inarticulate sound 'mmmm' made with closed lips and conveying no information. This use was first recorded in 1540 but may well be two centuries older than that.

mumbo-jumbo • *confusing and obscure language; meaningless ritual; involved activity*

This probably originated as an anglicised approximation to a Mandingo term for an idol or god venerated by certain West African tribes. The word has a long pedigree, having been first recorded in English in the early eighteenth century, after which it came to mean an object of foolish veneration. The shift in meaning to the modern sense was obviously influenced by the idea of gibberish and ceremony associated with magic. For a different development of the expression see **jumbo**.

music, face the • *face the consequences of one's actions, especially punishment*

In the mid-nineteenth century this meant to meet a test without flinching; the modern sense emerged over half a century later. The origin is almost certainly military, either from forcing a cavalry horse to face the regimental band to accustom it to the noise, or from formally expelling a disgraced soldier to the beat of drums.

myrmidon • *follower or henchman, especially one who carries out orders unquestioningly or brutally*

In Homer's *Iliad* the Myrmidons were a warlike tribe from Thessaly who followed Achilles to the Trojan War. They were known for their fierceness in battle and their loyalty to their leader. According to Greek legend their name, which literally meant 'ant people', came from an earlier period of history when Peleus, who was to become one of the most famous heroes of Thessaly, needed an entourage and the god Zeus provided one for him by turning some ants into men.

N

nabob   • *man of great wealth*

This was the title, from an Urdu word, of a Muslim official acting as deputy governor of a region under the Mogul Empire or as governor of a town in India. The word was applied, with some contempt, to people returning to England from India in the eighteenth century after having made their fortunes as employees of the East India Company. Some of them set themselves up with estates and parliamentary seats and were rather looked down on as interlopers.

nadir   • *lowest point (of one's fortune, of degradation, etc.)*

An astronomical term, from Arabic, denoting a point in the heavens diametrically opposite to the zenith.

nail   • *expose (lie, rumour, etc.) as false*

Probably short for an older expression 'nail to the counter', which meant the same and was an allusion to the shopkeepers' practice of nailing false coins to the counter as a warning or to remind themselves to be watchful.

nail, (cash) on the   • *immediate (payment)*

Several attempts have been made to link this expression to a stand in the shape of a post or bollard, called a nail, on which payment was made at certain stock exchanges. The expression, however, existed before exchanges were created. The best explanation points to old expressions in French, German and Dutch that translate as 'on the nail [of the finger]' and mean 'precisely' (which relates to the modern English meaning) but are otherwise unfathomable.

nail one's colours to the mast: see *colours*

namby-pamby   • *insipidly or sentimentally childish*

The nickname of the minor poet Ambrose Philips (1674–1749) which was invented by one of his fellow writers, probably the dramatist Henry Carey whose *Namby Pamby* (1726) ridiculed Philips' pastoral poems. The nickname is of earlier date, however, and was based on the poet's Christian name and the infantile style of some poems he had written for children. In the closely knit and backbiting literary world of early eighteenth-century London the sobriquet would rapidly have become common knowledge; by the middle of the century it was standard English with its modern sense.

name, give a dog a bad

A catch-phrase meaning that if one has acquired a bad reputation one will never be able to lose it. The full proverb is 'Give a dog an ill name and hang him', which can be interpreted in two ways: 'If you can succeed in giving someone a bad name you will destroy him' and 'If someone has got himself a bad name he is as good as destroyed'. There is also another proverb: 'He that has an ill name is half hanged'.

name is mud: see *mud*

names, no pack-drill, no   • *if I (or you) mention no names (or break no confidences) there can be no question of offence or punishment*

Pack-drill used to be a military punishment in which an offender was forced to drill (i.e. parade, or march up and down) carrying a full and therefore very heavy pack of equipment—64 pounds in the Crimean War, for example.

narcissism • *excessive self-admiration*

In Greek mythology Narcissus, son of a river-god, was a beautiful youth punished by the gods for having spurned Echo, who died of grief. They made him fall in love with his own image and when he saw it reflected in the water of a fountain he became so enamoured of it that he remained there until he died of languor.

navvy • *labourer, often unskilled, employed on roadworks, building sites, etc*

In the eighteenth century a canal was called a navigation and a man employed to dig them was a navigator, later abbreviated to *navvy* and applied to other labourers who dug earthworks, such as those of railways in the following century. The word is now more generally applied to anyone doing heavy physical work, especially digging, in the construction industry.

neanderthal • *extremely reactionary, primitive (especially in political views)*

A jocular allusion to Neanderthal Man, a Palaeolithic species of early humans named from the bones discovered in 1857 in a cave in the Neanderthal, a valley near Düsseldorf, Germany.

neck

To *stick one's neck out*, as if inviting the hangman to slip on the noose, is to take a risk. To *get it in the neck* (be punished or reprimanded) derives from the same idea. If, as has been suggested, both expressions originate in the USA—where a different sort of capital punishment is preferred—the basic idea is more likely to be of rural origin: that of chopping off the head of a chicken with an axe.

In horse-racing a *neck* is a short distance (the length of a horse's head and neck) by which one horse beats another; hence *neck and neck* (absolutely level in competition) and *neck or nothing* (at any cost; literally, win by a neck or win nothing).

Neck is also used geographically to mean something—a stretch of land or water, for example—which is long and narrow like a neck. A *neck of the woods* (place where one lives) was originally an Americanism for a stretch of woodland in which there was a small settlement.

nectar • *delicious drink*

The name given by Homer and others to the drink of the gods in classical mythology. The word is occasionally used figuratively for something that is particularly welcome and refreshing, such as good news.

neither rhyme nor reason: see *rhyme*

Nelson touch • *capacity for inspiring leadership*

The hero of Trafalgar, the battle (1805) which decided the survival of Britain and the freedom of Europe, seems to have invented this phrase himself to describe his own ability. From what he wrote it is not clear whether he was referring to his battle-plan or to the magic of his name, but it is the latter that lies behind modern applications of the phrase.

nemesis (or **Nemesis)** • *retribution by fate for wrongdoing; doom*

The name in Greek mythology of the goddess of retribution who punishes or avenges any offence against the moral law.

nepotism • *showing favouritism to one's relations or close friends, especially in appointment to office*

Coined in the seventeenth century as a result of the practice of popes and other senior ecclesiastics who gave patronage, often in the form of promotion within the church, to a 'nephew' (Latin *nepos*) who was sometimes in fact an illegitimate son. The word is now used more generally but the stigma remains.

Nero: see *fiddle while Rome burns*

nest-egg

Literally an artificial egg placed in a hen's nest or nesting-box to induce laying, in the days before hens were kept in battery-cages. It is used figuratively of a sum of money hidden away or set aside, perhaps as an inducement to further saving.

new broom   • *newly appointed person in charge who can be expected to make changes, perhaps far-ranging or sweeping*

From the very old proverb 'A new broom sweeps clean'. A broom was originally made of (replaceable) twigs of broom, heather, etc. attached to a handle.

New Deal

Promised by Franklin D. Roosevelt (1882–1945) at a convention speech in Chicago during his first presidential campaign in 1932: 'I pledge you—I pledge myself—to a new deal for the American people.' During the first five years of his presidency (1933–45) various New Deal programmes were devised to overcome the effects of the great economic crisis of 1929; these included public works, the reduction of unemployment from 17 million to less than 10 million, unemployment relief and social reforms.

new Jerusalem: see *Jerusalem*

Newcastle: see *coals*

next of kin: see *kith and kin*

nicotine

The name is derived from the *nicotiana* plant, so called after Jean Nicot who introduced tobacco into France in 1560 when he was French ambassador to Portugal.

nightcap   • *late-night drink before going to bed*

Literally this is a cap worn in bed to keep one's head warm. The figurative use is often a jocular euphemism for something alcoholic, which also warms one, but it may have originally arisen simply because a late-night drink and the donning of a nightcap were both associated with preparing to go to bed.

nightmare   • *frightening dream*

The second syllable here is not a horse but an old word for a spectre or hag. A *nightmare* used to be an evil spirit, in the Middle

Ages thought to be a female monster, which was supposed to settle on people during their sleep and produce a suffocating effect. Only in the sixteenth century did the modern meaning emerge.

nine

As a mystic number, a trinity of trinities, *nine* features strongly in the folklore, religion and demonology of many civilisations as well as in mathematics and astronomy. Despite the explanations offered for the following expressions, there remains the possibility that *nine* is being used in this mystic sense rather than in the ones given.

Possession is nine points of the law means that in any dispute over ownership the person actually in possession has an overwhelming advantage, i.e. that nine legal points (out of a supposed ten) will be determined by the fact of his or her possession. Before the seventeenth century the expression referred to eleven points (out of a supposed twelve). The change from eleven to nine is unexplained.

A *nine days' wonder* is a sensation or scandal whose fame, or notoriety, is soon over. The earliest form of the saying appears in Chaucer's *Troilus and Criseyde* (about 1374): 'For wonder last but nine night never in town'. The number may have been arbitrary or alliterative, or perhaps an irreverent allusion to the Roman Catholic Church's novena, a nine-day devotion.

A person *dressed to the nines* is dressed as smartly as possible. Again *nine* here may be mystic, denoting perfection, or it may, like the nine points of the law, represent a score of nine out of ten and thus imply near-perfection. It is unlikely to be a variant of an Old English expression, as some have suggested, because it is unrecorded before the end of the eighteenth century.

See also **ninepence, nineteen** and **cat**.

ninepence, right as   • *in good health*

This has developed from an earlier expression, 'neat as ninepence', which seems to have owed more to alliteration than good sense. A *ninepence* was an Irish coin, actually a shilling (12 pence), which was worth nine pence in England in the early seventeenth century. Perhaps it was 'neat' because nine pence was the plain, honest value of the coin, as distinct from the nominal value. 'Neat as ninepence' simply meant 'very neat', which is obviously related to the modern meaning of *right as ninepence*.

There may be something in the suggestion that silver ninepences used to be popularly given as love-tokens; that would fit in with the general sense of satisfaction associated with *neat/right as ninepence*.

nineteen to the dozen, talk   ●   *talk at a great rate (and at length)*

That is to say, speak 19 words during the time most people would need for a dozen. There seems to be no special significance in the figure 19, except that it is more unexpected and therefore more vivid than a neat round figure such as 20.

nip in the bud   ●   *destroy or slow down the growth of, usually at an early stage*

From gardening: the growth of a plant can be checked by nipping off buds or shoots.

nipper   ●   *small child*

The original sense of *nip* was 'pinch', and this remains one of its current meanings. In mid-sixteenth century slang it came to mean 'arrest', from the idea of catching hold of someone painfully. Because an arrest often entails quick movement the verb later came to mean 'move swiftly and smartly', another sense it still retains. In workers' slang, from around 1850, a *nipper* was a boy or apprentice who 'nipped about' running errands. From this we get the modern meaning of the noun, no longer slang but still informal.

nirvana   ●   *place or state of bliss*

This word is borrowed from Buddhist theology, in which it is the Sanskrit name for the extinction of individual existence (desires, drives, passions, etc.), freedom from the cycles of reincarnation, and the attainment of perfect beatitude.

no holds barred: see *holds*

no love lost: see *love*

no-man's-land   • *area of indefinite character or ambiguous activity*

This modern meaning is a metaphorical application of the military term (1908) made famous during the First World War as the name of the unoccupied and dangerous strip of land between opposing trench systems. The expression is in fact first recorded in 1320 as the name of a piece of unowned land (hence 'no man's') used as a place of execution outside the north wall of London. It recurs in 1349–50 as the name for a mass burial ground near Smithfield, London, designed for victims of the Black Death (bubonic plague) which is reputed to have killed a third of the population of England in 1349. This designation of the burial ground indicated that it was communal. It is curious that an expression merely signifying lack of ownership should have been closely associated with three different types of death over almost seven centuries.

no names, no pack drill: see *pack drill, no*

no respecter of persons: see *respecter*

no place like home: see *home, there's no place like*

Noah's ark: see *ark*

nob   • *wealthy, influential or socially superior person*

The word has been variously described as an abbreviation of 'nobility', of the Latin word for nobility (said to have been used after the names of members of the aristocracy in Oxford and Cambridge class-lists, to distinguish them from commoners) and of **nabob**. Some dictionaries prefer a derivation from 'knob' or 'nob' as slang for 'head', therefore related to 'chief', or from the Scottish dialect 'nab' or 'knabb', meaning a rich or socially influential person. This last seems nearest the mark, though the claims of nabob are strong.

nod is as good as a wink, a

A catch-phrase acknowledging that a hint has been understood. Oddly enough, the original sense was the opposite: 'a nod is as good as a wink to a blind horse' means that whatever sort of hint one may give, whether a nod of agreement or a more secret wink of complicity, some people are unable to understand it.

nose, pay through the ● *pay excessively; be overcharged*

Three explanations of this expression have been offered. One traces it to a ninth-century Irish poll tax imposed by the Danes, who slit the noses of non-payers. If this is the origin it is odd that the expression did not appear in print until 1672. A second links 'rhino', slang for money, with the Greek word *rhinos* (nose). This is as far-fetched as the third, which connects a nose-bleed with the idea of being 'bled' of one's money.

A simpler and more plausible solution exists. There is an old and popular expression, found in sixteenth-century English as well as in Italian, Greek and Latin, which is *lead by the nose*. Literally this means 'control' or 'dominate', as an animal is led by the nose, perhaps by means of a ring through it. Figuratively it means 'make a fool of': Shakespeare has 'led by the nose, as asses are' (*Othello* I, 3, lines 399–400). A development of this into *pay through the nose*, with the same implication of being fooled, must be a strong possibility.

nose to the grindstone, keep one's ● *keep one(self) working hard*

The original meaning, some of the flavour of which survives in its current one, was to keep someone punished or oppressed. A grindstone used to be a common implement—a revolving stone disc used for sharpening tools, knives, etc.—and the effect of this on the nose can be easily imagined.

nosey parker ● *prying person*

Nosey has a long history as a nickname for a person with a prominent nose and as an informal adjective applied to an inquisitive person who pokes his or her nose into other people's business in order to get a closer look at it. *Parker* seems to have been added in the 1900s with the appearance of a character on a comic postcard who was named Nosey Parker. Perhaps Parker was chosen arbitrarily as the character's surname, or perhaps it comes from the dialect word 'pawk' (be inquisitive) or from *parker*, an old word for park-keeper, a person better placed than most for spying on what people get up to.

The traditional explanation that the name originated with Matthew Parker, Archbishop of Canterbury in Queen Elizabeth I's day and a zealous inquisitor, fails to take into account that there is no record of the term either in his lifetime or during more than 300 years following his death.

notch up: see *score*

nothing new under the sun, there's

From the Old Testament *Ecclesiastes* (fourth century BC): 'There is no new thing under the sun' (1: 9).

nth degree, to the   ● *to the utmost degree or extreme*

In mathematics 'n' represents an indefinite number, usually the greatest in a series. To do something for the nth time is to do it yet again, after performing it innumerable times already.

number is up, one's   ● *one is doomed, ruined, finished; one is dead or about to die*

Taken into general use from military slang, the *number* being one's personal, official military number always used with one's name and rank for identification. In military terms *one's number* is virtually synonymous with one's existence; if that is *up* it is over (as in 'the game is up'). There is a similar military phrase 'lose one's number' (die).

numbered, days are   ● *life or existence is drawing to an end*

This expression, in which *numbered* is used in its now rare meaning of 'reduced to a definite (small) number', has its origin in Wyclif's translation (1380) of the Old Testament book of *Daniel*. This contains Daniel's well-known interpretation of the **writing on the wall**: 'God hath numbered thy reign and finished it' (5: 26).

nutshell, in a   ● *concisely expressed*

A nutshell is small enough to be a symbol for anything brief. There is no need for further explanation, though there are curious stories of attempts to copy substantial documents, such as the entire Bible, in letters so small that the resultant document will literally fit in a nutshell. Roman literature has a reference to the writing out of the whole of Homer's *Iliad* (17,000 lines) in this way.

O

oar in, put one's • *interfere*

A shortened version of an expression that can be traced back almost 500 years and may even originate in Latin or Greek: 'to have an oar in every man's boat' meant to have a hand in everybody's affairs.

odour of sanctity • *sanctimonious manner; simulated holiness*

A medieval term for the sweet odour said to have been given off by the bodies of saintly people at their death or when exhumed for appropriate reburial after official translation into sainthood. It was felt to be evidence of saintship. From being a metaphor for a reputation for holiness it has degenerated into one for hypocrisy and given rise to *in bad odour* (in disfavour).

odyssey • *long, eventful journey*

An allusion to the great epic Greek poem *The Odyssey* which describes the adventures of Odysseus during his ten-year return journey from the Trojan War to his kingdom of Ithaca; he was a warrior, counsellor and strategist known for his indomitable spirit and enquiring mind (though also capable of wiles). The work is generally thought to be by Homer (eighth century BC) and with *The Iliad* to constitute the finest poetry of western antiquity.

Oedipus complex • *male mother-fixation*

This popular definition is a rough-and-ready simplification of what the psychoanalyst Sigmund Freud had in mind when choosing the term to describe certain features of infant sexuality. His theories had to do with the unconscious sexual desires of a child, especially a male one, for the parent of the opposite sex in a way that aroused the jealousy of the other parent; this condition was held to be responsible for certain personality disorders in adults. In the Greek story, dramatised by Sophocles (496–406 BC), Oedipus was fated to kill his father, King of Thebes, and marry his mother Jocasta, both of which he unknowingly did. When he discovered his guilt, Jocasta hanged herself and Oedipus put out his eyes.

offing, in the   ● *about to happen*

Offing is one of a number of English words that are found only in a single expression. It means 'that part of the sea visible from (i.e. *off*) the shore'. A ship that was *in the offing* was therefore within sight.

oil on troubled waters, pour   ● *use tact, soothing words, etc. to calm a quarrel or upset*

The Roman author Pliny (first century AD) gave an account of the practice of contemporary seamen who used oil to still turbulent waves, but the idea is more likely to have reached English from Bede's *Ecclesiastical History* (731). This contains the story of a priest escorting a lady on a sea journey to become the bride of a king. St Aidan gave the priest a cruse of holy oil to pour on the sea if it became rough, and the oil was used with success. The expression, however, became metaphorical only in the nineteenth century and this may have been because Benjamin Franklin, the American polymath, took an interest in Pliny's story and wrote about it late in the eighteenth.

OK

The most universally known English expression and perhaps the most widely discussed. Originally American, it has been attributed to President Andrew Jackson, who is said to have annotated official documents with these initials in the belief that they stood for 'orl korrect', and to the nickname of President Martin van Buren, who was born in Old Kinderhook; both of these references are from 1839–40. Out of at least a dozen explanations the best is that the expression originated much earlier, either in the Wolof language of West Africa which was spoken by many American slaves or—more likely—in the Choctaw language of Native Americans, who appear to have had a word *oke* or *okey* to express assent. By the nature of things there is no contemporary documentation of either theory, but this view is now widely held.

old bat: see *bats*

old Bill, the: see *Bill*

old order changeth the: see *order*

old wives' tales: see *wives*

olive branch   ● *offer of peace*

The olive branch is a very ancient symbol of peace. In Greek mythology, for example, the olive tree is sacred to the great goddess Athene—in some legends she is said to have created it—and one was caused to sprout on the Acropolis at the naming of Athens. In the Bible the return of a dove bearing an olive leaf signalled to Noah the subsiding of the Flood that represented God's anger (*Genesis*, 8: 11). See also **ark**.

Olympian   ● *godlike; loftily detached*

Mount Olympus rises to a height of some 9,500 feet in a detached mountain chain near the Aegean coast of north-west Greece. Its south face is dominant and craggy, while its huge plateau, cloudy peaks rounded like a great amphitheatre, and huge boulders, put the ancients in mind of gigantic seats arranged for the use of supernatural beings. In legend it is the home of the gods, with Zeus as sovereign ruler, and the source of divine punishment and favour.

In modern use the adjective has overtones of majesty and wisdom but with strong suggestions of remoteness, aloofness and indifference to mere mortals.

once in a blue moon: see *blue moon*

one fell swoop, (at): see *swoop*

one over the eight, have   ● *be drunk*

From a military superstition that eight beers were safe to drink. See also the first paragraph of **nine**.

open sesame   ● *means, opportunity or secret way of gaining access to something otherwise inaccessible or unobtainable*

Originally 'Open, Sesame!', the words used by the 40 thieves to open a rock door into a cave, in the story of Ali Baba in the *Arabian Nights Entertainments*. Ali Baba used the same password to gain entry to the cave, which he found full of treasure. *Sesame* was presumably the name of a magic spirit. The story first appeared in English in the eighteenth century and the password became a metaphorical noun soon after.

oracle   ● *person giving wise or authoritative guidance or advice, especially in regard to future action*

This word had three meanings in Greek and Roman antiquity: it was the name for the mouthpiece of a deity; the message or prophecy given by the mouthpiece, usually a priest or priestess; and the shrine or other place where such divine utterances were delivered. These pronouncements were often ambiguous or obscure, sometimes misleading, and even now the adjective *oracular* means mysterious or ambiguous as well as wise or prophetic, though a person regarded as an *oracle* is not obscure. See also **Delphic**.

order changeth, the old

From Tennyson's *Idylls of the King* (1842): 'The old order changeth, yielding place to new' ('The Passing of Arthur', line 408).

original sin: see *Adam*

Orwellian

Although George Orwell (Eric Blair, 1903–50) wrote about many subjects, this adjectival use of his name is reserved to epitomise the nightmarish vision of his most famous novel *1984* (1949). This is the story of a man's hopeless struggle against a totalitarian police state which ruthlessly suppresses personal privacy, historical truth and independence of thought, and cruelly enforces soulless conformity, poverty of body and spirit, and communistic worship of **Big Brother**.

ostrich-like   ●   *refusing to face reality*

Like **Canute**, the **crocodile** and the **lemming**, the ostrich is persistently misrepresented in popular saying. There is no evidence that when pursued it buries its head in the sand in the belief that because it cannot then see its enemy it cannot itself be seen. The myth came into English in 1579 with the publication of North's widely read translation of Plutarch's *Lives*, but as Plutarch, the Greek biographer and moralist, was born in 50 AD it is clearly much older than that. Its origin, like that of some other travellers' tales, can only be guessed at.

ours not to reason why   ●   *it is not our place, job or whatever to question the orders of a superior, the way things are done, etc*

An adaptation of a line from the well-known poem by Tennyson, *The Charge of the Light Brigade* (1854):

Their's not to make reply,
Their's not to reason why,
Their's but to do and die:
Into the valley of Death
   Rode the six hundred.

This odd punctuation of 'their's', which as a possessive pronoun has no apostrophe, indicates that it is an abbreviation of 'their duty is'.

The charge was at Balaclava (see **balaclava**), near Sebastopol; 272 of the 673 Brigade members were killed or wounded in the charge because of a misunderstood order.

out-Herod Herod   ● *outdo in evil, extravagance or violence*

Shakespeare coined the phrase and put it into the mouth of Hamlet in the opening speech of III, 2, where he advises some strolling players not to shout and overact in the play he has written for them to perform. King Herod was commonly portrayed as a fearsomely blustering tyrant in old plays depicting biblical events, and Hamlet did not want his actors to behave as if they were trying to outdo him. Herod was also a cruel man, chiefly remembered for ordering the massacre of children in the hope of killing the infant Jesus; hence the modern adaptation of Shakespeare's term.

over the moon   ● *ecstatically happy*

Recorded as early as the middle of the nineteenth century, probably as a reference to the popular nursery ryhme *Hey diddle diddle* (about 1765), in which the 'cow jumped over the moon'— though there is no evidence that it did so out of happiness. The expression does not seem to have achieved any popularity until 1962 when the football manager Alf (later Sir Alf) Ramsey said, in an uncharacteristically colourful moment during an interview, 'I feel like jumping over the moon'. After that it rapidly became a resounding cliché that has survived much mockery.

over the top   ● *excessive*

Usually *go over the top* (behave without sufficient moderation or restraint). First World War infantry required to attack or raid enemy trenches had first to climb out of their own trenches and go forward over the top of the parapets. Going *over the top*—an occasion of mingled excitement and dread—became a well-known expression, or euphemism, for going into highly dangerous action. The shift to its present meaning, via showbusiness slang for 'over-act', is an odd one.

own goal, (score an)   ● *(do or say something that causes) self-inflicted damage*

In association football the object is to score by putting the ball through the opponents' goal. A player who accidentally puts the ball through his or her own side's goal, thus registering a score in favour of the opposition, is said to *score an own goal*.

oyster: see *world is one's oyster*

P

p's and q's, mind one's ● *be careful of one's behaviour*

This sounds as if it is a warning to children and it probably
originated as a classroom admonition in the days when children
learnt to write by copying the letters of the alphabet from a model
(see **criss-cross** and **copybook**): *p* and *q* were adjacent letters, both
had tails and so it would have been easy to confuse the two. A
teachers' catch-phrase advising care and correctness in writing
might readily have become generally adopted as one advocating
similar virtues in behaviour.

A more fanciful suggestion is that *p's* and *q's* were abbrevia-
tions of the pints and quarts recorded on a blackboard by a
publican keeping a tally of a customer's drinking (see **chalk up**).
The expression then becomes a customer's warning to the inn-
keeper to get the sums right.

paddle one's own canoe ● *make one's way by one's own efforts*

This saying, American in origin, was first recorded in 1828. It was a
favourite expression of Abraham Lincoln, for whom it epitomised
the American spirit of self-help; popularised in a poem by Sarah
Bolton in *Harper's Magazine* (1854), it was finally brought into
general currency when her words were set to a very popular song.

paint the town red ● *go on a spree*

Several attempts have been made to explain this. The most
persuasive locates its origin in an actual piece of drunken vandal-
ism by the Marquis of Waterford and a bunch of his chums who,

as an aristocratic joke, actually painted parts of the local town red in the area of Melton Mowbray, Leicestershire, in 1837. The incident created sufficient stir to be recorded in contemporary verse and engraving.

pale, beyond the   • *unacceptable, intolerable*

A pale used to be an area within certain bounds, subject to a particular jurisdiction. Its name came from a now obsolete sense of pale—a wooden stake used in enclosing an area with a fence. There were English Pales in France in the fifteenth century (the territory of Calais) and in Ireland, around Dublin, from the Middle Ages until the sixteenth century. Those beyond the Pale were held to be beyond the limits of civilised jurisdiction. The modern expression, with a small p, retains this colouring.

palm off   • *get rid of (usually something unwanted or inferior) by tricking someone into buying or receiving it*

From the trickery of conjuring, in which something may be concealed in the palm of the hand and apparently made to disappear, or—less likely—from cheating at cards or dice by sleight of hand. The adjective 'underhand' (not straightforward) comes from the same idea.

pan

In the language of American gold-prospectors to *pan* was to wash and agitate gravel in a pan in order to separate it from gold. To *pan out* was to get a good result from this process; it now means to work out or result. For *pan* in the sense of criticise see **dish one's chances**.

pandemonium   • *tremendous uproar and confusion*

The word, originally with a capital P, was invented by John Milton in his *Paradise Lost* (1667) as the name for the capital of Hell, containing the council chamber of the Evil Spirits. The pronunciation disguises the fact that the second and third syllables spell *demon*; the prefix means 'all'. Now spelt with a small p, the word is in general use but indicates a state or condition rather than a place.

235

Pandora's box • *seemingly innocuous situation but actually a profuse source of trouble to come*

In Greek legend Pandora was the first mortal woman, created by Zeus to bring calamity to men. Sent as a beautiful gift to Epimetheus, but with treachery in her heart, she brought with her a great vase (popularly described as a box) filled with afflictions; when she opened the lid these escaped and spread over the earth, though Hope remained at the bottom. The original idea, therefore, was that the first woman brought misery to the earth.

Panglossian • *taking an absurdly over-optimistic view of the world*

Dr Pangloss is the absurd and pedantic tutor to the hero of Voltaire's *Candide* (1759). He persists in his incurable optimism despite numerous misfortunes, which include an unsuccessful attempt to hang him. His philosophy is summed up as, 'All is for the best in the best of possible worlds' (chapter 30).

panjandrum, (the great) • *powerful or self-important person*

The actor and dramatist Samuel Foote (1720–77) invented this word in 1755. An actor called Macklin claimed that his memory was so good that he could repeat anything after hearing it once. Foote composed a nonsensical paragraph including a list of imaginary people, ending with *the Grand Panjandrum*, but Macklin refused the challenge. The word is still used in a jocular way.

pantechnicon • *large van*

An invented word, from two Greek ones: the first syllable means 'all' and the remainder 'belonging to the arts'. It was coined in London in about 1830 as the trading name for a bazaar in Motcomb Street, Belgrave Square, which sold all kinds of works of art. When the business failed, its premises became a furniture warehouse which retained the name; the vehicles used by the firm for removing furniture became known as 'Pantechnicon vans', from which the modern word and its meaning are derived.

pantheon   • *highly select group of individuals eminent in a certain sphere of activity and honoured as in a 'hall of fame'*

As the original Greek implies (*pan* meaning all and *theios* divine), in classical antiquity this was a temple sacred to all the gods. The word is best known from the Pantheon built by Hadrian in Rome (120–4 AD) on the site of the one built by Agrippa; it is now the church of Santa Maria Rotunda. In Christian times a *pantheon* changed from being a shrine of all the gods to a burial place of a nation's heroes, as indeed Santa Maria Rotunda is for Italy, and this is the sense that has given rise to the broader modern metaphorical use.

pants

Short for 'pantaloons', the old name for a style of trousers, which in turn came from Pantaloon, the Venetian character in popular Italian comedy who wore them. His name was an adaptation of the Italian *pantalone*, the characteristic mask used for the Venetian character in a particular sort of play, so called after St Pantaleone, a favourite saint of the Venetians.

paper tiger   • *person (occasionally thing) outwardly powerful but in fact weak*

Translation of a Chinese expression which first became generally known when it was indirectly applied to the USA as a term of abuse by the Chinese communist leader Mao Tse-tung in 1946.

par for the course   • *what one would expect; normal; average*

A misuse of a golfing term which denotes the score that a good player, not an average one, should reach when going round a particular course. It enables golfers to measure their standards against an officially recognised one.

paraphernalia   • *miscellaneous things*

Originally a legal term for the personal goods such as clothes and jewellery which a married woman was allowed to keep as her own—i.e. they were not included in her dowry, which passed into the ownership of her husband. The word literally means 'beside or beyond the dowry' and the modern meaning comes from the idea of personal belongings being a miscellany of articles.

pariah   • *outcast; person shunned*

Although in southern India, where it was of Tamil origin, this word denoted a person of low caste, the Europeans who exported it extended it to mean a person of no caste at all, i.e. a social outcast. It literally means a drummer, this being a function that the original pariahs were permitted to undertake at certain festivals.

Parkinson's law   • *work expands to fill the time available*

A facetious law of economics formulated by the English historian C. Northcote Parkinson in an essay in *The Economist* in 1955 and subsequently in his book *Parkinson's Law* (1957), a humorous but deadpan study of public and business administration based partly on his experience as a staff officer in the Second World War. An important corollary of this law is that 'subordinates multiply at a fixed rate regardless of the amount of work produced' and it is this notion of ever-increasing bureaucracy that is now normally in people's minds when they refer to Parkinson's law.

part and parcel of   • *very much part of*

Both words used to mean the same thing—an integral portion—though *parcel* no longer has this sense except in this expression. It was originally a legal formula used in defining ownership, the contents of estates, etc., and was merely emphatic, the second noun reinforcing the first, as is often the case in the jargon of legal documents.

Parthian shot   • *pointed or wounding remark made on departure, giving no time for reply*

The idea of having the last word may now imply flouncing bad temper but the original phrase did not. Parthia was a non-Greek kingdom which emerged in about 238 BC in what is now northeastern Iran, west of Afghanistan. It became the object of a number of campaigns by the Romans, notably Crassus in the first century BC, and it was then that the Parthian horsemen became noted for their skill at discharging their missiles backwards while in real or pretended retreat.

parting of the ways • *place or time at which separation occurs*

Originally biblical: 'the King of Babylon stood at the parting of the way' (*Ezekiel*, 21: 21).

parting shot • *final word or action (usually unfriendly) before leaving, so that response is impossible*

Formerly a **malapropism** for **Parthian shot**, but now an acceptable and clear idiom in its own right.

pass the buck: see *buck, pass the*

past master • *person expert or much experienced in a particular activity*

This could be derived from the old expressions 'to pass master' and 'passed-master', both of which referred to graduation as a Master (of Arts, etc.) from a university. A more likely explanation is that it is from the later variant 'past-master', a former master of a guild (see **masterpiece**), freemasons' lodge, etc. Mastership was an office to which one was elected in recognition of one's adeptness in a particular craft.

pasteurise • *destroy bacteria in liquids by heating*

After Louis Pasteur (1822–95), the French chemist whose researches into fermentation led to the establishment of the science of bacteriology.

pastures new: see *fresh fields*

patch on, not a • *nowhere near as good as*

A not very intelligible variant of an older and clearer expression 'but as [i.e. no more than] a patch on', meaning 'inferior to'. The idea is that a patch is inferior in that it spoils a garment.

Pavlovian • *automatic, unthinking*

Usually applied to human behaviour, especially to a change in behaviour as a result of stimulus. A *Pavlovian reaction* is a conditioned reflex.

Ivan Pavlov (1849–1936) was a distinguished Russian physiologist who conducted a famous series of experiments using dogs. He trained them to salivate at the sound of a bell, whereas normal salivation is a reflex produced by food. He did this by measuring in laboratory conditions the saliva produced by dogs when presented with food: such salivation is an unconditioned (i.e. normal) reflex. When he caused a bell to be rung a few seconds before food was presented to the animals, he found that (after due repetition) the dogs salivated at the sound of the bell alone— a conditioned (i.e. induced) reflex.

Pavlov's experiments had an important influence on the development of modern psychology, including educational psychology, though his findings are now regarded as oversimplified.

pay through the nose: see *nose, pay through the*

pays the piper calls the tune, he who • *whoever pays for something has the right to control it*

'Paying the piper' is an old figure of speech for 'bearing the cost': the idea was that of paying a musician to play for dancing, the pipe being either a sort of recorder, or any of the forerunners of modern woodwind instruments, or the bag-pipes. The second part of the expression, 'calling [choosing] the tune', is a late-Victorian addition.

There may be an allusion to the story of the Pied Piper of Hamelin, who led away the town's children because he had not been paid for ridding the town of rats, but *pay the piper* was, in its early appearances, always used in connection with dancing, not with any less orthodox use of music.

pearls before swine, cast • *offer something valuable to those unable to appreciate it*

Proverbial in English since the fourteenth century—it occurs for example in Langland's poem *Piers Plowman* (1362)—and popularised by its use in the Bible: 'neither cast ye your pearls before swine' (*Matthew*, 7:6 in the Authorised Version of 1611 and previously in Tyndale's translation of 1526).

pearly gates • *entrance to heaven*

A popular adaptation of the biblical description of the Christian paradise: 'the twelve gates were twelve pearls; every several gate was of one pearl' (*Revelation*, 21: 21).

pecker up, keep one's • *show courage or good spirits*

Pecker means 'beak'; if it is held up, so is the head. The whole phrase has therefore to do with holding one's head up and not allowing it to droop in despair or tiredness. A similar expression is 'keep one's chin up'.

pecking order • *hierarchy based on rank or status*

This alludes to behaviour originally recognised among hens, and later among other groups of animals, in which those of high rank in the group attacked (by pecking) those of a lower rank without provoking an attack in return. The term was first used in twentieth-century studies of animal behaviour and was rapidly adopted as a popular metaphor for an aspect of human be-haviour.

Pecksniff • *hypocrite*

The name of a mean, treacherous and bullying arch-hypocrite in Dickens' *Martin Chuzzlewit* (1843–4) who preaches morality and social duty while behaving wickedly and selfishly himself.

peeping Tom: see *Tom*

peg

To *take someone down a peg* is to humble him or her. The *peg* here is the pin around which is fixed one of the strings of a musical instrument. It is turned to loosen or tighten the string, thus changing its pitch when tuning the instrument. To 'let/bring/take down a peg', thus lowering the pitch, has for several centuries been a figure of speech for lowering someone's self-importance.

To *peg out* (slang for die) is from cribbage, where the score is kept by putting small pegs in holes on a board. It literally means to finish a game by reaching the last holes.

Peg away (work persistently) is from the action of hammering away to drive a peg into the ground, etc.

Peter Pan   • *eternal little boy*

A disparaging term for a man who does not behave in an adult way. The original is the central character in J. M. Barrie's popular play (later also a book) of the same name (1904); he is a little boy who never grew up and lives in a fairy-tale world of make-believe.

pharisaic   • *hypocritically self-righteous*

The Pharisees were a strict Jewish sect who advocated rigid adherence to their own interpretation of the Mosaic law, especially to the outward forms of religion and morality, and who assumed their own superiority in this regard. They were frequently criticised by Jesus for their literalism and hypocrisy, notably for their dedication to doctrine and ritual without the true spirit of piety or humility. It is these condemnations (see for example *Matthew*, 23: 13–33) that lie behind the modern adjective.

philippic   • *bitter denunciation, often a speech full of invective*

The first Philippics were the famous orations of Demosthenes denouncing Philip of Macedon, the enemy of Athens, in the fourth century BC. The same name was later given to the speeches of Cicero, the Roman lawyer and statesman, against Mark Antony. In the singular and with a small p the word is now applied to written as well as spoken invective, and to that directed against a cause as well as a person.

philistine, philistinism

In the Old Testament the warlike people of Philistia in south-west Palestine were the constant enemies of the Israelites, contesting their possession of Palestine: see for example **David and Goliath**. Because of the frequency of scriptural references to them as a heathen enemy their name became used in sixteenth-century English, usually though not always jocularly, to denote any threatening enemy such as bailiffs or literary critics. There was a similar development in Germany, where university students used the word *Philister* to denote someone not at the university, a townsman, deficient in liberal enlightenment and culture. This sense was introduced into English by the Victorian poet and critic Matthew Arnold in an essay on the German poet Heine (*Essays in Criticism*, 1865) and developed in his influential *Culture and Anarchy* (1869), which describes the English middle classes as predominantly Philistine. By this he meant that they were inveterately inaccessible to ideas and preoccupied with material gain. Modern uses of *philistine* and *philistinism* imply indifference or hostility to aesthetic (or intellectual) values or activity.

philosopher's stone   ● *panacea*

Before the word 'philosopher' settled down into its modern sense it meant, among other things, a practitioner of occult science, including alchemy. The alchemist's or philosopher's stone was, in medieval times, the solid or preparation reputed to be able to turn all base metals into gold. The discovery of it was a supreme objective.

phoenix from the ashes   ● *something that grows anew out of the destruction of its predecessor*

The phoenix is a legendary bird. In Egyptian mythology, in which it may have been sacred, it resembled the eagle in shape and size and appeared in Egypt only once every 500 years, flying from its birthplace in Arabia with the body of its father, which it buried in a temple. In later Greek legend it had gorgeous plumage, was the only one of its kind and lived for 500 or 600 years in the Arabian desert, after which it built a nest as a funeral pyre, sometimes in Egypt. From the ashes of this it emerged with renewed growth to live through another cycle.

picket   ● *group of striking trade-unionists stationed outside place of work to persuade non-strikers to support them*

Borrowed by the trade-union movement from army terminology, in which a *picket* is a group of men on watch for the enemy. The army usually spelt it 'piquet', true to its origins as a French word for a pointed stake as used in making a defensive stockade.

Pickwickian • *using words in a sense different from the commonly understood one; odd, unusual use of language*

Improper language, especially when insulting, may sometimes be explained away as having been used only *in a Pickwickian sense*—i.e. as not having the meaning it would normally have. The allusion is to an incident in Dickens' *Pickwick Papers* (1836–7) in which Mr Pickwick, an honourable and accident-prone gentleman who is sometimes unguarded in what he says, has a quarrel with Mr Blotton which is resolved when both agree that they had used offensive language in an inoffensive way. *Pickwickian* is also sometimes applied to a person to signify benevolence or naiveté, which are other traits in the personality of Dickens' creation.

pidgin English • *English with the pronunciation, spelling or grammatical construction of another language*

The development of trading contacts between Britain and China led to the emergence in nineteenth-century China of a trading language consisting of basic English and some Chinese with Chinese pronunciation and some Chinese grammatical forms. The Chinese called this hybrid language 'business English', but as they had difficulty in pronouncing 'business' this came out as 'bidgin' or *pidgin*, which is now a standard English word.

By a curious and misguided tidying-up process, 'that's not my pidgin' (that's not my business) entered written English as *that's not my pigeon*. The familiar *that's your pigeon* (i.e. your responsibility) is from the same error.

pie in the sky • *foolish and illusory hope of future benefit*

Usually credited to the American trade-union organiser Joe Hill, who wrote in *The Preacher and the Slave* (1906):

> You will eat, bye and bye,
> In the glorious land above the sky!
> Work and pray, live on hay,
> You'll get pie in the sky when you die.

This bitter advice to tolerate inhuman social conditions in order to earn rewards in heaven is a parody of 'We shall meet by and by', a popular hymn in the Moody and Sankey hymnbook, *Sacred Songs and Solos* (see **hold the fort**). Contemporary evangelical or revivalist sentiment promised a better life to come, but implied resigned acceptance of one's place in society in the meantime.

Pie in the sky was seized on and much used by the militantly radical Industrial Workers of the World, a potentially revolutionary American labour movement, who used it to taunt the conventionally minded religious and industrial establishment and idealistic socialists alike. It may even be that Hill did not invent the phrase but merely utilised an existing ironical slogan of this organisation.

pig in a poke: see *cat out of the bag, let the*

pig's ear, make a   ● *blunder; make a mess*

Probably from the sixteenth-century proverb 'You cannot make a silk purse out of a sow's ear' (you cannot make something good out of inferior materials), in which the sow's ear is synonymous with something useless, valueless, etc.

pigeon, not one's: see *pidgin English*

pigeonhole   ● *place into a category, often one that is too restricted; defer for later consideration (often with the implication of indefinite postponement)*

Both meanings come from the placing of papers in the open box-like compartments of a bureau or in the similarly shaped racks where documents are filed for collection by individuals in a large organisation. These compartments are called *pigeonholes* because of their resemblance to real pigeonholes, the often extensive ranges of holes or recesses made for nesting pigeons in the times when these birds were commonly used for food.

pikestaff: see *plain as a pikestaff*

Pilate: see *Pontius*

245

pillar to post, from   • *in a state of being harassed and badgered*

Usually thought to be from real (royal) tennis, an old indoor version of the game, which involves toing and froing as *pillar to post* may imply: *pillar* and *post* were features of the court and may have figured in a technical term for a certain type of shot. But the expression is ancient (at least early fifteenth century) and more common than one would expect of a phrase originating in limited aristocratic circles. For these reasons it may well have come rather from the medieval punishment of the pillory (pillar) and whipping-post; these were more in the public domain than real tennis and imply greater inconvenience.

pin money   • *small earnings (especially from part-time job), usually of wife; pocket-money*

Formerly a sum of money allotted, often by legal settlement, by a man to his wife for her personal expenses. The phrase reflects an earlier period when pins, needed for dressmaking and sewing, were neither cheap nor plentiful, their manufacture being controlled by a Crown monopoly. *Pin money*, therefore, while incidental to the main household running costs, was something that needed to be reckoned.

pinch of salt: see *salt*

ping-pong   • *table-tennis*

Invented as a trademark, though now in general use, and a good example of onomatopoeia: the first element captures the light sound of ball on bat, and the second the hollower one of ball on table.

pink, in the   • *in good health*

A pink is a popular garden flower. Shakespeare was the first to use it as a metaphor for a perfect embodiment of a particular quality: 'I am the very pink of courtesy', says Mercutio playfully (*Romeo and Juliet*, II, 4, line 36). The image was copied and spread, most notably in 'the pink of [good] condition', of which the current expression is a shortened version.

pipe down   • *stop talking*

In nautical language this was a command given on a bosun's pipe, last thing at night, for silence and lights-out.

pipe-dream   • *impossible fanciful hope or plans*

Despite its comfortable modern associations this was originally a reference to the pipe-smoking of opium and to the fantasies it produces. Opium used to be a legal drug in the form of laudanum.

pit   • *set (wits, strength, etc.) in opposition or competition*

From the *pit* or depression, chosen for the convenience of spectators, in which cocks, dogs, pugilists, etc. used to fight.

pit, bottomless   • *inexhaustible supply*

Originally biblical for hell (see for example *Revelation*, 20: 1), but now used in a quite different sense.

pitched battle   • *fierce encounter*

Literally a battle of which the plans, site, etc. are chosen in advance, as distinct from a running battle or skirmish, and therefore likely to be more murderous. *Pitched* means established, fixed, set up in a place.

plain as a pikestaff   • *very obvious*

Originally 'plain as a packstaff', the staff to which a pedlar strapped his pack. *Plain* meant either simple (in appearance) or smooth (of surface).

plain sailing   • *unobstructed progress*

Formerly *plane sailing*, navigation by plane charts which represented the earth's surface as plane (i.e. flat) instead of spherical. This form of navigation was simpler and left less room for errors; hence the modern sense of the term which is, roughly, 'easy'.

platonic   ● *having no element of sexual desire*

The adjective is usually used in conjunction with words like *relationship, friendship* or *love*. The allusion is not to the sexuality of Plato (427–347 BC), the Greek philosopher, but to his *Symposium*, a dialogue on the nature of love in which one of the characters is Socrates, his own teacher. Socrates describes how human love, including that for someone of one's own sex, can take an intellectual form and lead to the highest form of love, that for beauty in itself.

In English studies of Greek philosophy 'platonic love' came to denote male homosexual love as a union of minds and souls only, and especially the abstract love of beauty and wisdom for its own sake. It is the first of these senses which persists, as a degraded and simplified synonym for 'sexless', in modern usage.

play ball   ● *cooperate*

An Americanism meaning simply to play baseball. This being a team game, an invitation (e.g. in a school playground) to *play ball* is also an invitation to join in with others, hence the general meaning.

play by ear   ● *make decisions in the light of the way things develop rather than by advance planning*

Not a very apt expression. In music, from which it is taken, to play by ear is to play from memory, i.e. without reading the music, not to make something up as one goes along.

play fast and loose   ● *treat carelessly; behave unreliably or deceitfully*

Fast-and-loose was one of several names for a medieval cheating game or fairground confidence trick played with a skewer-like stick and a belt or piece of string. The player was invited, for a wager, to pin the folded belt or coiled string to a table with the stick so as to hold it fast. The operator, who had of course arranged the folding or coiling in the first place, then showed that it was not 'fast' but 'loose' and so won the wager. The game has been superseded by the three-card trick and other sleights of hand but its name—and its associations of shiftiness—remain familiar.

play possum • *lie low; dissemble; feign ignorance (sleep, etc.) to deceive someone*

From the habit of the common American marsupial (properly 'opossum') of lying as if dead when under threat.

play second fiddle • *be subordinate (to another person)*

In an orchestra, string quartet, etc. the second fiddle plays music which, although important, tends to have less of the melody and more of the supporting harmony than the first fiddle, which is generally more prominent. In non-musical figurative use the expression implies a greater element of subservience and relative unimportance than is literally the case.

play to the gallery • *behave, speak or write in a manner designed to attract popular favour*

In a theatre the gallery is the highest part of the auditorium and the most distant from the stage. It has the cheapest seats and therefore in former times, when the possession of money was equated with merit, was thought to accommodate the least discerning spectators. A performer who 'played to the gallery' used a vulgar, exaggerated style designed to please this coarser element.

pleased as Punch • *very pleased*

In the old story of Punch and Judy he is a happy character; indeed he is usually presented as unduly self-satisfied, and duly punished, though neither of these ideas is present in the modern phrase.

plonk • *cheap wine*

Originally 'plink-plonk' or 'plinkety-plonk', soldiers' facetious slang for the French 'vin blanc', during the First World War.

ploughman's lunch • *bread and a piece of cheese*

Despite its agreeably rustic if not medieval feel, this expression actually belongs to 1970 when it made its first appearance in a contribution to *Cheese Handbook* by Richard Trehane, chairman of the English Country Cheese Council. As an astonishingly successful piece of marketing it was promptly adopted by virtually every public house in Britain. Whether any ploughman ever actually ate one—or what his language would be on contemplating one after several hours' hard labour behind the horses—is another matter.

plumb the depths　　● *sink as low as possible (metaphorically)*

A nautical term meaning to use a mariner's plumb or plummet—a piece of lead (etc.) attached to a line—to measure the depth of water from a ship, especially when in a channel or close to shore, in order to avoid running aground. The expression was originally quite factual, without the sense of despair or baseness it now carries.

Podsnap　　● *self-satisfied and self-important person, usually starchy*

After the similar character, Mr Podsnap, in Dickens' *Our Mutual Friend* (1864–5).

poetic justice; poetic licence

Neither of these has much to do with poetry; they are popular expressions, not technical terms of literary criticism, though *poetic justice* used to be. 'Poetic justice' is now simply good justice; it used to mean the rightness, sweetness or carefulness associated with poetry, or the sound morality of great epic poems and verse drama. *Poetic licence* is a rather tongue-in-cheek expression meaning fanciful exaggeration or even harmless dishonesty in describing something or stating a case. The idea is that poets use language in an uncommon but forgivable way to make their effects.

pogrom

From a Russian word meaning 'destruction'. It came into English only in 1905, applied to an organised massacre such as those directed against Jews. It is still used in this sense, but also more generally of any sweeping, brutal change in which people are punished for their beliefs or lose their livelihood.

point-blank

Literally, from such a close range as to be sure of hitting the target. Figuratively, plain(ly) or blunt(ly).

Blank derives from the French *blanc* (white). The white spot in the centre of an archery-target was therefore called a blank and to aim *point-blank* was to point the weapon straight at the blank. The modern meanings, both literal and figurative (e.g. *a point-blank refusal*), stem from this idea of directness.

poisoned chalice   ● *something apparently cordial but actually deadly*

A quotation from Shakespeare (*Macbeth*, I, 7, line 11), where it is Macbeth's image for his murdering of the king while giving him hospitality (a chalice is a drinking cup). Shakespeare may have got the idea from the tradition that the enemies of St John once tried to kill him by offering him a poisoned cup (*Acts of St John*, third century) and from medieval depictions of the saint holding a chalice with a serpent around it as an image of death.

Pollyanna   ● *irrepressible optimist*

Pollyanna is the girl heroine of children's books by the American writer Eleanor Potter (1868–1920) and unfailingly looks on the bright side of even disastrous things. Though doubtless an irreproachable model for children of her time, as the years have passed she has become synonymous with tedious, saccharine and even self-deluding optimism.

Pontius Pilate   ● *person who refuses to take responsibility for his or her own actions, especially wrong ones; person in authority who is weak, hypocritical or given to self-deception*

The Roman governor in Jerusalem at the time of Christ's crucifixion, Pilate believed Jesus to be innocent of the charges brought against him but gave in to the demands of the Jews and delivered Jesus to them. He washed his hands publicly in front of the crowd, saying 'I am innocent of the blood of this just person: see ye to it' (*Matthew*, 27: 14). See also **wash one's hands**.

Pooh-Bah • *person, often self-important, holding many public or private positions, not all of them necessarily important or well discharged*

Pooh-Bah was the name of the Lord-High-Everything-Else in the popular comic operetta *The Mikado* (1885); the librettist was Sir William Gilbert (1836–1911). The name is now applied jocularly or derisively.

pooh-pooh • *express disdain or contempt for*

An exclamation resembling *pooh* is first recorded in Shakespeare (*Hamlet*, I, 3, line 101) but may well be much older. It was later doubled for emphasis and turned into a verb.

posh • *smart; expensively elegant; upper-class*

Popularly supposed to be from the intitials of 'port out, starboard home', an abbreviation used in booking the most desirable cabins on the shadier side of ships sailing to and from the east in the days before air-conditioning. Neither the main carrier, P and O, nor anyone else has ever been able to produce evidence to support this explanation, but if it is fictitious it is certainly ingenious and why anyone should invent it is difficult to understand.

An alternative explanation is that the word used to be slang for 'money' (from the Romany); it later became a term for a dandy. Both these meanings are obviously related to the modern one, which belongs to the early twentieth century.

An early (1903) sighting occurs in a work by P. G. Wodehouse, who describes a brightly coloured waistcoat as 'quite the most push thing'. This may simply be a mis-hearing and consequent misspelling of a then unfamiliar word, or it raises the possibility of an origin in the idea of something ostentatious pushing itself on one's attention.

possession is nine points of the law: see *nine*

possum: see *play possum*

post-haste • *very quickly*

From the old direction written on letters: 'Haste, post, haste'. 'Post' here meant 'postman'; it earlier meant the horsemen stationed at intervals along post-roads, whose duty was to convey mail to the next stage.

posted, keep one ● *keep one supplied with the latest information*

From the jargon of book-keeping. To 'post' was to transfer into a formal central ledger the information provided by various employees, such as counter clerks, about their day-to-day transactions so that an official and authoritative account was kept of otherwise miscellaneous or auxiliary business. Something 'posted' was therefore transmitted to and entered in a central record.

As often happens when a technical expression passes into metaphorical or colloquial use, this meaning changed: nowadays a person who is *posted* receives rather than transmits information.

pot

Anything that has *gone to pot* or is *all to pot* is ruined, destroyed, not functioning. The allusion, as various sixteenth-century references make clear, is to the cutting up of meat into pieces ready for the cooking-pot.

The pot calling the kettle black is a catch-phrase used of people who blame others for faults that they themselves are also guilty of. It goes back to the days when both pot and kettle were equally likely to be blackened by the smoke of fires used for cooking, and grew out of another homely and more vivid expression *the kettle calls the pot black-brows* (ugly, scowling) or *burnt-arse*.

To *take pot-luck* is to take whatever happens to be available. The expression is still used in its original literal sense as well—to take one's chance or luck as to what may be in the pot, cooked for a meal, as distinct from what is specially cooked for a guest. There may also be an allusion to the use, in peasant cookery, of a stew-pot or stock-pot to which is added each day whatever happened to be ready from the garden or market.

Anything that is *in the melting-pot* is liable to change. The metaphor is not from cookery but from the use of a crucible to melt pieces of metal, often scrap or damaged articles, for pouring into a mould to make something new.

pottage, sell one's birthright for a mess of • *accept a (trivial) material advantage in exchange for something of higher (moral) worth*

The story of how Esau sold his birthright (his rights and privileges as the first-born) to his brother Jacob in exchange for 'bread and a pottage [soup] of lentils' is in *Genesis*, chapter 25. The word *mess* does not appear there, but it is an obsolete word meaning 'dish'; *mess of pottage* would once have been an everyday phrase. As such it is found in the heading to chapter 25 of *Genesis* in the Bibles of 1537 and 1539, and by this route it became part of the semi-biblical expression that has remained fixed in the language.

At one time *mess* also meant a company of people eating together, a sense which survives in *officers' mess*, etc.

pound of flesh • *exactly what is due*

Made famous by Shakespeare in *The Merchant of Venice* (1596–8) as the forfeit demanded by the moneylender Shylock if his loan to Antonio, against whom he bears a grudge, is not repaid by the appointed day. Antonio agrees the terms but in the event is unable to repay the debt in time. In court his advocate, Portia, turns the tables on Shylock by pointing out that the agreement referred only to a pound of flesh, but not to a single drop of blood. Since it would clearly be impossible to take his exact due of flesh alone, Shylock's case collapses.

While Shakespeare certainly popularised the term he did not actually invent it. He found it in the source he used for his play, an Italian short story from a collection written in the late fifteenth century and published in Milan in 1558.

pour oil on troubled waters: see *oil*

power corrupts, (all)

Lord Acton's famous dictum 'Power tends to corrupt, and absolute power corrupts absolutely' (*Historical Essays and Studies*, 1907) is not an original thought but his expression of it is the most frequently quoted, or rather misquoted.

powers that be • *those in authority*

Now sometimes used sarcastically or with a helpless shrug. The original expression is scriptural: 'Let every soul be subject unto the higher powers. For there is no power but of God: the powers that be are ordained of God' (*Romans*, 13: 1). St Paul's advice, condoning or even sanctifying civil authority, perhaps owes more to good contemporary politics than to good theology.

powwow • *conference, meeting, consultation, conversation*

A jocular word from an Algonkin term for a priest or medicine-man of the North American Indians, and for a magic ceremony, a feast or a conference. American settlers adopted the word in the last two of these senses; the last one passed into British English in the nineteenth century, a time when many Americanisms crossed the Atlantic.

press-gang • *force to do something (especially to join in) against one's will*

The press-gangs, who kidnapped civilians for service in the army or navy, usually the latter, were feared for centuries until an improvement in servicemen's pay and conditions in the 1830s made them redundant. *Press* has nothing to do with 'pressure' here: it is from the obsolete *prest* (French *prêt*, or loan) meaning the money advanced on enlistment.

pretty kettle of fish: see *kettle of fish*

pride goes before a fall

The modern version of an old proverb originating in the Bible: 'Pride goeth before destruction, and a haughty spirit before a fall' (*Proverbs*, 16: 18). As this makes clear, 'pride' here means rash conceit, not justifiable self-respect.

prima donna

This is Italian, as many musical terms are, for 'first lady', and applied to the principal female singer in an opera. Because such singers were popularly—and sometimes rightly—thought to be prone to dramatic tantrums, sulks or other uncooperative or selfish behaviour, the term has come to mean a person, of either sex, who has a temperamental nature.

primrose path   • *pleasurable way of life*

Shakespeare was the first to use the attractive spring flower as a metaphor for freedom from care: Ophelia teases her brother not to tread 'the primrose path of dalliance' (*Hamlet*, I, 3, line 50) and the drunken porter in *Macbeth* sees 'the primrose way' as leading to 'th'everlasting bonfire' of hell (II, 3, line 18).

procrustean   • *enforcing conformity*

The adjective implies arbitrariness or even violence, the allusion being to Procrustes, the giant and robber in Greek mythology who forced his victims to lie on a bed; if they were too long for it he chopped off the parts of their bodies that overhung the edge, and if they were too short he stretched them to make them fit exactly.

The word may be spelt with a capital P because it comes from a person's name, or with a small one because it is now well established in the language in its own right. The latter is more usual.

prodigal son   • *lavishly wasteful (young) man*

The young man in Jesus' parable (*Luke*, 15: 11–32) wastes his fortune until he has nothing left, whereupon he repents of his ways, returns to his father and is made welcome: see **fatted calf**. Scripture does not actually call him 'the prodigal son' but a chapter heading in the English translation does. *The prodigal returns* is a jocular catch-phrase of welcome from the same source.

Promised Land or **promised land**   • *place or state of affairs believed to offer final realisation of hopes*

In the Old Testament this is the land of Canaan promised by God to Abraham and his descendants (*Genesis*, 12: 7; 13: 15, etc.) and a persistent theme of Jewish history. In Christian vocabulary, such as that of hymns, it signifies paradise.

propaganda   • *tendentious information*

A modern Latin word which came into use in 1622 when Pope Gregory XV set up the *Congregatio de propaganda fide* (Committee for propagating the faith), a group of cardinals responsible for overseeing foreign missions. The word was initially used to mean the propagation of doctrine but was later applied to any (biased) opinions, ideas, allegation, etc. spread around to help the cause of a government or other body, or to damage enemies.

pros and cons   ● *reasons or arguments for and against*

Not to be confused with 'pro's' as an abbreviation for *professionals*. It is an adaptation of the Latin *pro et contra* (for and against).

protean   ● *readily taking on different shapes, forms or roles; very varied*

Proteus, a seagod in Greek mythology, was herdsman to Poseidon, god of the sea (called Neptune in Roman mythology). He had the ability to change his shape at will.

protocol   ● *code of etiquette*

From two Greek words meaning 'first' and 'glue', this was originally the term for a fly-leaf glued to a manuscript or its case and giving particulars of the contents. Then it came to mean a minute summarising a negotiation (e.g. legal or diplomatic) and forming the basis for later and more detailed agreement. This sense is still retained in the language of international diplomacy, where *protocol* also means a summary of an agreement. In the nineteenth century the French applied it to an official statement of the way in which state ceremonial was to be observed, whence its current and more general sense.

pull all the stops out   ● *use all available means*

At an organ keyboard the knobs which a player pulls out to bring different pipes into use are called *stops*, though modern organs have more sophisticated control mechanisms. If all the stops are pulled out the instrument makes its loudest and fullest sound.

pull one's leg   ● *tease one*

This innocuous activity was previously less so; the origin is the Scottish 'draw [i.e. withdraw] the leg(s)' from under a person by tripping him up either literally, perhaps in order to rob him, or figuratively in the sense of putting him at a disadvantage to make him appear foolish.

pull one's weight   •   *do what one is capable of, especially in a group effort*

From rowing; if one member of the crew does not pull the oar with a force appropriate to his or her weight, the rower then fails to make the contribution expected by the rest of the crew.

pull strings: see *string*

pull the wool over one's eyes   •   *deceive or delude one, especially by giving misleading or confusing information*

Attempts have been made to interpret 'wool' as a wig, which if pulled forward over the wearer's eyes prevents him or her from seeing what is going on. There are two objections to this explanation: the first is that a wig is not made of wool; the other is that the earliest recorded uses of the expression (in the USA in the mid-nineteenth century) have other verbs besides 'pull', including 'spread'—hardly appropriate to a solid object like a wig. A better explanation is that 'wool' has been jocular standard English for the hair of the head since the seventeenth century. Just as you can be *hoodwinked* if someone covers your eyes with your hood, the same effect can be achieved if someone covers them with your own hair.

Pullman   •   *luxury*

Applied to seating or accommodation on various means of transport and named after the American George Pullman (1831–97), who helped to design—and later set up the Pullman Palace Car Company to manufacture—a well-appointed railway carriage in the form of a furnished room, usually incorporating sleeping facilities.

pundit   •   *expert; authority*

One of several words that have entered English as a result of British rule in India. It is a variant of a Hindi word for a Hindu learned in religion, philosophy and law. Its use in English was originally jocular, or even patronising, and something of this colouring still remains because a pundit is sometimes, though by no means always, self-appointed.

pup: see *cat*

purdah, in   ● *isolated from others (often by disgrace)*

In the original Urdu and Persian a *pardah* was a curtain, especially one to screen women to prevent their being seen by men. It came to be the name for the whole custom of secluding women in some Muslim and Hindu communities, but the modern metaphorical use in English has a far more general application.

purgatory   ● *anything extremely painful*

In the formulations of doctrine by the early church, purgatory was the place where the souls of the dead are 'purged' (the origin of the word) by suffering and prepared for heaven. Authority for this notion was found in some Jewish beliefs and, it was claimed, in some New Testament passages. The Church of England rejected the doctrine in 1562, declaring in its Articles of Religion (No. 22) that it was a 'Romish doctrine . . . a fond thing vainly invented, and grounded upon no warranty of Scripture, but rather repugnant to the Word of God'.

puritan   ● *person with rigorous moral code, especially opposed to indulgence in physical pleasures*

This word was coined towards the end of the sixteenth century and rapidly became a derisive term. It was used of a Protestant—usually a **Calvinist**—who believed that the establishment of the Church of England by breach from the Roman Catholic Church at the Reformation was an incomplete break requiring further 'purification' of both doctrine and ritual in order to ground them on the sole authority of the Bible. In this historical sense the word is spelt with a capital P; in its more general modern sense it is not.

purple patch or **passage**   • *florid, ornate piece of writing; period of ostentatiously erratic or bad behaviour*

The second of these meanings derives from the first, which in turn goes back to the Latin poet Horace (65–8 BC). In his *Ars Poetica*, a work of literary criticism that exercised some influence on later English writers, he described an obtrusively ornate passage of composition designed for show as a 'purple patch' sewn on a garment for display. His choice of colour showed wit: 'purple' was the synonym of the rank of the Roman emperor as well as the colour of his robe (and that of other high notables). To wear a purple patch was therefore comically pretentious.

purse-strings: see *string*

pussyfoot (around)   • *avoid committing oneself to a course of action*

This meaning is an obvious development from an earlier and still current one: to proceed timidly, evasively or warily. Although this makes sense in terms of the gentleness and lightness of a cat's normal movement, it originates in an even earlier piece of American slang which had to do with sly behaviour, as of a cat creeping up on its prey—quite different from the current meaning.

put a sock in it: see *sock*

put paid to   • *put an end to*

Simply from the practice of putting the word 'paid' on a bill after it has been settled.

Pyrrhic victory   • *victory won at too great a cost to oneself*

Between 280 and 275 BC Pyrrhus, king of Epirus in Greece, who had crossed into southern Italy to help the Greek city-states against early Rome, won a number of costly victories over the Romans. The well-known phrase derives from these, notably from the Battle of Asculum (279) after which Pyrrhus exclaimed: 'One more such victory and we are lost'. In due course he was defeated and returned across the Adriatic.

Q

QED

Abbreviation of the Latin *quod erat demonstrandum* ('which was to be demonstrated'), placed at the end of a piece of mathematics to indicate that one had successfully demonstrated the truth of the proposition with which one had been required to deal.

quack

A jocular term for a doctor, but not jocular when used to mean a charlatan, medical or otherwise. It is an abbreviation of the obsolete 'quacksalver', in which 'quack' was the sound of a duck and 'salver' had to do with salve (healing ointment). A quacksalver made false claims to medical knowledge and skill and was often an itinerant seller of 'cures' at fairs and markets. The 'quack' in the name is a mocking comparison between what the quacksalver said and the harsh, meaningless noise made by a duck.

quarter (asked or given), no   • *no mercy (requested by or shown to a person who is being defeated)*

The reference is to military quarters (accommodation) to which prisoners of war are entitled. Originally the command 'give no quarter' would have meant 'take no prisoners', i.e. 'show no mercy'.

queer one's pitch   • *put difficulties in one's way*

As a verb, *queer* is old slang for spoil or ruin. *Pitch* was a costermonger's or entertainer's word for (a place of) sale or performance, from the idea of pitching a tent. The whole expression would have been heard in market or fairground disputes between stallholders.

Queer Street or **queer street, in** • *in difficulties, usually financial*

The use of a place name to signify the people who work there is a familiar figure of speech: thus Fleet Street used to mean journalists or newspaper people, Whitehall means civil servants, etc. By the same token Queer Street is an imaginary place which accommodates people with difficulties. Though originally London slang of the early nineteenth century, the expression is now standard.

quixotic • *idealistic, optimistic, chivalrous, but in a rash, improbable or impractical way*

The hero of the satirical romance *Don Quixote* (1605–15) by the Spanish novelist and dramatist Cervantes (1547–1616) is a poor, dignified and amiable gentleman whose wits have been so affected by too much reading of ballads and romances of chivalry that he has lost any sense of reality. He sets off, in rusty armour and on an ancient horse, in search of adventure. His attempts to right the wrongs of the world involve him in absurd escapades, and he is finally persuaded to return to his village. The book, intended as a burlesque of popular tales of chivalry, is actually a rich and affectionate celebration of the common man, even though modern uses of *quixotic* are often pejorative. See also **tilt at windmills**.

Rabelaisian   • *characterised by bawdy humour, satire and bold caricature*

These are certainly features of the writings of François Rabelais (c.1494–1553), but this adjectival use of his name does not do justice to his extraordinarily broad erudition and the humanism that informs his opposition to dogmatism and tyranny. See also **gargantuan**.

rack and ruin   • *destruction; destitution*

Rack here is a variant of the archaic 'wrack', now 'wreck'.

rack one's brains   • *make great mental effort (to remember something, think of a solution, etc.)*

Literally, to stretch one's brains on the *rack*, an instrument of torture which stretched a victims' joints when its wheels and rollers, to which the limbs were attached, were turned by the operator. Its use in England was abolished in 1640.

radio-ham: see *ham*

rag: see *chew the rag, red rag*

railroad   • *force (through) hastily and without proper or fair consideration*

An allusion to the attitude of American railway companies whose construction programmes in the nineteenth century often showed as much disregard for local feeling or private ownership as for natural obstacles.

rain cats and dogs   • *rain very heavily*

Of many explanations the most popular is that cats and dogs used to drown as a result of heavy rainfall on medieval towns that had no street drainage. Some commentators add that superstitious folk may have assumed that the dead animals had fallen from the sky.

Apart from the fact that medieval superstition is normally not entirely witless, and that cats—if not dogs—are perfectly capable of looking after themselves in a flood, the first recorded appearance of the expression in a play of 1653 is 'It shall rain . . . dogs and polecats'. The latter are hardly town animals.

A better explanation, or at least a clue, is to be found in a quotation from Chaloner's translation of Erasmus' *In Praise of Folly* (1549): 'Rather should we let all the world go to wreck both with dog and cat (as they say)'. This indicates that there existed a popular expression 'with dog and cat', that it was used of a disaster, and that it meant 'completely and utterly', down to the last dog and cat (as when Noah took refuge from disaster in the **ark**?). A downpour reminiscent of the **Flood** might thus have become known as a rain 'with dog and cat', like the end of the world.

rain-check, take a

In America the meaning is clear: a *rain-check* is a counterfoil or ticket which, if an outdoor sporting event is rained off, gives admission to the postponed game. Metaphorically, an American who *takes a rain-check* on something is refusing it while promising later action, acceptance, reconsideration, etc.

In Britain, where spectators are expected to tolerate bad weather and no such booking system exists, the expression is known from American films but not always understood. It is therefore used with differing meanings, including 'check the facts', 'take time to consider' and 'postpone a decision'. This last is the most usual, and nearest to the American original.

raise Cain: see *Cain and Abel*

rank and file ● *the main body of members of an organisation, excluding officials, leaders, etc*

Originally military: in parade-ground terminology a *rank* is a line of troops standing shoulder to shoulder and a *file* is one in which they stand one behind the other. The *rank and file* are therefore the whole body of ordinary troops in a formation. Officers on parade stand outside it.

rap, not care (give) a ● *not care in the least*

The original *rap* was a virtually worthless counterfeit halfpenny coin in eighteenth-century Ireland. Its name seems to have been an abbreviation of an Irish word.

rap, take the; beat the ● *accept blame; avoid blame*

An Americanism. A *rap* here is a criminal charge, a rebuke or an adverse criticism, simply a figurative use of a literal rap—a blow or knock.

raspberry, blow a ● *express contempt*

Literally, make a noise of breaking wind. Cockney rhyming slang: raspberry = raspberry tart = fart.

Rastafarian

Ras Tafari (1891–1975) is better known as Haile Selassi, emperor of Ethiopia from 1930 to 1974. Because of his special symbolic significance as a crowned black man his name was adopted by a Jamaican 'Back to Africa' movement which later spread to other areas, including Britain, as a cult. Its title may now imply one or several of a number of attitudes: recognition of the emperor as God; religious puritanism; desire for a homeland in Ethiopia; seclusion, frugality and vegetarianism; redemption of the black race; the wearing of plaited hair and wispy beards, use of a distinctive vocabulary and cultivation of a particular sort of music.

rat race • *competitive struggle to maintain one's position in life, especially in work*

Before acquiring its current meaning this was the name, now obsolete but never much known in its day, of a low-grade form of dancing to jazz practised by American teenagers in the 1930s; the name sounds like a parody of the bizarre animal-names of earlier dances such as the turkey trot, bunny hug and fox trot. It is impossible to say whether the phrase as now used (since about 1939) took over the previous one and gave it a new meaning or whether it is an entirely separate development. What must be very likely is that there is a common source in the traditional image of rats being used in laboratory experiments, e.g. placing them in mazes to test their learning ability, or on treadmills to measure their energy under certain conditions, etc. The idea of being on a treadmill is certainly part of the modern meaning.

rats leave a sinking ship

The earliest versions of this proverb go back at least as far as Pliny (first century AD) and have to do with mice leaving a house because they can detect, before humans can, the very first creaking noises that indicate its imminent collapse. Thus the proverb initially was no more than a sensible injunction to be observant and look to the future. Shakespeare appears to have been the first to supply the modern twist: 'a rotten carcass of a boat . . . the rats instinctively have quit it' (*The Tempest*, I, 2, lines 146–8). The expression continued in use with its previous meaning but it is Shakespeare's more vivid image that prevailed. The rats that leave a sinking ship are the disreputable people who desert, as soon as it runs into trouble, a cause they have previously gone along with and been sustained by.

read the Riot Act: see *Riot Act*

red herring • *irrelevant matter, usually one that diverts attention from the subject under discussion*

A red herring is one that has been smoked, its colour having become reddish-brown in the process. It makes its first metaphorical appearance (late nineteenth century) in such expressions as 'draw a red herring across the trail' (introduce an irrelevance), which implies that its strong odour is capable of leading hounds away from a scent if one is drawn across the trail between them and the fox. This may be a purely fanciful picture (unrelated to hunt sabotage, which came later) or it may be because herrings were used when hunters were training hounds to follow a scent, with the result that hunts were sometimes sidetracked if hounds encountered and followed such a trail previously laid for training purposes.

red, in the • *in debt*

In the days before computerisation, the bank statements of customers included figures printed in red when an account was overdrawn.

red rag to a bull, like • *infuriating*

The persistent belief that bulls are maddened by anything red is part of unfathomable folklore (perhaps even Greek or Roman in origin) reinforced by the traditional use of red-lined capes by bullfighters. In fact all the evidence suggests that what causes bulls to charge is something that moves, irrespective of its colour.

To *see red* (become very angry) is a variant of the same idea.

red tape • *bureaucratic procedures causing complications, delays, etc*

Red tape (actually more pink than red) became synonymous with the complexities of bureaucracy because it was used by government officials to tie up bundles of documents. It is still used in the legal profession, but the frustrations associated with it are usually thought of in the context of officialdom, especially the civil service, rather than the law.

267

red-handed, catch   • *detect in the very act of wrongdoing*

That is to say, before there has been time to wash off the victim's blood. The word was an adaptation by Walter Scott (in *The Lay of the Last Minstrel*, 1805) of older Scottish expressions 'redhand' and 'with red hand', both legal terms and both now obsolete.

red-letter day   • *memorable or lucky day*

A reference to the old custom of printing saints' days and the names of other major festivals in red ink in ecclesiastical calendars.

respecter of persons, no   • *not someone who singles out people for unduly favourable attention (e.g. out of respect for their wealth or position)*

A quotation from *The Acts of the Apostles*, 10: 34–5: 'God is no respecter of persons: But in every nation he that feareth him, and worketh righteousness, is accepted with him.'

rhyme nor reason, neither   • *no good sense*

Strictly speaking this means a lack of good expression (rhyme) as well as of good sense, but it is used invariably of lack of reason, the 'rhyme' being merely emphatic. Shakespeare coined the phrase (*Comedy of Errors*, II, 2, line 49), though rhyme and reason are coupled in earlier phrases in a less pithy way.

riddle: see *sphinx-like*

ride roughshod over   • *treat inconsiderately; act without regard for another person's feelings, interests, etc*

A horse is said to be *roughshod* when it has shoes with the nailheads projecting so that it can get a better grip, in icy weather for example.

rift in the lute   ● *sign of disharmony between people, especially the first evidence of a quarrel that may become worse*

A *rift* is a crack, a *lute* is a musical instrument (symbol of harmony), and the whole phrase is from Tennyson's *Merlin and Vivien* (1859), lines 388–90):

It is the little rift within the lute
That by-and-by will make the music mute,
And ever widening slowly silence all.

right as ninepence: see *ninepence*

right-hand-man   ● *chief assistant (of either sex), especially an indispensable and trusted one*

The right hand is normally the stronger of the two. It has therefore traditionally been held out as a symbol of friendship and trust. The right-hand side is also the position of honour: see, for example, the biblical quotation at **sheep from the goats**. All these ideas come together in this old expression.

rigmarole   ● *long, complicated procedure*

This meaning is a fairly recent development from an earlier one which still exists: a rambling, confused or pointless statement, account, explanation, etc. Both stem from the idea of a list or catalogue derived from the obsolete 'ragman roll' of which *rigmarole* is a colloquial adaptation.

Ragman was an old game played with a written roll. Strings were attached to various items contained in the roll and the players drew a string at random. In one version (1290) the game seems to have been a simple amusement, the items in the roll being verses describing personal character; perhaps it was a children's rhyme consisting of a list (i.e. a roll, as in roll-call) of characters described in verse and beginning with '[King] Ragemon le bon'. The French implies an origin before the Norman conquest, and the name of the game is therefore an anglicisation of this French name (perhaps a demon's). In another version (1377) the game is a method of gambling and also illegal.

There is another historical Ragman Roll, a set of documents recording the pledges of homage paid by Scottish nobles to

Edward I of England, but this (unexplained) name comes later; it may even have been adopted from that of the earlier game, which should be regarded as the true origin of the modern *rigmarole*.

Riley, live the life of   ● *live a comfortable and carefree existence*

First found in *My Name is Kelly*, a music-hall song with an Irish flavour written in 1919 by H. Pease:

> Faith, and my name is Kelly, Michael Kelly,
> But I'm living the life of Reilly just the same.

This would not have made much sense unless the audience was expected to recognise or be amused by the mention of Reilly. The reference is probably to an earlier popular song, *Is that Mr Reilly?*, which describes what Reilly would do if he ever made his fortune:

> Is that Mr Reilly that owns the hotel?
> Well if that's Mr Reilly they speak of so highly
> Upon my soul, Reilly, you're doing quite well!

ring a bell   ● *remind one of something*

Said of anything that awakens a response in the memory, as a successful shot makes a bell ring when a marksman hits the bull's eye in a shooting-gallery. Originally American.

ring the changes   ● *vary the ways in which a series of actions is carried out*

'Change' is a technical term in bell-ringing for the order in which a peal of bells is rung. When bell-ringers ring changes they play a succession of tunes.

ring true; have the ring of truth   ● *give the impression of being true*

A counterfeit coin could be identified by letting it fall on a hard surface such as a marble counter or stone floor. A genuine silver coin would give out a ringing sound (thus *ringing true*); a forged one would not.

Riot Act or **riot act, read the** ● *strongly reprimand, especially with a view to putting a stop to unacceptable conduct*

The actual Riot Act of 1715 provided that if 12 or more people assembled unlawfully or riotously a specified portion of the Act was to be read aloud to them by a magistrate or other competent authority. If they failed to disperse within one hour they were to be considered as felons liable to arrest.

Rip van Winkle ● *person who is very much behind the times*

This is the name of the happy-go-lucky character in a story by Washington Irving (*The Sketch Book*, 1820) who takes refuge from his scolding wife by taking a ramble in the Catskill Mountains north-west of New York, falls asleep after drinking too much and awakens twenty years later to find that things have changed. For example, he goes to sleep as a subject of the king of England and wakes up as a citizen of the USA.

rise out of someone, take a ● *raise a laugh at someone's expense to provoke him or her (often to irritation or bad temper) by teasing, etc*

An adaptation of an angling term for the action of causing a fish to be attracted to a bait so that it rises to take it and gets caught.

river, sell down the ● *betray the faith of*

Originally American, associated with the history of slavery. The river was the Mississippi, and 'down' implied the transfer of slaves from north to south: there was a slave-market near the mouth of the river at New Orleans, among others. Such transfers took place either because of increased or seasonal demand in the cotton or sugar-fields of the south, as distinct from the more northerly tobacco-plantations, or because the harsher slave-owners of the deeper south were not choosy about accepting—and dealing with—troublesome slaves whom northern owners wished to offload, or domestic ones who could be turned into profit.

The modern sense comes from the loss of security, often including home and family, that this traffic entailed, together with the humiliation or breach of faith it implied.

271

rob Peter to pay Paul • *take away from one person in order to give to another*

Not in the sense of robbing the rich to pay the poor but of behaving illogically or failing to solve a problem by merely creating another. Early appearances of the proverb (first found in about 1380) show that the reference is to St Peter and St Paul as two men of equal sainthood.

Robin Hood • *champion of the poor against the rich*

The legendary English outlaw has been variously identified and described but he is most commonly said to have been Robert Fitz-Ooth of Nottinghamshire, perhaps the Earl of Huntingdon, living from c.1160–1247 and dying by being bled by a treacherous nun in Yorkshire. With his supporters he lived in Sherwood Forest, robbing the rich, sparing and supporting the poor, killing only in self-defence, protecting the honour of women and displaying much daring, courage and generosity.

robot

Introduced into English in 1923 with the first London production of *R.U.R.* (Rossum's Universal Robots) by the Czech novelist and dramatist Karel Capek (1890–1938) in which it is the name, from the Czech *robota* (drudgery), for a mechanical automaton. In the play, a remarkable early example of science fiction, several of these robots acquire human emotions, rise up against their servitude, and destroy the humans who have enslaved them.

rod of iron, rule with a • *rule very inflexibly and sternly*

From *Revelation*, 2: 27, alluding to Psalm 2: 9. A rod is a staff symbolising authority, as in the name of the British parliamentary officer Black Rod, but the predominant image is that of a rod as an instrument of punishment—as in **spare the rod** and 'make a rod for one's own back'.

Rome

St Ambrose, the fourth-century Bishop of Milan, was responsible for the conversion of St Augustine who recorded in his *Epistles*

(No. 36) the bishop's advice when asked about the Roman practice, not observed in Milan, of fasting on Saturdays. This has come down to us as *When in Rome do as the Romans do* (conform to the customs of the people you live or work among).

Another saying, *Rome was not built in a day*, a rather obvious comment on the greatest city of the ancient world, was proverbial in French in the twelfth century and has been common in English since the sixteenth.

See also **fiddle while Rome burns**.

Romeo

There have been many other young, romantic and dashing male lovers in literature, some of them less accident-prone, but it is Shakespeare's hero of *Romeo and Juliet* (1595, though based on a fifteenth-century story by the Italian Bandello) who has caught the popular imagination as the archetype because of his ardour and poetry, the tragedy of young love caught up in a family vendetta, and suicide that brings the families to a reconciliation.

rookie: see *blackleg*

room to swing a cat, not: see *cat, not room to swing*

root and branch   •   *entirely*

Specifically, the thing itself (*root*) and all its effects (*branch*). The phrase became well known from the wording of the London Petition (1640), much supported by the **Puritan** cause, for the total abolition of the episcopacy of the church 'root and branch', an expression borrowed from the Old Testament book *Malachi*: 'the day that cometh shall burn them up, saith the Lord of hosts, that it shall leave them neither root nor branch' (4: 1).

rope in   •   *coerce into taking part*

An Americanism, from the use of the lasso in ranching.

ropes, know or **learn the**   ● *know or learn how to carry out a task*

A nautical term from the days of sail when an understanding of the complexities of ropes, knots, rigging, etc. was essential for a seaman.

rose

Because of its beauty, fragrance and colour, the rose figures prominently in literature, often indicating a person—especially a woman—of peerless beauty, virtue and excellence. It is also an emblem of England, a heraldic device and an element in Christian symbolism. Common expressions include *bed of roses*, a position of ease and comfort, and *roses all the way* (a quotation from Robert Browning's poem *The Patriot*, 1855), which means pleasing or triumphant progress.

rough-and-tumble

Originally boxing slang, but now standard English for the fairly minor inconveniences and upsets inseparable from some forms of activity.

round table

If King Arthur existed, he was probably a warlike but Christian British chieftain or general in the fifth or sixth century. Armed with his sword Excalibur he gained victories over the heathen in Scotland, Ireland and Iceland. He declared war on Rome rather than pay tribute, but was forced to return home because of the treachery of the nephew he had left in charge of his kingdom. In the ensuing battle with his nephew's supporters, Arthur prevailed but was mortally wounded and conveyed to the island of Avalon.

This story was very much embroidered and added to in several languages, gathering a mass of legend notably about the exploits and courtly loves of several chivalrous and holy knights, such as **Galahad**, and about the quest for the **Holy Grail**. The Round Table is first mentioned by a Norman writer in 1155 as a device for avoiding disputes over precedence among the 150 knights who had the right to be seated at it with Arthur in his court. Even today a *round table conference* implies a meeting of equals committed to reach agreement.

round-robin   • *petition passed round for signature*

The expression first occurs, as 'round Robin', as a blasphemous name for the Sacrament in sixteenth-century religious controversy: 'Robin' may have been an allusion to Robin Goodfellow, a hobgoblin that led people astray, and 'round' was the shape of the communion wafer. The Roman Catholic doctrine that the Sacrament denoted the real presence of Christ in the Mass was repudiated by the emerging Church of England as superstitious, which would explain why a denunciation of it contains a reference to a hobgoblin.

The expression recurs much later, in nautical use and with the modern meaning. When naval petitions were signed, the signatures were appended in circular form, like the spokes of a wheel, to signify the unity of those signing (and, more importantly perhaps, to disguise the identity of the organiser who presumably signed first). This explains *round* but not *robin*. Perhaps the older expression, if not its meaning, had remained in folk memory and was adapted for a new function.

Adjectivally the expression is now also used of a tournament in which all the participants play each other in turn, i.e. all are treated alike—as in a round-robin—and are not subject to the luck of a draw.

rub, there's the   • *that is the problem, obstacle, difficulty, etc*

A quotation from Hamlet's soliloquy 'To be or not to be' (III, 1, line 65), though the use of *rub* as a metaphor for difficulty is earlier. It comes from the game of bowls, in which a *rub* was any impediment which hindered a bowl or diverted it from its course.

rub up the wrong way   • *irritate (person) by tactless handling*

As a cat arches it back, normally a sign of roused feelings, if it is stroked against the lie of its fur.

Rubicon, (cross the)   • *(make a) fateful decision from which there is no turning back*

The Rubicon was a small river, little more than a stream, which formed part of the boundary between ancient Italy and the province of Cisalpine Gaul (now northern Italy). In 49 BC Julius

Caesar took the decision to cross this from his province of Gaul to march on Rome. In the political circumstances of his day this precipitated war between him and Pompey and led to his dictatorship and eventual assassination.

rule of thumb　● *rough measure, guide or approach, often based on experience*

From the use of the upper joint of the thumb to make a measurement when precise accuracy is not needed.

rule the roost　● *be in a dominating position over others*

This conjures up a picture of a cock lording it over a group of hens (a roost) but it is more likely to be a relatively modern corruption of the older 'rule the roast', a reference to the joint of meat that would be carved by the master of the house or be the principal dish at the table he presided over (ruled).

run for one's money, have a (good)　● *be in an enjoyable contest, competition or event*

From racing slang, said of a horse on which one has bet money and which runs well, though without winning.

run of the mill: see *mill*

run to earth　● *find (something or somebody hidden) after a search*

A metaphor taken from fox-hunting, in which the prey is chased (*run*) to its burrow or hiding-place (called its *earth*) so that it cannot escape.

Ruritania　● *idealised or make-believe place of romance or adventure, usually thought of as a small central European state with a royal court subject to* **cloak-and-dagger** *intrigue*

Invented by Anthony Hope (1863–1933) as the setting of his novel *The Prisoner of Zenda*, later more widely known as a popular film.

S

sabotage • *malicious damage done to stop something working*

This word became known in Britain shortly before the First World War. At that time there was a railway strike in France; in order to cause disruption the railway workers were reported as loosening or removing the shoes (*sabots*) that held the railway lines to the sleepers. This, according to many commentators, accounts for the origin of the word *sabotage* and for its appearance in English.

They may be right on the second count but not on the first. *Sabotage* existed as a French word long before this. A *sabot* was a large, heavy wooden clog made of a single piece of wood and worn by workers. The verb *saboter* (literally, to wear *sabots*) meant to clatter about in clogs and, figuratively, to do something ham-fistedly. *Sabotage* was therefore clumsy workmanship, tools that were no good, low levels of skill, broken down vehicles, etc.—all related to the clog's clumsiness and lack of refinement. From this general sense of botched workmanship it was a short step to deliberate botching, the sense eventually taken over into English.

sack, get the • *be dismissed from employment*

Journeymen mechanics used to provide their own tools and carry them from job to job in a bag ('get the bag' and 'get the canvas' are earlier versions of this expression). Perhaps an employer looked after the bag or sack and literally handed it back to a workman when he was dismissed.

sackcloth and ashes, wearing or **in**   • *expressing contrition*

The Hebrew custom of wearing coarse and uncomfortable sack-cloth and sprinkling ashes on the head, as a sign of penitence or grief or as appropriately abject attire at certain religious cere-monies, is frequently referred to in the Bible (see for example *Jonah*, 3: 6 and *Luke*, 10: 13) and is alluded to in the name of Ash Wednesday. Modern use of the expression, which became well known from scripture, is of course metaphorical.

sacred cow   • *belief, custom or institution held to be unalterable and beyond criticism*

There is a powerful Hindu **taboo** against killing cows or eating beef: the cow is regarded as a symbol of life and a sacred animal. Use of the expression in English implies some scorn, however.

sadder but/and wiser

In the penultimate line of Coleridge's *Rime of the Ancient Mariner* (1798) the wedding-guest is described as 'a sadder and a wiser man' after hearing the mariner's tale. See also **albatross**.

sadism; sado-masochism

The first is a love of cruelty, especially of the act of inflicting it on others, and is named after the Marquis de Sade (1740–1814) in whose pornographic novels it amounts to a sexual perversion. The second is a blend of this with **masochism**. In popular use the first, though not the second, has no sexual connotation.

sail close to the wind   • *take a risk; go to the very extremity of what is legal, decent, acceptable, etc*

Taken from nautical terminology: if a boat under sail heads directly into the wind it will be stopped by the backward pressure of the sails against the masts. Sailing 'close to' the direction from which the wind is blowing is therefore risky but makes for more rapid progress than sailing at a more oblique angle.

salad days   • *time of youthful inexperience*

Coined by Shakespeare, whose Cleopatra speaks of

My salad days,
When I was green in judgement . . .

in *Antony and Cleopatra*, I, 5, lines 73–4. A salad uses vegetables which are raw, and it is this characteristic that provides the metaphorical sense.

salary: see *salt*

salt

A person who is *the salt of the earth* is the best of people, especially the most dependable. The expression comes from the Bible, where Jesus describes his disciples as 'the salt of the earth [i.e. of mankind]' in *Matthew*, 5: 13. He meant something different, however: salt has preserving and purifying qualities (newborn babies in the east were rubbed with salt to promote health) and so the disciples were being described as the agent by which mortal souls were to be purified and preserved. The modern meaning, though related, is untheological.

To *salt away* something, usually money, is to preserve it for future use. This stems from the days before refrigeration, when salt was widely used to preserve meat and fish for later consumption.

Anything which is *taken with a pinch of salt*, as a piece of gossip may be, is treated with caution or reservation, just as a dish is treated with salt to make sure that it is to one's taste.

It is interesting to note that the word *salary* is closely connected to salt. The Roman soldier's *salarium*, from the Latin *sal* for salt, was an allowance for the purchase of salt and passed into English as a word for 'pay'. Even today to be *worth one's salt* is to be worthy of one's pay and of respect.

Samaritan, good   • *charitable person, especially one who helps someone in distress*

Speaking of the need to love one's neighbour and answering the question 'Who is my neighbour?', Christ told the parable of a Jewish man who was beaten and robbed, then ignored by two holy men passing by, and finally rescued by a man from Samaria who gave first aid and cared for the victim at an inn before going on his way, leaving money for further assistance. In view of the traditional hatred of Jews for Samaritans the parable teaches that good neighbourliness is independent of national or religious differences. The story is in *Luke*, 10: 30–7.

Samson

A popular Hebrew hero of prodigious strength which he frequently used against the **Philistine** enemy and which has given rise to speculation that his story and that of the Greek hero Hercules (see **Herculean**) have a common source. Delilah, his Philistine mistress, was bribed to betray him: she discovered that the source of his strength was in his long hair and cut it off while he slept, as a result of which he was captured and blinded. In modern use Samson is a personification of physical strength; a Delilah, less frequently, is a seductress who brings ruin.

sandboy: see *happy as a sandboy*

sands of time (running out)   ● *time (passing)*

An allusion to the hour-glass, an old device for measuring the passage of time. It consisted of two glass vessels linked by a narrow neck, and contained a quantity of sand that took exactly an hour to pass from the upper to the lower chamber.

sandwich

Not invented by but named after the disagreeable John Montagu, fourth Earl of Sandwich (1718–92), who is reputed to have spent 24 hours at the gaming-table while eating nothing but slices of beef in bread so that he could carry on playing without breaking for a meal. The snack was given his name for this or some similar act of devotion, and the word spread from London clubland into standard English and indeed into other languages.

sanguine   ● *hopeful, confident, cheerful*

According to medieval physiology the human body contained

four chief fluids or 'humours'—blood, phlegm, choler and melancholy—and the relative proportions of these in one's body determined one's temperament, among other things. If blood (*sanguis* in Latin) predominated, this gave a ruddy complexion and a hopeful, brave character. A person with these attributes was therefore said to be of a *sanguine* disposition. The word used to have some other meanings but this is the one that has survived.

saxophone

Musical instrument invented by the Belgian instrument-maker Adolphe Sax (1814–94) and patented by him in 1846.

scandalmonger: see *warmonger*

scapegoat   • *person (occasionally thing) made to carry the blame for the faults of others*

The ceremonies prescribed for the Jewish Day of Atonement (Yom Kippur) by the Mosaic Law in *Leviticus*, chapter 16, included the bringing of two goats to the altar, one for God and one for Azazel (a devil, perhaps Satan). The former was sacrificed; the latter, to which the priest transferred the sins of the people, was led to the wilderness and allowed to go free, taking the people's sins with it.

When William Tyndale translated the Old Testament into English (1530), he either mistook or misinterpreted the Hebrew *Azazel* as *ez ozel* ('goat that departs') and invented the word *scapegoat* as a translation, *scape* being a variant of 'escape'. By this accident he added a useful new word to the language.

scarlet woman   • *sexually promiscuous woman*

This rather dated term comes from the whore 'arranged in . . . scarlet colour' and seated on 'a scarlet coloured beast' in St John the Divine's prophetic vision (*Revelation*, 17: 1–5). He was probably referring to pagan Rome, though in later theological controversy the *scarlet woman* became an abusive epithet for the Roman Catholic Church. In secular vocabulary she lacks these theological dimensions.

score, settle a; settle scores   • *avenge a wrong*

A *score* is originally a notch cut (scored) into a stick to mark an addition when keeping accounts. It therefore came to mean a bill and to *settle a score* was simply to pay a debt. The relationship between this and the modern meaning is clear.

It is interesting to note that this old sense of *score* as a notch survives in *notching up* (i.e. registering) a victory, goals or runs scored in a game, etc.

scot-free   • *without penalty or loss*

Nothing to do with the Scots. This *scot* is an old and now obsolete word for a payment and was specially used of a municipal tax and of the bill (or one's share of the bill) for entertainment at an inn. A drink on the house was therefore *scot-free*. The meaning has shifted over the years.

Scotch mist   • *rain, drizzle*

The English have rain; the Scots, either from pride or to assert their hardiness, merely have mist. The expression is generally used as an impatient description of something obvious which another person has failed to recognise, find, grasp, etc.

Scott!, great

An exclamation of surprise or disgust, originally American and said to be a reference to General Winfield Scott (1786–1866). Those who identify it as an expression of admiration point to his popularity after his victorious Mexican campaign of 1847. Others believe it to have been originally ironic and to refer to his notorious fussiness and pomposity as a presidential candidate.

scratch

An old sporting term for a starting-line, probably because it was originally scratched on the ground. To *start from scratch* is therefore to start from the beginning. To *come/be up to scratch* (be of the required standard) may have the same origin or be more specifically from prize-fighting: before the modern rules laid down that there should be a certain number of three-minute rounds, a round lasted until one of the contestants was knocked down; there was then a 30-second interval at the end of which he was allowed eight seconds to come unaided *up to scratch*, a line marked in the centre of the ring.

screws on, put the ● *exert strong and uncomfortable pressure on (person)*

From the thumbscrew, sometimes called 'the screws', an instrument of torture formerly used to compress a person's thumb.

Scrooge ● *person who is very mean with money; killjoy*

An allusion to the miserly and mean-spirited man of business in Dickens' much loved *Christmas Carol* (1843) who experiences ghostly visions that turn him into a genial old man.

Scylla and Charybdis ● *two equally dangerous alternatives*

In Greek legend these were two redoubtable sea-monsters who lived on opposite sides of the Straits of Messina which separate Italy and Sicily. Scylla, on the Italian side, was specially associated with a rock on to which she lured sailors who came too close. Charbydis, on the other coast, was a dangerous whirlpool. In avoiding the one, seamen were in danger of destruction by the other. The earliest reference is in Homer's *Odyssey* (XII).

sea, (all) at ● *bewildered; unable to understand*

Originally a nautical expression to describe the condition of a ship out of sight of land and having lost its bearings.

sea-change

A vogue expression meaning 'considerable change', though it is now used so often and unthinkingly that it is in danger of becoming no more than another word for any change. The origin is the song 'Full fathom five' sung by Ariel, a spirit in Shakespeare's *The Tempest* (I, 2, lines 399–407), describing the drowning of the king:

Of his bones are coral made;
Those are pearls that were his eyes:

Nothing of him that doth fade,
But doth suffer a sea-change
Into something rich and strange.

This sea-change, a mysterious transformation into rich or rare substances of the sea, is a metaphor of redemption through death, one of the great themes of the play, and it is unfortunate that the modern use of the term has become so debased.

sea-lawyer

Literally a sailor who, like his **landlubber** counterpart the barrack-room lawyer, is disposed to raise awkward points about rights and wrongs, as lawyers are prone to do. In other words he is an insubordinate nuisance, sometimes even more troublesome by virtue of having right on his side. Now used of both men and women.

seal

A seal is a device, such as a heraldic design or monogram, impressed on a piece of melted wax which then hardens. It is attached to or used to close up a document as evidence of genuineness, or as a mark of ratification or approval. Its use, once everyday, is now rare but is recalled in *one's lips are sealed* (one reveals nothing, one's mouth being closed as with a seal), *seal one's fate* (decide it irrevocably) and *set the seal on* (mark or distinguish with a final characteristic act).

seamy side   • *sordid or least pleasant aspect*

In tailoring, dressmaking, etc., seams are the junctions where the edges of two pieces of material are sewn together. Like a turned-up hem, these are on the inside of a garment and are not seen when it is worn. This *seamy side* is sometimes rough, usually unsightly and best left unseen. Hence the seamy side of a city, etc.

see red: see *red rag*

see the light   • *realise the truth*

An allusion to St Paul's conversion to Christianity: see **Damascus**.

sell down the river: see *river*

sell one's birthright: see *pottage*

sere and yellow, the　　● *old age*

An allusion to Macbeth's lament (V, 3, lines 22–3):

> I have lived long enough: my way of life
> Is fall'n into the sere, the yellow leaf . . .

The metaphor compares Macbeth's life with a leaf that has become dried up (*sere*) and withered (*yellow*), ready to fall in autumn.

serve two masters, (no one can)

'No man can serve two masters: for either he will hate the one, and love the other; or else he will hold to the one, and despise the other. Ye cannot serve God and **mammon**' (*Matthew*, 6: 24).

set the Thames on fire, not: see *Thames*

seven deadly sins　　● *pride, wrath, envy, lust, gluttony, avarice, sloth*

This is not a biblical list but one that arose from the writings of the Fathers of the Church, the notable Christian theologians who formulated doctrine in the first twelve centuries AD, especially the first six. Strictly speaking, a deadly or mortal sin was unpardonable, unlike a mere venial one. The first reference to the expression in English is in a devotional manual of 1340, a translation of a French moral treatise of 1279.

seven years' bad luck

This supposed penalty for breaking a mirror is said to originate in a Roman superstition that if one broke a mirror one also damaged the last person who looked in it, assumed to be oneself. *Seven years* used to mean no more than 'a long period', seven being a mystic number as in the previous and following entries.

seventh heaven, in (the)   • *in a state of blissful happiness*

The Jewish religion recognised seven heavens of which the highest, the seventh, was the abode of God. The seven heavens of Islam—the seventh being a place of divine light and pure ecstasy—come from this. The division was of Babylonian origin, founded on astronomical theories. Despite this antiquity the expression was not used in its modern secular sense until the nineteenth century, probably as a result of increased British familiarity with Islam during the period of empire.

shake the dust off one's feet: see *dust off one's feet*

shakes, be no great   • *be nothing very special*

From gambling: if one makes no great (i.e. no very successful) shakes of the dice, one achieves no great score.

shambles, a   • *a place or condition of great disorder*

Like the Latin and then Old English words from which it is derived, a *shamble* was a bench. It came to be specially used of a bench or stall for the sale of meat. In the plural it therefore meant a meat market or row of butchers' shops, which is why there are still areas of old cities called the Shambles. Later, and understandably enough, it meant a slaughter-house and thus, figuratively, a scene of bloodshed and carnage such as a massacre or fierce battle. The modern meaning is a weakening of this.

shamrock

This became the national emblem of Ireland because according to legend St Patrick, the apostle and patron saint of the country, used its three leaves as a visual aid to explain the doctrine of the Holy Trinity.

shanghai   • *trick into doing something unwanted, unpleasant, etc*

Originally the American equivalent of to **press-gang**, except that drink or drugs were often used to render men more amenable to kidnap as involuntary crew members for voyages to the orient. Shanghai, an important Chinese port, was a likely destination for such voyages.

Shangri-la • *remote, imaginary earthly paradise*

James Hilton invented this as the name for an ideal community of immortal beings, located in the Tibetan Himalayas, in his novel *Lost Horizons* (1933), later a popular film. The word became even better known after it was adopted as the name of the US presidential retreat in Maryland, now called Camp David.

Shanks'(s) or shanks'(s) pony, on • *on foot*

Shanks is both a surname and an old word for 'legs', so the expression is a jocular punning metaphor for 'on a means of conveyance consisting of one's own legs'. It was originally Scottish, first recorded in the early sixteenth century and probably older even than that. The USA has retained the earlier form, *Shanks's mare*.

shape of things to come, the • *(usually ominous) indication of what things will be like in the future*

The title of a popular work of political and scientific speculation by H. G. Wells (1933).

sheep from the goats, separate the • *divide or pick out good, superior or meritorious people from the rest*

An allusion to Christ's prophecy of the **Last Judgement** when the good are to be saved and the evil doomed: 'The Son of man shall come . . . And before him shall be gathered all nations: and he shall separate them one from another, as a shepherd divideth his sheep from the goats: And he shall set the sheep on his right hand, but the goats on the left' (*Matthew*, 25: 31–3).

sheet anchor • *chief support, especially in a difficulty*

A nautical term for a large anchor used only in an emergency. *Sheet* may once have been 'shoot' (ready to shoot out in a crisis), or it may be the seafaring term for a means of attaching something (see **three sheets in the wind**), i.e. the *sheet anchor* was not simply a replacement anchor but an emergency one and was therefore always kept ready with its own *sheet* attached.

shekels • *money*

The *shekel*, the chief silver coin of the Hebrews, became familiar in English because of frequent references to it in the Old Testament, though its true origin has been traced back to Babylon in the fifteenth century BC. The modern use is jocular slang or colloquialism.

shell, come out of one's: see *draw one's horns in*

shell out • *pay*

To shell something, peas for instance, is to remove the shell, pod or husk. To *shell out* money is to remove its casing (purse, wallet, etc.) and hand over the contents. The term has been colloquial for nearly two centuries.

shenanigans • *mischief; trickery*

Originally American, probably an approximation to the Irish *sionnachuvighim* (I play tricks) introduced into the USA by immigrants.

shibboleth • *worn-out and discredited belief*

According to the Bible story in *Judges*, chapter 12, when the Ephraimites wished to cross the fords of the River Jordan, which were in the hands of their enemies the Gileadites, they tried to deny that they were in fact Ephraimites. They were then required to pronounce 'shibboleth' as a test, because it was known that Ephraimites could not say the sound 'sh'. Those who failed the test were killed. Thus *shibboleth* (Hebrew for stream and for ear of corn) came to mean a password known only to certain people, and later signified a belief, custom or principle clung to by a particular group. This is the source of the modern meaning.

shindig • *enjoyable or boisterous party or social occasion*

A recent development of **shindy**, which used to have this meaning, among others, and according to some dictionaries still does. A more colourful explanation is that a *shindig* is so called because it also meant a lively dance in which one was likely to get a kick (*dig*) on the *shin*.

shindy • *quarrel; row; commotion*

An adaptation of 'shinty', a rough game (which explains the present meaning) but an enjoyable one (which throws light on the meaning of **shindig**). It is a sort of hockey. Its name, which used to be 'shinny', is apparently from the cry 'shin ye' used in the game. Whether this meant 'use your legs', and if so what for, cannot now be determined.

A frequent expression is *kick up a shindy* (make a noise or fuss); perhaps this too was once a term used in the game.

ship

Shipshape (in neat order) is a tribute to the traditional high standards of good order on board sailing ships, especially in the Royal Navy. The second syllable is a shortening of 'shapen', the old form of 'shaped', i.e. fashioned. *Shipshape and Bristol fashion* means the same: before the growth of Liverpool, Bristol was the major British west-coast trading-port with a high reputation for the standards of equipment and service needed for long voyages.

When my ship comes home is a catch-phrase meaning 'when I finally make my fortune'. It harks back to the days when an individual's investment or livelihood might well depend on the safe arrival of a trading-ship from a distant port.

Ships that pass in the night are chance acquaintances met only once. The words are from Longfellow's 'The Theologian's Tale' in *Tales of a Wayside Inn*:

Ships that pass in the night, and speak each other in passing,
Only a signal shown and a distant voice in the darkness;
So on the ocean of life we pass . . .

See also **spoil the ship**.

shirty • *bad-tempered; irritable*

A development from the slang expression, 'have one's shirt out' (be or become angry), the idea being that the clothing of a person in a rage becomes dishevelled.

shoddy • *of poor quality*

Shoddy was a cheap yarn made by shredding woollen rags, often cast-off clothes, and adding some new wool to make a kind of cloth. The word has lost its connection with dress, though not with inferior quality, and is now generally an adjective.

shoestring, on a • *at very little cost; on a small budget*

Literally, for the price of a *shoestring*, the old word for shoelace, one of the cheapest commodities one can buy.

shoot one's bolt: see *bolt from the blue*

short shrift of, make • *deal with or dispose of rapidly or inconsiderately*

'Short shrift' was a brief time allowed by law to a condemned person to make a confession to a priest before execution. *Shrift* is an obsolete word now used only in this expression. It comes from the verb 'shrive', another obsolete religious word, which meant to hear a confession and pronounce absolution of sins. It survives in *Shrove Tuesday*, so called because, as the day before the Christian fast of Lent, it is an occasion for preparatory confession.

short straw, (draw) the: see *straw, (draw) the short*

shot

A *long shot* (vain attempt, unlikely prospect, wild guess) is originally military, from the lack of success to be expected when firing at a distant target. *By a long shot* (by a considerable amount) comes from the same source. A *shot in the dark* (guess) is related, perhaps a coinage by George Bernard Shaw (1895). A *shot in the arm* (stimulus, encouragement) is medical, from a hypodermic injection, while a *shot across the bows* (warning, sometimes called a *warning shot*) is naval, from the practice of firing across a ship's course to warn, intimidate or bring to a halt, but not to damage.

shoulder to the wheel, put one's   • *make a major effort*

No particular wheel, merely a general reference to horse-drawn transport. In the days when this was common, wagoners might literally have put their shoulders behind a cart-wheel so as to bring to bear the full weight of their bodies to help the horses extract the cart from the mud, etc. The first recorded appearance of the term in English (in Robert Burton's *Anatomy of Melancholy*, 1621) occurs in the context of a reference to an Aesop's fable (sixth century BC) in which a wagoner whose cart is stuck and who cries out to the god Hercules for help (see **Herculean**) is advised by a cynical friend to depend rather on putting his own shoulder to the wheel.

show a leg   • *(a jocular call to) wake up, get out of bed or become active*

In the days when seamen were refused shore-leave in case they deserted, 'wives' were allowed on board a berthed ship and permitted to lie in longer than the men. In the morning the bosun's mates had to check whoever was still asleep and did so by requiring them to *show a leg* over the side of the hammock. If a leg was hairy it was presumably male and its owner was ordered to get up and begin work.

After the abolition of this amiable custom in 1840 the expression continued in use as a general injunction to get moving.

show(-)down   • *final confrontation to settle a disputed matter*

The term derives from poker, in which players finally reveal the strength of their hands of cards by placing them *down* on the table face-upwards to *show* what they are.

shrapnel

From the name of General Henry Shrapnel (1761–1842) who as a young officer invented a shell containing bullets or ball-shot that were scattered when a time-fuse burst open the shell-casing. The word is now also used of the fragments of metal from the case of an exploded bomb, etc.

Shrove Tuesday: see *short shrift*

Shylock   • *extortionate moneylender*

An accurate though oversimplified description of the central character in Shakespeare's *Merchant of Venice* (1596–8): see **pound of flesh**.

side of the angels, on the: see *angels*

sideburns   • *side-whiskers*

These were known colloquially as *sideboards* in England and as *sideburns* in America from the latter part of the nineteenth century. The American term came from General Burnside (1824–81), who fought in the Civil War. He was distinguished by his side-whiskers and by little else; he resigned his commission after a court of enquiry into his ability.

Side-whiskers became *sideburns* either by a simple pun on 'Burnside's' or because it seemed more natural to transpose the syllables of the general's name to put the adjectival *side* in a conventional position in front of the noun *burns*. The American term became standard English after 1945, probably because British servicemen imported it after contact with US servicemen during the Second World War.

silhouette   • *shape of person or things as it appears against a lighter background*

This sense comes from an earlier and still current one: an outline drawing, often a portrait, filled in with black or cut from black paper, set against a lighter background.

Etienne de Silhouette (1709–67), a French politician and Controller of Finance, made himself unpopular by tax measures which reduced the wealth of the better-off. He was caricatured in drawings which consisted of a few strokes, said to be 'à la Silhouette', the joke being that the artist was exercising economy and the resultant figure lacked substance—as Silhouette's victims did. *À la silhouette* (economically) actually passed into general French.

The type of outline drawing and portraiture already described was extremely popular between about 1750 and 1850. It too lacked the substance of a normal painting and, being cheaper, was also suitable for the less prosperous. It was natural that it should be given Silhouette's name, though the original light-hearted reason for doing so has long been forgotten.

silk purse: see *pig's ear*

silly Billy   • *foolish person*

The nickname of William, Duke of Gloucester (1776–1834): he was King George III's uncle and of weak intellect.

silver

Thirty pieces of silver is the price of treachery, from the betrayal of Christ by **Judas**. He was given this sum (literally, 30 pieces of money) by the chief priests in return for identifying Jesus so that he could be arrested (*Matthew*, 26: 15).

    See also **cloud has a silver lining**.

silver spoon in one's mouth, born with a   • *born into affluence*

Unlike ordinary children, that is, who have to wait until their christening before they receive the traditional gift of a silver spoon from their godparents.

sinecure   • *paid job involving little work*

From an ecclesiastical term *beneficium sine cura*, a benefice without the cure of souls, i.e. a paid position without any spiritual responsibility for a congregation.

siren voices or **song**   • *attractive-sounding invitations or propositions which if accepted lead to disaster*

Homer's *Odyssey* describes the Sirens as malevolent female sea-monsters having the head and bust of a woman and the body of a bird. They sang sweetly to attract men and then destroyed them. Odysseus had been warned about them, so when he came in sight of the rocky islet where they lived he had himself lashed to the mast of his ship, having previously stopped up the ears of his companions with wax so that they could not hear the enchanting music. He therefore escaped the danger, but the bones scattered about the island were proof of the failure of previous voyagers.

Siren in the sense of warning signal is from the same source.

sirloin

Despite the old joke about this joint of meat being a loin that was once knighted by an appreciative king of England—variously identified as Henry VIII, James I and Charles II—who placed his sword on it and said 'Arise, Sir Loin', the truth is more pedestrian. The word is a variant spelling of *surloin*, meaning 'above [French *sur*] the loin', which is where the meat comes from. This is not to deny that a king may once have made a joke, but it would have been after, not before, the word had come into existence.

Sisyphean task ● *endless, fruitless and therefore futile task*

Sisyphus, a cunning hero in Greek legend, died as a result of offending Zeus but fabricated an excuse to return temporarily to earth from the underworld. He then refused to go back, and was punished for his breach of faith by being required eternally to roll a great boulder up a mountain; the boulder slipped down again each time he got it nearly to the top.

six, hit or knock for ● *wrecked, defeated*

In cricket a ball that is hit over the boundary without touching the ground scores six—exceptional enough for the bowler of such a ball to feel a sense of failure. A person who is said to have been *hit for six* is seriously upset: a thing *hit for six* has been badly damaged.

sixes and sevens, at ● *in a state of confusion*

The pips on a dice, and later on playing-cards, used to be numbered in an approximation to French: ace (which is still used in card-playing), deuce, trey (both of which persisted into the twentieth century), quatre, cinq(ue) and sice. To *set (all) on cinque and sice* meant literally to gamble on the highest numbers and figuratively to behave recklessly.

In the course of time the literal meanings of *cinque* and *sice* were forgotten: *cinque* (pronounced 'sink') was incorrectly anglicised as *six*, so *sice* became *seven* and the whole phrase gradually assumed its familiar form. From the earlier association with reckless behaviour came the idea that things in disorder were *at sixes and sevens*.

skeleton in the cupboard or at the feast

The first phrase means a secret personal or family disgrace, problem, discreditable fact or scandal from the past. It has been said to date from the nineteenth century, when corpses were much sought after for medical research or teaching but were unobtainable legally, with the result that a skeleton would have to be kept hidden. This is unlikely: a skeleton can be copied in other materials. The origin is more probably an old saying or joke comparing a person's secret with a murder he or she has committed and hushed up.

A *skeleton at the feast* is somebody or something that in the midst of pleasures acts as a reminder of life's troubles. The expression alludes to the practice among the ancient Egyptians of displaying a skeleton at a celebration in order to remind guests of their mortality. The Greek biographer and moralist Plutarch noted this custom in his *Moralia*, first published in English in 1603 but well known before then.

skin of one's teeth, by the • *by the narrowest of margins*

'I am escaped with the skin of my teeth' (*Job*, 19: 20). The earlier translation by Coverdale (1535) is 'only there is left me the skin about my teeth'. *Skin* here means 'outer covering'. See also **Job**.

skylarking: see *lark*

slapstick • *(comedy) of an exaggerated, knockabout style*

The original slap stick, in American pantomine or low comedy, was a split rod or two flat pieces of wood hinged at one end; when it was used to hit someone it gave an unexpectedly loud crack. Sometimes a small explosive charge was hidden in the stick to make a bang of the sort associated with clownish circus-comedy.

slate

The use of slate as a writing surface on which one could **chalk up** scores in games or debts in a shop or pub has given rise to a number of current expressions. Something that has been *put on the slate* is on credit. To *wipe the slate clean* is to prepare for a fresh start, either by paying off debts or by expunging the score of the previous game to make room for the next. To *start with a clean slate* is a similar expression. The verb *slate* (criticism) may derive from the practice of recording debts on a slate or from a northern English dialect word meaning to use or encourage a dog to attack or to herd animals.

The former use of slate as a writing surface in schools may have given extra currency to expressions about *clean slates* or may be the origin of them. It has also been suggested that *slated* (condemned) may have originated in a practice of writing the names of disgraced pupils on a publicly displayed slate used as a notice-board.

slaughter: see *lamb*

sleep like a top   • *sleep very soundly*

Unlikely as it may seem, the *top* referred to here is the child's toy which seems not to be moving when it is spinning, though it wobbles when being set in motion or when running down. It is this period of apparent stillness (accompanied by a quiet and steady sound?) that gave rise to the simile, first used by Shakespeare or his collaborator Fletcher in *Two Noble Kinsmen* (1613) and common ever since.

sleeve, up one's   • *held (secretly) in reserve*

From conjuring, in which the performer may use his or her sleeve for concealment, though the mystery is often compounded by the conjurer showing that there is 'nothing up my sleeve'. A longer expression *have a few tricks up one's sleeve* (have some surprises in store) is from the same source.

See also **laugh**.

slipshod   ● *untidy; careless*

The sixteenth-century 'slip–shoe' was a loosely fitting shoe or slipper that was thought to be unsmart; there are lines in Shakespeare and Jonson suggesting that slip-shoes were suitable for folk with chilblains. They became synonymous with down-at-heel poverty and finally with slovenliness.

slough of despond   ● *state of despair*

In his allegorical *Pilgrim's Progress* (1678) John Bunyan dreams of a figure, called Christian, who journeys to the Celestial City and encounters various people and places symbolising aspects of human and spiritual life. Part of his pilgrimage takes him through the Slough of Despond (the latter is an archaic word for despondency), a place of fears, doubts and discouragements.

Slough (pronounced 'slow') used to be a common word for a bog or stretch of muddy ground, and this is its meaning in the story, though it was already a common metaphor for a state of moral degradation.

small beer   ● *matter(s) or person(s) of no importance*

Not a reference to the size of a glass of beer but to its strength: *small* meant 'of low alcoholic strength' as early as 1440. The whole expression has been used in its current metaphorical sense since the eighteenth century.

smell a rat   ● *become or be suspicious*

In less hygienic days, when rats were common household and urban pests and carriers of disease, dogs were prized for their ability to smell out and destroy them. A dog which began to sniff around might well have smelt a rat, and this idea was transferred to a person who had cause to feel that something was not as it should be.

snake

A *snake in the grass* is a secretly treacherous person. The image was first used in writing by Virgil (70–19 BC) in his *Eclogues* (III, 93). The now familiar English formulation emerged only in the late seventeenth century but earlier approximations to it are common, the earliest being in Chaucer's 'Summoner's Tale', line 1994, in the *Canterbury Tales* (about 1387), the popularity of which must have been responsible for making the idea generally known. Its persistence is curious in a country where poisonous snakes are not part of common experience.

A *snake/viper in one's bosom* is also a person who is not only treacherous but ungrateful too. The origin here is Aesop's fable (sixth century BC) of the farm-hand who took pity on a snake frozen stiff by the cold, put it in his bosom to warm it, and received a fatal bite when it revived.

sneezed at, not to be   • *not to be underrated or treated lightly*

Taking snuff may induce sneezing. 'Snuff' also used to be a word for anything of little value, so anything of greater value was 'not snuff', i.e. not a sneezing matter.

soap (opera)   • *television (or radio) serial in popular style*

This name was coined in the USA in the 1930s because the earliest examples of such serials were sponsored by soap manufacturers in a form of direct financing forbidden in Britain until recently. A specific origin may have been *Amos and Andy* (1927), sponsored by Proctor and Gamble. The word *opera* is added derisively: the preoccupations of these programmes are normally well below the level of high drama associated with grand opera. Cowboy films were sometimes called 'horse-operas' at the time of the first *soaps*—perhaps a little earlier, in which case it is likely that *soap opera* was a borrowing.

The term is sometimes now used of any long-running state of affairs.

sock in it, put a   • *stop talking*

The most common explanation for this expression is that it dates from the early days of the gramophone when, in the absence of a volume control, a sock was stuffed into the horn of the machine to deaden the sound. This seems improbable: in the sort of household that alone could have afforded such a novelty it is unlikely that a sock would be used in the drawing-room.

In a barrack-room, however, socks would certainly be lying

around at night and one can imagine a heavy snorer being shouted at and told to 'put a sock in it' (his mouth). Some such military origin is far more likely.

Sodom and Gomorrah   ● *places regarded as centres of vice or depravity*

These two ancient cities were in the plain to the south of the Dead Sea. As told in *Genesis*, chapters 18 and 19, they were destroyed by God because of the great wickedness of their inhabitants. Their names recur in both the Old and New Testaments as bywords for sinfulness.

soft pedal   ● *treat (more) gently or cautiously*

On a piano the soft pedal, operated by the left foot, is used to reduce volume either by causing the hammer to strike only one instead of the usual two or three strings, or by bringing the hammer closer to the strings to lessen the impact.

soft soap   ● *flatter; persuade or cajole with charming talk*

An Americanism, used also as a noun, and familiar in British English since the middle of the nineteenth century. It is an obvious reference to the lubricant qualities of soft soap but appears to be based on the older 'soft sawder', a variant of the much earlier 'soft solder'. This was a common form of solder made from tin and lead and was used for uniting pieces of metal and, metaphorically, for uniting people. The development of 'solder' into 'sawder' is easily explained because the letter l in 'solder' is often unpronounced.

sold a pup: see *cat out of the bag*

sold down the river: see *river*

Solomon, wisdom or **judgement of**

When Solomon, the third king of Israel (tenth century BC), was offered a gift by God he asked for an understanding heart and thus became 'wiser than all men' (*I Kings*, 4: 31). Required to

299

adjudicate between two harlots who claimed maternity of the same baby he called for a sword and ordered that the child be cut into two, with each woman to receive a half of the child, whereupon one of the women renounced her claim, showing herself to be the true mother. The *judgement of Solomon* is therefore a harsh but necessary choice between equally strong competing claims; the *wisdom of Solomon* is proverbial. See *I Kings*, chapter 3, for the whole story.

song, (going) for a   • *(available) for a small amount of money*

The first printed comparison between a trifle and a song is found in 1601 in Shakespeare's *All's Well that Ends Well* (III, 2, line 9) but there is evidence that 'sold for a song' was already proverbial. Sheet-music was very popular and the stationers who printed and sold ballads employed vagabonds to peddle them up and down the country for small sums.

sop   • *something offered as a concession or bribe*

A sop was a piece of bread soaked in liquid. Its modern metaphorical use originated in an incident from Virgil's *Aeneid*, written in the first century BC and known in English since 1513, in which Aeneas was able to pass into the underworld because Cerberus, the monstrous dog guarding the entrance, had been drugged with a sop. This sense of pacification has now displaced the literal sense. See **milksop**.

SOS

This appeal for urgent help has nothing to do with the abbreviation of 'Save our Souls'. The combination of letters was chosen merely because in morse code (in which it is represented as three dots, three dashes, three dots) it was simple, unmistakable and easy for use in an emergency by a radio operator.

sound and fury

A quotation from Macbeth's comparison of life to a tale 'Told by an idiot, full of sound and fury,/Signifying nothing' (V, 5, lines 27–8).

sour grapes   ● *disparagement (of merit, ownership, success, etc.) by someone who is incapable of such an achievement; sulkiness stemming from envy, animosity, etc*

From Aesop's fable (sixth century BC) of the hungry fox who, unable to reach some grapes from a vine because they were too high, comforted himself by saying that they were not ripe anyway.

sow one's wild oats   ● *indulge in youthful vices or excesses*

The wild oat looks like the cultivated one but is actually merely a tall grass: to spend time and energy sowing it is therefore unprofitable.

The expression sometimes implies sexual activity, probably as a result of the (implied) obsolete sense of 'seed' (semen; also, in scripture, offspring).

Spanish Inquisition

Now used in jocular reference to any severe cross-examination, this was an infamous ecclesiastical court of the Roman Catholic Church in Spain from 1479–1834. Like Inquisitions elsewhere it was intended to prosecute heretics, was held in secret, used torture as a means of extracting evidence, and had the power to refer its findings to the secular authorities, which usually resulted in the victim's execution by burning.

spare the rod (and spoil the child)

The precise words are first found in Samuel Butler's satirical poem *Hudibras* (1664) but different expressions of the same sentiment go back to about the year 1000 and originate in the biblical *Proverbs*, parts of which are earlier than the eighth century BC: 'He that spareth his rod hateth his son' (13: 24).

Spartan   ● *austere, frugal, simple, hardy, bare of comfort*

That is to say, having some of the qualities associated with Sparta, the ancient capital of Laconia in south-west Greece. It was the most efficient military power in the ancient Greek Empire; children were taken away from their homes from the age of five and subjected to military discipline until they were 30; courage, cold-bloodedness and a capacity to endure hardship were rigorously cultivated. See **laconic**.

sphinx-like • *inscrutable*

There are two famous sphinxes. One is the colossal statue (c. 2620 BC) of a lion with a human head near the El-Gizeh pyramids in Egypt. The other is the monster of Greek mythology with the head and shoulders of a woman, the body of several animals and the wings of a bird, who killed those who failed to answer its riddle: 'What animal has four feet, then two, then three, but only one voice?' **Oedipus** answered correctly: man, who crawls as a child, then walks, then uses a stick for support in old age. Deprived of its secret the Sphinx killed itself, and Oedipus thus saved the citizens of Thebes from its terror.

It is the sphinx of legend that has given rise to modern uses of the word: an inscrutable person is *sphinx-like* in being mysterious, enigmatic and incomprehensible—something of a riddle, in fact.

spick and span • *neat and clean*

Spick exists nowhere else in English, nor does *span* as an adjective. The original form was 'span-new' (perfectly new), from an Old Norse term; this changed to 'spick-and-span new' as little more than an emphatic extension, and finally shortened to its present version. It is an interesting example of how any expression can change its form and meaning over the centuries for no obvious reason.

spike somebody's guns • *thwart somebody's opposition*

A metaphorical adaptation of an old military term meaning to render a (heavy) gun unserviceable (often one's own, prior to retreat) by driving a spike into the touch-hole.

spill the beans: see *bean*

spirit is willing, the

An apology for inaction, the full quotation being 'the spirit indeed is willing, but the flesh is weak' (*Matthew*, 26: 41), a reproach to the disciples who fell asleep while Jesus was praying in Gethsemane shortly before his arrest and crucifixion.

spitting image   ● *exact likeness*

There is a very old expression (c. 1400) 'as like one as if he had been spit out of his mouth' (meaning 'very alike'); Jonathan Swift, for example, wrote much later 'She's as like her husband as if she were spit out of his mouth'. Later variants were 'he's the very spit of . . . ' and 'he's the spit and image of . . . ', and this last one developed into the modern version.

splice the mainbrace   ● *have a celebratory drink*

In the days when sailors had a rum ration, the order to *splice the main brace* (two words) meant serving an additional tot as a pick-me-up after special exertion. After the introduction of steamships had made the sailors' lot less exhausting, the order was given when any special celebration was due.

In naval parlance a brace is a rope and splicing it is a form of repair. The main brace was connected to the main sail; splicing it was not only obviously important but also dangerous in a storm. But there is no very clear link, except a jocular one, between an (unwelcome?) order to do this work and a welcome one to serve extra drink.

spoil the ship for a ha'porth of tar   ● *spoil something by economising on a small detail*

This was originally, from at least 1600, 'lose the sheep [often 'hog'] for a half-pennyworth of tar'—i.e. let the animal die for want of spending a trivial sum on tar to protect its sores or wounds from infection by flies.

'Ship' was the dialect pronunciation of 'sheep' over much of England, and non-countryfolk obviously assumed that the expression referred to a ship, the assumption being reinforced by the reference to tar, which was widely used on wooden ships to coat and preserve the timbers. To complete this transformation of a rustic expression into a nautical-sounding one, the rather extravagant and unconvincing idea of 'losing' an entire ship for the sake of a small economy was changed to 'spoiling' and the now familiar version emerged in the mid-nineteenth century.

A person who is *tarred with the same brush* has the same faults as someone else being referred to. It is probable that this image also comes from the application of tar to animals, either for the purpose already described or to mark them out as members of the same flock.

spoke in one's wheel, put a • *thwart one's actions or plans*

This has nothing to do with a wheel-spoke in its modern sense, as part of a bicycle wheel for instance. It refers to a wooden bar, called a *spoke*, which used to do service as a braking-device on horse-drawn vehicles. Thrust into a specially provided hole, it acted on a wheel to prevent a vehicle going out of control down a hill.

sponge: see *towel, throw in the*

spoonerism • *accidental transposition of initial letters or syllables of words, producing comic effect*

This quirk is so called after the Revd William Spooner, Dean and later Warden of New College, Oxford, between 1876 and 1924. Spooner was prone to making such slips, though some of the most frequently quoted examples, such as his description of Jesus as a 'shoving leopard', are apocryphal. He seems to have been more given to the sort of absent-mindedness exemplified by 'fifty miles as the cock crows' and 'such a sad death—eaten by missionaries'.

spots off, knock • *beat or surpass easily*

Perhaps from the use of playing-cards as targets at shooting galleries, the spots being the pips one is required to hit.

spout, up the • *ruined; lost*

In a pawnship, resort to which obviously implies financial trouble, the lift for sending deposited articles up for storage used to be called the *spout*. If anything—or, by transference, anybody—is *up the spout*, there are difficulties.

spur

In former days a boy of noble birth might do service as a page and squire and later be raised to the (military) rank of knight by the sovereign or some other authorised person, perhaps after good service in battle. He would be presented with a pair of gilt spurs to mark this achievement. Today *to win one's spurs* is to gain recognition or be raised from junior to senior status as a result of one's own efforts.

A *spur* is used to urge a horse forward. Figuratively, the word signifies a stimulus or incentive. Something done *on the spur of the moment* is done without premeditation, the moment alone acting as the *spur* to action.

square one, back to   ● *back to where one started, having wasted time*

The most usual explanation refers to the diagram of a football pitch divided into numbered squares, printed in *Radio Times* from 1927 until about 1940 to help listeners follow radio commentaries on matches. The commentator referred to these squares when describing the progress of play, enabling the listener to visualise it more clearly.

While it may be true that commentators used the phrase 'back to square one', it would not have meant what it now means: soccer is a game of rapid movement and there is little sense of starting again after useless effort. There is, however, an alternative origin in board games such as Snakes and Ladders in which certain throws of the dice do indeed take players back to square one, wiping out the progress they have made. This is the more likely origin of the phrase, though football commentators may have popularised it.

Stalinism

Joseph Stalin (1879–1953), leader of the USSR after the death of Lenin (1924), was seen as an avuncular ally during the Second World War, but the reality was quite different. He is now remembered as a ruthless dictator who distorted the idealism of the first communists, imposing strict uniformity and centralisation on the Soviet people, exterminating dissent with dreadful purges and imprisonment, and forcing rigid conformity on Eastern European countries from 1945 until their liberation in the late 1980s.

stalking horse   • *person, occasionally thing, put forward to mislead, mask intentions, etc*

Literally, a horse specially trained to allow a hunter, especially a fowler, to hide behind it in order to stalk, i.e. to get within easy reach of game without alarming it in the way that a hunter alone on foot would.

stamping ground   • *habitual place of resort*

Some cloven-footed animals, sheep and deer for example, stamp the ground to express warning of an invasion of their territory. For this reason the term, originally an Americanism, was coined to mean the place where particular animals could be found, and it is now commonly applied to people.

star, hitch one's wagon to a   • *set oneself high aspirations*

In its original formulation by the American philosopher and poet Ralph Waldo Emerson (1803–82) in *Society and Solitude* (1870), *star* is used in its vague poetic sense of something distant and beautiful that guides human destiny, while *hitch your wagon* is a homespun Americanism for securing a wagon to whatever draws it along. The whole expression meant hitching one's wagon (i.e. life) to someone else's star, i.e. aspiring to the admirable example set by that person, though it has now rather degenerated into a sense of throwing in one's lot with someone who is apparently successful.

steal a march on   • *gain an advantage over, usually by stealth*

In military terminology a *march* used to be the distance that troops could cover in a day. Any war of movement entails calculations of how far or how quickly an enemy may travel. Gaining a day's advantage, for example using skilful, daring or rapid manoeuvre to get to a place and be ready for an enemy earlier than he expected, was therefore tantamount to stealing a day (i.e. a *march*) from him. The expression was later applied to other sorts of military advantage.

steal someone's thunder • *reduce the effect of someone's action or ideas by using them as one's own or before she or he does*

John Dennis (1657–1734), best remembered as a critic but also an ineffective poet and dramatist, wrote a dismal tragedy called *Appius and Virginia* (1709) for which he invented a device for making stage thunder. His bitterness at the play's early demise was enhanced when he heard his own thunder-device being used in a subsequent production of someone else's play. The closely knit and often malicious literary world of Queen Anne's London would have enjoyed his complaint that his thunder had been stolen—and was in greater demand than his play.

stentorian • *very loud*

Apart from giving this word to the language, Stentor is known only as a Greek warrior in the Trojan War who, according to Homer, 'could raise a shout like that of fifty men together' (*Iliad*, V, 783).

stick to one's guns: see *guns*

sticky wicket, on a • *(in an) awkward position*

A cricketing term for a wet batting-pitch, difficult for batsmen because of the advantage it offers to spin bowling.

stiff upper lip • *courage and self-control in the face of adversity*

This term has been traced back to J. Neal's *Down Easters* (1833) as a development from a number of earlier expressions in which control of the lips (prone to quiver with grief, anger, etc.) is equated with the repression of emotion—thought by the British to be a virtue.

still small voice • *conscience*

A secular borrowing of a term which in religious contexts means the voice of God, *still* here signifying quiet and tranquil. The origin is scriptural, from Elijah's encounter with God on Mount Horeb (*I Kings*, 19: 11–12).

sting in the tail • *unexpected hurt, shock, etc. at the end of an otherwise painless process*

St John's prophetic vision in *Revelation* includes an account of monsters who 'had tails like unto scorpions, and there were stings in their tails: and their power was to hurt men' (9: 10). The expression acquired its modern metaphorical meaning early in the sixteenth century.

stocks, on the • *in preparation*

Not the device in which people used to be placed for punishment, but the wooden framework on which a ship used to be supported while under construction.

stoical • *showing no response to discomfort, pain, inconvenience, etc.; fatalistic*

The Greek word *stoa* means a porch or roofed colonnade and was the name specially given to a great Athenian hall where Zeno (c. 333–262 BC) lectured and from which his disciples took their name. *Stoicism* is a complex philosophy with a long history but its central tenets may be summarised as the cultivation of virtue, denial of pleasure, suppression of the passions and withdrawal from the external world.

stone, cast the first • *act self-righteously*

When Christ was asked if an adulterous woman should be stoned in accordance with Mosaic law he replied, 'He that is without sin among you, let him first cast a stone at her' (*John*, 8:7), at which the crowd of accusers melted away.

stone unturned, leave no • *search everywhere; try by all means*

This was the advice of the **oracle** at Delphi when consulted by Polycrates, who had failed to find the hidden treasure of the Persian general defeated at the Battle of Plataea (479 BC). The advice was successfully followed.

stonewall   • *behave obstructively, usually by refusing to give answers or respond to demands*

Metaphorical uses of 'stone wall' as an image for anything strong and solid can be traced back to several old expressions such as 'hunger breaks stone walls' (fourteenth century) and 'run one's head against a stone wall' (sixteenth century). *Stonewall* as a single word is found as cricket slang (to bat defensively) and as the nickname of General Jackson, a Confederate hero in the American Civil War, who in the words of a fellow officer stood 'like a stone wall' at the first Battle of the Bull Run (1861).

    The current meaning originated in Australian politics (1867), where *stonewalling* became the term for parliamentary obstruction by means of lengthy speeches and other delaying tactics. The Australians almost certainly borrowed the word from cricket.

stony broke   • *without money*

Originally 'stone-broke'. There are a number of parallel expressions—clean/dead/flat-broke—and perhaps *stone* suggested itself by analogy with 'stone-deaf' or 'stone-cold', where *stone* has the force of 'very' (though originally these expressions were compressed similes: deaf as a stone, cold as a stone).

stony ground   • *person or place unreceptive to one's ideas, etc*

In Christ's parable of the sower, some seed 'fell on stony ground . . . and because it had no root, it withered away' (*Mark*, 4: 5–6); the seed here is God's word and the parable is about the different ways people respond to it.

stops: see *pull all the stops out*

straight and narrow   • *strictly correct path of behaviour, legally and morally*

An alteration, probably as a result of misunderstanding or misspelling, of a section from Christ's Sermon on the Mount: 'Enter ye in at the strait gate: for wide is the gate, and broad is the way, that leadeth to destruction . . . strait is the gate, and narrow is the way, which leadeth unto life' (*Matthew*, 7: 13–14). Here 'strait' means 'narrow'; it is archaic in this sense (although it survives as a noun—dire straits, Straits of Gibraltar, etc.) and has often changed its spelling to *straight* (straightjacket, **straight(-)laced**), much as purists may object. In fact *straight* (not crooked) *and narrow* (strict) makes good sense even though its biblical origin was slightly different.

straight bat, with a   ● *very correctly, not loosely or wildly*

A cricketing term: keeping the bat in a vertical position when playing certain strokes is held to be correct style.

straight from the horse's mouth: see *gift-horse*

straight from the shoulder   ● *with full force; directly, frankly*

From boxing: if the fist is brought to the shoulder and then punched forward, the full length and power of the arm is behind the blow.

straight(-)laced   ● *prudish*

An alternative spelling of the more correct strait(-)laced, where 'strait' is an archaic word (see **straight and narrow**) for 'tight' or 'narrow' and 'laced' refers to the string that fastens a bodice or corset.

The very tight fastening of a bodice or corset to which the word refers used to be fashionable, though it was often uncomfortable or even unhealthy. It has been metaphorical for excessive rigidity of conduct since the sixteenth century.

strain at a gnat   ● *be unduly fussy about tiny detail*

Railing against the Pharisees (see **pharisaic**), Christ described them as 'blind guides, which strain at a gnat and swallow a camel' (*Matthew*, 23: 24). He meant that their obsession with legalistic minutiae was like carefully straining gnats (mosquitoes) from their drink while being oblivious to the fact that they were eating whole camels (unclean meat to the Jews), i.e. they were missing the whole point of religious observance. Later translations of the Bible have 'strain out', which is more accurate than *strain at*.

strait: see *straight and narrow* and *straight(-)laced*

straw, final or **last**   ● *in a series of calamities, the final (perhaps small) blow which makes matters insupportable*

A quotation from chapter 2 of Charles Dickens' *Dombey and Son* (1848): 'As the last straw breaks the laden camel's back, this piece of underground information crushed the sinking spirits of Mr Dombey.' This colourful variant of the older 'last feather that breaks the horse's back' is now proverbial as 'it is the [last] straw that breaks the camel's back'. The reference is to the carrying of loads by animals.

straw, draw the short   ● *(be allocated to) a disagreeable task*

From an old method of drawing lots, using several pieces of straw of equal length and one that was shorter. They were held in the hand so as to conceal the length of all the straws, and whoever *drew the short straw* was the loser.

straw in the wind: see *straws, clutch at*

straw that broke the camel's back: see *straw, final* or *last*

straws, clutch at   ● *desperately resort to any inadequate remedy to get help or support*

A modern reference to the old proverb 'A drowning man will catch at a straw'. Earlier versions, which go back to the sixteenth century if not before, refer to a stick or a twig; no doubt these were replaced by a straw because of its even greater inadequacy as a means of support. *Clutch* replaced 'catch' in the nineteenth century.

A number of expressions use *straw* to typify anything having negligible importance, substance or value. A *man of straw* is weak, like a straw dummy, and a *straw in the wind* is a small hint or fact which may indicate a more important coming event. This last is from the proverbial 'Straws show which way the wind blows': just as one may drop a straw to check the direction or strength of the wind (some rugby players about to make a place-kick still do this, using a piece of grass), so one may learn about something significant from small signs.

streets paved with gold   • *place where one may find one's fortune*

The story of Dick Whittington, first published in 1605, refers to a historical figure who was a liberal benefactor and three times Lord Mayor of London in the late fourteenth and early fifteenth centuries. Parts of the legend, however, especially the role of the cat which helps its owner to become wealthy, may belong to remoter times or countries. It is now a traditional feature of the story that Dick goes to London, to enter the service of a merchant, because he has been told that it is a place of such great richness that even the streets are paved with gold.

strike while the iron is hot   • *act while the time is favourable*: see **hammer and tongs**.

string

This means, among other things, a cord for leading an animal, especially a horse, and is therefore found in a number of expressions having to do with the exercise of control. They include *no strings attached* (without restrictions), *string along* (join the 'string' of horses, i.e. accompany, often reluctantly; mislead), and possibly *pull strings* (exercise influence), though the latter may derive from puppetry. 'String' is also short for *bowstring*: to have *more than one string to* (i.e. for) *one's bow*, a sensible precaution for archers, is to have more than one expedient, including a *second string*, a second resource in case the first should fail. *Holding the purse-strings* (controlling expenditure) is a reminder of the days when a purse was a small bag, the neck of which was held tight by a drawstring. See also **shoestring**.

stumbling block   • *impediment*

At first glance this is a curious term because a block is ordinarily thought of as something which bars progress, not merely causes a stumble. The explanation is that *block* is also an obsolete word for a tree-stump. When William Tyndale translated the New Testament from Greek into English (1526) he was the first to use the term (as one word) in print, as a translation of a Greek word meaning 'cause of stumbling': 'that no man put a stumbling block or an occasion to fall in his brother's way' (*Romans*, 14: 13). The word was retained in the later Authorised Version and has passed into everyday use as a metaphor.

'Stumble at a block' (trip over a tree-stump) is found in a book of about 1450 and was probably everyday English at a time when England was predominantly rural and tree-stumps or roots were far more likely to cause a pedestrian to stumble than they are today. *Stumblingblock* may also have been current, or may have been coined by Tyndale.

stumped: see *stump up*

stump up   • *pay money (often reluctantly or with difficulty)*

Originally, to stump (up) was to dig up tree-stumps by the roots in order to clear land for cultivation. The expression, an American one from the days of settlement, became figurative with the idea of digging deep into one's pocket to get money out.

The same verb has given rise to *stumped*. Farmers were said to be *stumped* if they encountered hidden roots when ploughing land that had been imperfectly *stumped (up)*, i.e. cleared. Consequently the word came to mean 'nonplussed, puzzled, held up by a difficulty'. There is no good reason for the view that this sense comes from cricket, where being stumped means something quite different (i.e. dismissed).

Stygian   • *hellish*

Usually applied to nouns such as gloom and darkness, this is the adjective from Styx, the river around the underworld of Greek mythology, a place of shadows and mystery. The ghosts of the dead were ferried across the Styx, and the gods swore their most solemn oaths by it.

sublime to the ridiculous, from the

Adapted from Tom Paine's influential *The Age of Reason* (1793): 'The sublime and the ridiculous are often so nearly related that it is difficult to class them separately. One step above the sublime makes the ridiculous, and one step above the ridiculous makes the sublime again'. Napoleon may have helped to popularise this idea in its more succinct modern form: he is reported as saying, in the year of the retreat from Moscow (1812), 'From the sublime to the ridiculous there is only one step'.

suffer fools gladly • *show patience towards the foolish (i.e. the incompetent, self-important, etc.)*

This phrase is usually found in the negative, as an attribute of intolerant people. It is from St Paul: 'For ye suffer fools gladly, seeing ye yourselves are wise' (*II Corinthians*, 11: 19).

sure as eggs is eggs, as: see *eggs is eggs*

survival of the fittest

Not coined by Charles Darwin, as is usually assumed, but by Herbert Spencer in *Principles of Biology* (1864–7), though Darwin later acknowledged the appropriateness of the phrase. Spencer used *fittest* in the sense of 'most suitable'; he was referring to animals' adaptability to an environment. In modern use, however, it is taken to mean 'most strong' and the whole expression is used of people fighting for survival or exercising strength in order to prevail over others.

Svengali: see *trilby*

swallow does not make a summer, one • *a single or isolated happy event does not mean that all one's troubles are over*

The annual migration of swallows to Europe from southern climes at the end of winter was the subject of a Greek proverb recorded by Aristotle (384–22 BC) in his *Nicomachean Ethics* (I, 7, line 16): 'One swallow does not make a spring'. The English version has been common since the sixteenth century, the basic metaphor being that the end of winter is the end of hard times but that more than one piece of evidence is needed to prove that it has been reached.

swan-song • *final performance*

The belief, which has no foundation in fact, that a swan sings for the only time in its life just before it dies is first recorded in Aesop (sixth century BC) and is also found in Latin literature and in English from the fourteenth century onwards. This song is generally described as melodious, but is variously identified as a dirge and a song of joy at the prospect of death. In Greek mythology, for instance, the swan was sacred to Apollo and Aphrodite and its dying song was one of happiness at the imminence of joining them.

sweep the board: see *board, above*

sweet Fanny Adams or **sweet FA**: see *Fanny Adams*

sweetness and light   ● *(unexpected) agreeableness or cooperation*

Popularised by Matthew Arnold, for whom 'sweetness and light' were among the gifts of culture (*Culture and Anarchy*, 1869), though Swift had earlier referred to the same pair, calling them 'the two noblest of things' which the ancient writers had given to mankind (*Battle of the Books*, 1697). Modern use of the quotation is merely jocular.

swim, in the   ● *in the mainstream (especially of fashion and events)*

The *swim* is what countryfolk and anglers call a section of river much frequented by fish. A person who is *in the swim* is therefore where everyone else is—i.e. doing what everyone else is doing.

swing the lead   ● *malinger, evade duty, often by inventing an excuse*

Originally twentieth century military slang. Despite what some authorities say, it is unlikely to be nautical; it is true that a rope weighted with lead was used to measure the depth of sea beneath a ship, but this involved no swinging and was so crucial—and so closely supervised—that it cannot have become a metaphor for malingering.

There was, however, a nautical expression 'swing the leg', an allusion to the pretence of having a damaged leg so as to avoid work: malingerers 'swung' it when walking so as to appear crippled. This expression may have been misheard or misunderstood during its transference to more general military vocabulary.

swings and roundabouts

What you lose on the swings you gain on the roundabouts is a catch-phrase originating in fairground language. It is an optimistic assertion that, all things considered, matters tend to turn out satisfactorily if you take the rough with the smooth. Swings go up and down, and roundabouts go round and round, but taken both together they add up to the same thing—a way of giving amusement and making a living.

swoop, (at) one fell   •   *(with) a single effort; all at once*

A *swoop* is a sudden descent, like the pouncing of a bird of prey on its victim. *Fell* is an old adjective meaning 'savage'. The whole expression is from Shakespeare: Macduff, struggling to come to terms with the murder of his children and wife on the orders of the 'hell-kite' Macbeth, cries 'What, all my pretty chickens and their dam/At one fell swoop?' (*Macbeth*, IV, 3, lines 218–9). In modern use the expression does not generally carry this sense of savagery, though it sometimes does.

sword

They that live by the sword will die by the sword is the modern adaptation of Jesus' warning against violence: 'all they that take the sword shall perish with the sword' (*St Matthew*, 26: 52).

The *sword of Damocles* was, according to the Roman orator and philosopher Cicero, a sword hung from the ceiling by a single hair. It was so placed at a banquet above the head of the sycophantic courtier Damocles by Dionysius the Elder, ruler of Syracuse from 405 to 367 BC, to remind Damocles of the precariousness of the power and privilege which he envied. It is still a popular metaphor for any great and threatening evil that may befall one at any time.

sybarite   •   *sensualist; devotee of luxury and self-indulgence*

Derived from Sybaris, a Greek city and colony founded in southern Italy in 720 BC and noted for its luxury and voluptuous pleasures.

T

T, to a   ● *exactly*

Despite what some commentators have alleged, this does not come from the draughtsman's T-square which brought precision to drawing. The expression, explained under **jot and tittle**, existed before the T-square was invented.

T- or **tee-shirt**

So called from its shape when laid out flat.

tabloid journalism

The word *tabloid* was invented in 1884 by Burroughs, Wellcome, the pharmaceutical company, as a trademark for concentrated drugs and chemicals in tablet form. The newspaper proprietor Lord Northcliffe was the first to apply the word to half-size newspapers; Burroughs, Wellcome successfully applied for an injunction to prevent this use but had to give way three or four years later and accept that *tabloid* had become common property. At the time, the word was intended to mean no more than 'concentrated' or 'compressed'; if anything it was complimentary, implying that *tabloid journalism* (1901) was as good, handy and beneficial as tabloid medicine. In the light of experience it has become a term of abuse meaning 'oversimplified, superficial, bigoted and nasty'.

tables, turn the   • *cause a reversal of fortunes or circumstances*

The *table* here is the board on which certain games such as chess or backgammon are played. If the position of the board is *turned* (reversed), so are the relative fortunes of the two players.

taboo   • *forbidden*

This was originally a Tongan word which came into English as a result of the Pacific explorations of Captain Cook in the eighteenth century. It meant something consecrated for and restricted to a specific purpose, especially a sacred one, and therefore untouchable and banned from general use. The system of prohibition, social as well as religious, extended throughout Polynesia and applied to many aspects of behaviour, including certain actions, food, words and contact with others. In its modern use *taboo* remains a strong word, but usually carries no religious implications.

tack, on the right/wrong   • *in the right/wrong direction; following the (in)correct course of action or line of thought*

From sailing, in which *tack* means 'direction'. More specifically it means the direction given to a ship's course by the act of tacking, i.e. moving in a zig-zag fashion by adjusting the sails so as to move into the wind but obliquely to its direction.

take a leaf from/out of someone's book: see *leaf*

takes all sorts to make a world, it

First recorded in this form in D. W. Jerrold's *The Story of Feather* (1844) though the same sentiment in different words goes back at least another two centuries.

talk the hind legs off a donkey, can   • *talks volubly or excessively*

During the history of this expression numerous other animals have featured in it: a horse, a dog, a cow and a bird (which of course has no hind legs). It was originally an expression of admiration for a person's powers of successful persuasion—a suggestion that one could bring about the impossible by talking. Nowadays, though sometimes said of a person admiringly, it is more usually a complaint.

talk turkey • *discuss (business) bluntly and practically*

The large bird which is now commonly eaten originated in the USA, where it was domesticated by the American Indians before Europeans reached the country. The settlers called it *turkey* from confusion with the fowl they had known in Europe; this was actually guinea-fowl (a native of Africa) but called *turkey* at the time because it was thought to come from Turkey. Such was the settlers' taste for it (it is still the national dish on Thanksgiving Day) that serious barter with the Indians, on whatever subject, became known simply as 'talking [about] turkey'.

Tammany Hall

Now a byword for political corruption, especially municipal, this was a building on 14th Street, New York, which belonged to the Tammany society. The group was notorious for its influence on the city's politics in the nineteenth century. The building was leased to the Democratic party of the city, an equally corrupt and powerful force not only in New York City and State but in the party as a whole, and its name came to epitomise the activities of its tenants.

The Tammany societies, patriotic and anti-British, originated during the War of American Independence, taking their name from an American Indian chief who is said to have signed a treaty with William Penn, the founder of Pennsylvania.

tank • *armoured and armed combat-vehicle*

Invented by Colonel Ernest Swinton in 1914 and first used in the late stages of the Battle of the Somme in 1916, this vehicle was initially a secret weapon; a codename had to be found for it that would mislead any spy, especially when it was being moved through France. From a list of possible codenames that included 'reservoir' and 'cistern', *tank* was chosen and has remained. The original intention was to give the impression that it was a bulk water-carrier.

tantalising • *desirable but inaccessible*

In Greek mythology Tantalus, king of Phrygia and son of Zeus, offended the gods by stealing their food when invited to dine with them. By taking it away he revealed their secrets to mortals. When he returned the gods' invitation he served to them the body of his son, in order to test their divinity by seeing if they would realise what the meat was. For these offences Tantalus was cast into the deepest underworld and made to stand waist-deep in a lake surrounded by trees bearing delicious fruit. When he stooped to drink, the water receded; when he raised his hand to pick the fruit, the branches drew back.

tarmac

From the name of John McAdam (1756–1836), surveyor-general of roads in Bristol and later in the London area, who invented a road-surfacing system which used layers of stones of uniform size. His method became so successful and general that it became known as *macadamising* (1825). The addition of tar to the process occurred later, giving rise to the word *tar-macadam* for the new material. Abbreviated to *Tarmac*, it was registered as a tradename in 1903 but is now a general word, no longer distinguished with a capital letter.

tarred with the same brush: see *spoil the ship*

Tarzan • *muscular, agile, acrobatic hero, though sometimes naive*

This character was invented by Edgar Rice Burroughs (1875–1950), the American novelist, as the central figure in a series of adventure stories beginning with *Tarzan of the Apes* (1914). He became very widely known from film versions of the stories as well as from radio stories and comic strips. According to the novels, Tarzan was the son of a British aristocrat abandoned in the jungle as a baby and brought up by apes, growing into a strong, honourable man of simple virtues who continued to live in the wild.

teach one's grandmother to suck eggs: see *eggs, teach one's grandmother to suck*

teddy bear

There is general agreement that the name comes from that of Theodore Roosevelt, US president from 1901–9, Teddy being the pet form of Theodore. However, there are conflicting accounts of how his name became attached to the popular toy which was introduced to the American market at the turn of the century. One is that Roosevelt was a keen hunter, closely associated with bear-hunting in the minds of Americans, with the result that his name came to mind when parents were asked by children to name their toy. Another is that the soft toy was named after him as a clever marketing ploy. A more circumstantial story is that the president once refused to shoot a bear-cub and that this incident was recorded in a popular cartoon depicting the toy in place of the real cub. This produced a craze for the toy that was so specifically associated with the president's own sympathies, to the point that it acquired his name.

teetotal   • *totally abstaining from alcohol*

English authorities date the word to 1833 and credit it to Richard Turner, a working man from Preston, Lancashire, in a speech advocating total abstinence as distinct from mere abstinence from spirits. Where he got the word from is not known. Perhaps he had in mind some such ideas as 'total with a capital T' or 'T for Total' (some commentators unkindly speculate that he had a stutter). Perhaps he knew that some American temperance societies kept registers of those who signed the pledge of abstinence, recording OP (old pledge) against the names of those who promised to refrain from spirits and T against those pledging total abstinence. The total of the latter was thus the T-total (1807). Be this as it may, the documentary evidence is that *teetotal* as an adjective with the now familiar spelling was first used by Turner; indeed his invention of the word was such a source of pride that it is even referred to on his gravestone.

tenterhooks, on   • *in a state of tension, anxiety or suspense*

From the literal tension applied to newly woven cloth in order to stretch it evenly and allow it to dry without shrinking. The wooden framework used for this operation was called a tenter; the word 'tent' comes from the same Latin origin, *tendere* (stretch). The hooks to which the cloth was attached were therefore called *tenterhooks*.

tether, at the end of one's   ● *at the limit of one's endurance*

A *tether* is a fixed rope or chain to which an animal is tied, enabling it to move or graze within a limited area but preventing it from straying. The earliest metaphorical use (sixteenth century) has to do with living 'within one's tether', i.e. within one's resources. The sense of frustration at being restricted by a *tether* is a later development.

Thames on fire, not set the   ● *not do anything notable in life*

An English version of a similar Latin tag about the Tiber. There are also French and German versions referring to the Seine and the Rhine. Some authorities offer an explanation in terms of a pun on an obsolete word 'temse'; this appears to be guesswork.

there but for the grace of God (go I): see *grace of God*

thereby hangs a tale   ● *certain consequences, conclusions, etc. flow from that*

A formula used to draw attention to the implications of something that has just been said. It is first found in Shakespeare, meaning simply 'about that there is a tale to tell'. The fact that he used it four times (e.g. *The Taming of the Shrew*, IV, 1, line 60) may indicate either that he was proud of the phrase or that it was already commonly in use in his day as a story-telling device.

there's no place like home: see *home, there's no place like*

Thespian   ● *actor*

Thespis, a Greek poet of the sixth century BC, has been called the father of Greek tragedy, and thus of drama more generally. He was the first to introduce a monologue, to be spoken by an individual actor, into an art form which until then had consisted of choral speaking and dancing.

Both *Thespian* and *thesbian* (dramatic) are now thought to be pompous and their use is facetious.

they also serve who only stand and wait

This is the last line of John Milton's sonnet *On his blindness*, in which he finds comfort in the reflection that God may be served in passive as well as active ways. Milton (1608–74) began to go blind in his thirties and was totally blind by 1651.

thick as thieves • *very friendly*

The reference is to the closeness of association and interdependence existing in a gang of thieves. *Thick* is used in its sense of 'densely arranged', as in thick undergrowth, grass, hair, etc.

thin end of the wedge • *small beginning that will lead to something more significant*

Although now usually thought of as a device for holding something in place, a *wedge* was originally a tool for splitting wood or stone: the sharp (thin) end was used to make the first crack, which was then widened by driving in the remaining and increasingly thickened part of the wedge until a complete split occurred. Thus the *thin end of the wedge* is inevitably followed by something greater.

thinking cap, put on one's • *take time to consider carefully*

Said to be an allusion to the official cap donned by a judge when the time came to deliver judgement or pass sentence. The cap was later worn only for the passing of the death sentence and has now passed out of use altogether.

However, the allusion may be less specific. In the days when everyone wore headgear, caps denoted a wide range of professions, trades and status. It would have been natural for someone who was asked to think about something to be jocularly invited to 'put on your thinking cap'. Additionally, from the sixteenth to the eighteenth century the normal term was 'consideration cap', an alliteration which may imply popular metaphor rather than specific reference to a professional thinker such as a judge.

323

third degree   • *vigorous questioning (to extort confession)*

In medieval natural philosophy, *degrees* were the successive stages of intensity in which the elementary qualities of bodies (hot, cold, moist, dry) were described. The *third degree*, out of a normal total of four, was very intense; Shakespeare humorously describes one of his characters as lying 'in the third degree of drink'. The terminology survives in *third degree burns* (the deepest variety) and in the (originally American) idea of *third degree interrogation*, though this may owe something to Masonic ritual in which initiation into the third or highest degree of membership is said to be rigorous.

third world   • *poor, less developed countries*

Coined by the French diplomat Georges Baladier in 1956. He was referring specifically to the 29 African and Asian countries which came together at the Bandung Conference (1955) to discuss matters of common concern, though his term is now used more generally. As originally formulated it applied to those countries not belonging to the two 'worlds' or spheres of influence dominated by the superpowers, the USA and USSR, in the Cold War of that time.

thirty pieces of silver: see *silver*

thorn in the flesh   • *source of continual trouble*

In a mysterious passage in his second letter to the Corinthians, St Paul says that he suffers from a certain 'thorn in the flesh, the messenger of Satan to buffet me' (12: 7), which he has asked God to remove but which he has been told he must endure so that he never becomes too proud of the favours God has shown him. What it actually was can only be guessed at, but his metaphor has become commonplace.

thrash out   • *settle by discussion, often vehement*

Thrash is basically the same word as 'thresh', i.e. to separate the grains of a cereal from their husks and straw, especially by beating with a flail. The figurative use of this idea is very old: the image is one of getting at what is important (essential, true, etc.)

by vigorously getting rid of what is not, through a process of argument. In the course of time *thrash* has come to be associated with hitting or winning, while thresh has remained a farming word, but *thrash out* retains the old agricultural sense.

thread, hang by a   • *exist precariously*

Originally 'hang by a hair', an allusion to the **sword** of Damocles.

three R's, the   • *reading, writing and arithmetic*

Reputed to have been proposed, in all seriousness, as a toast by Alderman Sir William Curtis (1752–1829), an illiterate lord mayor of London, at the end of a speech in favour of elementary education for all. It has been common, as useful jocular shorthand, since 1828.

three score years and ten   • *normal life expectancy*

The number is proverbial rather than factual. The origin is Psalm 90: 10.

three sheets in the wind   • *very drunk*

In nautical parlance, *sheets* are ropes attached to sails and are let out or pulled in to adjust the sails' positions. If they (and therefore the sails) are flapping loose they are said to be *in the wind*; the result is loss of control. A drunken person, experiencing a similar disorientation, was therefore said to be 'a sheet in the wind'; if one was *three sheets in the wind* (now a rather dated expression) one's condition was more desperate.

throw in the towel: see *towel*

throw one's hat into the ring: see *hat*

throw the book at: see *book*

throw up the sponge: see *towel*

325

thumbs up (or down), give the ● *approve (or disapprove)*

According to contemporary observers such as Juvenal and Horace, the spectators at ancient Roman gladiatorial contests used to be called upon to determine whether or not a beaten gladiator should be killed. If their response was favourable they kept their thumbs clenched in their fists; if not, they turned their thumbs out. This is not what the modern expression says, but it appears to be the origin.

thunder: see *steal someone's thunder*

ticket, that's (just) the ● *that is exactly what is wanted*

Either an allusion to the winning ticket in a lottery or, more likely, a shortened version of 'that's the ticket for soup', a catch-phrase from the second half of the nineteenth century referring to the tickets given to poor people to enable them to get something to eat at a soup-kitchen. The original sense was 'that's all you're going to get', which is not what *ticket* means in the present saying, though it is common for expressions, especially slang ones, to change their meaning or emphasis as time goes by.

tilt at windmills ● *(ludicrously) fight imaginary evils or enemies*

In one of the absurder adventures of Don Quixote (see **quixotic**) he charges with his lance (i.e. tilts) at some windmills, imagining them to be evil giants whom it is his duty as a chivalrous knight to destroy (*Don Quixote*, Part I, 8). His lance gets caught in a sail and he is carried up in the air before being brought back to earth with a bump. The expression therefore implies a rather crazy action likely to end in ridicule.

tinker's damn or **cuss, not worth a** ● *worthless*

Also *not give/care a tinker's damn/cuss* (not care in the slightest). *Cuss* is modern (mid-nineteenth century American) for 'curse'. 'Not worth a curse/damn' is very old and means that anything so called is so worthless as not to justify even the expenditure of breath to swear at it. *Tinker's* was added later for emphasis: tinkers were usually itinerant menders of pots and pans whose position in society, like their language perhaps, was low.

tit for tat • *an equivalent given in retaliation (for an injury, etc.)*

A variation of the older and slightly more comprehensible 'tip for tap' in which both words signified a light blow, though the first is now obsolete in this sense. The expression therefore meant 'blow for blow', but its modern variant owes more to onomatopoeia than to English.

Titans or titans; titanic

The original Titans were, according to Greek mythology, the first race, born to Gaea (Earth) and Uranus (Heaven) after the creation of the universe. They were six male and six female giants of enormous power and strength and were deities of the early Greeks, to whom they represented huge natural forces and, in some cases, abstract qualities. After a mighty 10-year struggle for sovereignty they were overthrown by Zeus, who became supreme ruler and thus dominated the more familiar later mythology. The Titans themselves were cast into deepest hell. It is their gigantic strength and original eminence, however, not their revolt and downfall, that are remembered in modern uses of their name.

titch • *very small person.* Also **titchy**, *very small*

At the end of a famous court-case in the 1870s Arthur Orton was jailed for passing himself off as heir to the Tichborne baronetcy and estate. On his release the 'Tichborne Claimant', as he had become known, decided to profit from his celebrity by taking to the music-halls, where he recited his tale of woe to large audiences throughout the country until the novelty wore off. He was appearing at Greenwich when a certain Harry Relph, a dwarfish but podgy man, was entertaining the queues outside the theatre on his penny whistle. Relph was so natural an entertainer that the theatre manager invited him to join the bill as an extra turn. Needing to find a stage-name, as was conventional at the time, the manager thought it would be amusing to announce Relph as Little Tichborne in contrast to the other Tichborne, who weighed 20 stone. The name stuck: Little Tich (1868–1928), who remained hardly four feet tall, became one of the most celebrated music-hall performers of his day and his name—slightly re-spelt to fit the normal '-itch' sound—entered the language.

titfer • *hat*

Abbreviation of **tit for tat**, rhyming slang for hat.

tittle; tittle-tattle: see *jot*

toady • *sycophant; behave sycophantically*

Originally *toad-eater*, a charlatan's assistant who publicly ate toads, commonly but erroneously believed to be poisonous, in order that his master could exhibit his skill in effecting a 'cure'. The modern meaning stems from the assistant's extraordinary dutifulness, but it is a strong word and probably reflects people's general antipathy towards toads, not to mention the consumption of them.

tod, on one's • *alone*

Rhyming slang: on one's own = on one's Tod Sloan = on one's tod. Sloan was a famous American jockey who first rode in England in 1897 after several highly successful seasons in his homeland. He was very popular, and rode King Edward VII's horses, but faded from the public eye after being banned by the Jockey Club in 1901.

toe the line • *conform to a defined rule or standard*

Literally refers to the convention that all competitors in a race line up at the beginning, toes against the starting-line, so that no one has an advantage before the race starts.

Tom

Leofric, Earl of Mercia and one of the most powerful men in England during the first half of the eleventh century, imposed certain taxes which his wife, Lady Godiva, patroness of Coventry, asked him to remove. He promised to do so if she would ride naked through the city, which she accordingly did in 1040. This story, first recorded in a thirteenth century history, was subsequently embellished. A seventeenth century addition was that the people of Coventry stayed indoors behind drawn curtains in order not to offend her modesty, but that an inquisitive tailor called Tom peeped out, whereupon he was struck blind or, according to another story, done to death by more upright citizens. Thus *peeping Tom* became the name for a voyeur.

Any Tom, Dick or Harry is a dismissive term for any ordinary person. The list has included other names down the centuries, such as Jack and Will—Shakespeare has 'Tom, Dick and Francis' in *Henry IV, Part I*—but the current trio has been invariable since 1734. The names have no significance other than being common ones chosen at random.

The name of *Tom Thumb*, a dwarf of popular tradition in a nursery tale first published in 1629, though known previously, is sometimes applied to any small or insignificant person.

tomfoolery   ● *foolishness, buffoonery*

From 'Tom Fool', an old invented name for any foolish or half-witted person. This was probably based on the earlier 'Tom o'Bedlam', a sixteenth century name used either for a madman let out of custody with a licence to beg or for an itinerant lunatic, sometimes someone who feigned madness to attract sympathy while begging. Tom was the name such beggars often assumed; a character in *King Lear* adopts both the name and the disguise to escape danger. See also **bedlam**.

tooth and nail   ● *with ferocity; using all one's means*

Literally, biting and scratching.

top brass: see *brass, top*

Topsy, like   ● *growing of its own accord*

The original Topsy was the little slave-girl in Harriet Beecher Stowe's *Uncle Tom's Cabin* (1852):

'Do you know who made you?'
'Nobody, as I knows on,' said the child, with a short laugh . . .
'I 'spect I grow'd'.

Tory, tory

An anglicised spelling of an Irish word meaning a pursuer. It was originally applied to Irish (Roman Catholic) outlaws who plundered and killed English settlers and soldiers in Ireland in the seventeenth century. With a capital T it became the abusive nickname of the supporters of Charles II who wished to see the restoration of Roman Catholicism in England, and especially of those favouring the succession of the Roman Catholic James, Duke of York, to the throne. From 1689 it was the name of the political party which originated among these royalists, though after 1830 the term was superseded by 'Conservative', with which it is now interchangeable.

totem • *emblem; revered symbol*

From an American Indian word for the hereditary emblem or badge of a tribe or group of Indians. It was usually a representation of an animal, less commonly of a plant, which gave the group its name.

touch and go • *a risky state of affairs*

The original phrase was 'to touch and go', to deal with something very briefly, i.e. to touch if for a moment and then go away. As an adjectival phrase 'touch-and-go' therefore meant 'done quickly'. Only in the early nineteenth century did the expression develop its modern meaning, presumably from the idea of something so evenly balanced that even a mere *touch* would cause it to *go* crashing down.

touch wood

A catch-phrase used to avert bad luck by touching wood (jocularly one's head), especially to avoid misfortune as a result of boasting (of one's good fortune, success, etc.) or wishing for something. It is a vestige of an old superstition that certain trees had a sacred significance and would give blessing and protection if touched—a notion that may have its origin in the cult of Pan, a Greek god of nature. Alternatively the expression may date from medieval times when relics, including pieces reputed to be from Christ's cross, were hawked around, to be bought or touched for a blessing.

touchstone   ● *anything which tests the genuineness of something; criterion, standard by which something is judged*

This was originally a smooth dark-coloured variety of quartz or jasper used for testing alloys of gold or silver. If the alloys were rubbed against the touchstone they left a streak, the colour of which could then be compared with samples of known gold or silver content. The word is now widely used to mean any standard of judgement, often in a philosophical sense.

towel, throw in the; throw up the sponge   ● *surrender; give up*

Boxing rules are now such that a referee must stop a fight if he thinks one of the contestants has taken enough punishment. In earlier and rougher days a boxer's second could call a similar halt by throwing into the ring the towel or sponge normally kept ready to hand to refresh his man between rounds.

tower of strength   ● *dependable person offering support, comfort, etc*

Shakespeare was the first to use this expression—'the King's name is a tower of strength' (*Richard III*, V, 3, line 12)—but he may have known *Proverbs*, 18: 10: 'The name of the Lord is a strong tower'. Both quotations mean that someone's name or status can be helpful to others; the modern meaning is a natural extension of this sense.

traces, kick over the   ● *behave without restraint; defy control*

Traces are the leather straps, formerly ropes or chains, which connect the collar of a draught-horse to the pivoted cross-bar at the front of a plough, etc. A horse which gets a leg over these *traces* is able to *kick* out more freely and dangerously, or may be trying to loose itself from its harness.

trail, blaze a   ● *pioneer*

A *blaze* is a white patch on the face of a horse or other animal. The word was adopted to signify a prominent white mark made on a tree by chipping off a piece of the bark to indicate a path or trail. Its first recorded use as a verb in this sense is in the *Journals* (1750) of the American Thomas Walker, who explored land for speculative purposes. It obviously originated in the language of settlers.

tree, bark up the wrong ● *misdirect one's effort*

An Americanism first found in print in a book by Davy Crockett, the folk hero and Congressman, in 1833. It comes from the hunting of raccoon, a tree-climbing animal valued for its fur. Being a nocturnal animal it had to be hunted at night, which explains why the hunting dogs responsible for signalling in which tree a raccoon had hidden were prone to error and sometimes barked up (at) the wrong one.

tricks up one's sleeve: see *sleeve, up one's*

trilby ● *soft felt hat with brim and dented crown*

Named from *Trilby*, the heroine of the immensely popular novel of the same name written and illustrated by George du Maurier and published in 1894. She wore such a hat, which itself became popular after it was seen in the production of a dramatised version of the novel a year later.

Trilby, an artist's model, falls under the spell of Svengali, a German–Polish musician who trains and establishes her as a famous singer. Such is his hypnotic influence over her that when he dies she loses her talent, declines and dies in despair. A person who exercises a strong mesmeric power over someone through force of rather sinister will and personality is still sometimes referred to as *a Svengali*.

trip the light fantastic ● *dance*

A jocular adaptation of:

Come, and trip it as ye go
On the light fantastic toe

from John Milton's *L'Allegro* (1631), lines 33–4.

Trojan

The ten-year war in the mid-thirteenth century BC between Greece and Troy, an ancient city of Asia Minor near the

Dardanelles, derives its significance from being the subject matter of Homer's *Iliad* and part of Virgil's *Aeneid*. According to the latter, a huge statue of a horse was built by order of Ulysses, one of the principal Greek commanders, who let it be known that it was an offering to the gods for a safe return to Greece. The Trojans dragged it into their city, but it was filled with Greek infiltrators who stole out at night and destroyed the city. A *Trojan* (or *wooden*) *horse* is therefore a metaphor for a concealed danger, especially one designed to subvert from within.

The Trojans are described in literature as courageous, honest and energetic, but it is curious that the expression *work like a Trojan* (i.e. very hard) is not recorded before 1846.

Trotskyite,-ist

Leon Trotsky (1879–1940) took a leading part in the Russian Revolution of 1917 and founded the Red Army, but in the struggle for power that followed Lenin's death (1924) he was defeated by Stalin. He was exiled in 1929 and settled in Mexico, where he was assassinated with an ice-pick, probably at the instigation of Stalin.

One of Trotsky's central differences with Stalin was his advocacy of permanent worldwide revolution by the proletariat, whereas Stalin held that communism should be built within individual countries, with central authority concentrated in the USSR. **Stalinism** has been discredited but Trotskyism persists, even though *Trotskyite* (or *-ist*) is often used loosely as a term of abuse for revolutionaries thought to be extremist, anarchical and violent.

trowel, lay it on with a   • *flatter grossly; spread thickly*

An image from bricklaying, in which a *trowel* is used for laying on mortar. It was first used by Shakespeare (*As You Like It*, I, 2, line 94). The underlying idea is that mortar will not do its work if spread too thinly and that a *trowel* is a tool not used with much finesse.

trump

In card-playing this is the name (a corruption of 'triumph') for a suit which for the time being outranks other suits, thus putting

333

the holder of a *trump card* in a winning position. A related expression is *come/turn up trumps* (give help). *Trump* is also a verb meaning 'play a trump card': to *trump one's ace* is to score a victory over someone who had apparently already won as a result of placing an **ace**.

The last trump is quite different—the final trumpet call at the **Day of Judgement**: 'We shall not all sleep, but we shall all be changed, In a moment, in the twinkling of an eye, at the last trump: for the trumpet shall sound and the dead shall be raised incorruptible' (*I Corinthians*, 15, 51–2).

trumpet, blow one's own   ●   *boast*

Because of its penetrating sound, the trumpet has been used from ancient times to send signals (especially military ones), express celebration or draw attention to something. The arrival of an important person may even today be proclaimed by a fanfare of trumpets. In contrast, a person who has to blow his own trumpet lacks modesty and invites derision.

Tsar: see *Czar*

Turk: see *young Turk*

turn over a new leaf: see *leaf, turn over a new*

turn the other cheek: see *cheek*

turn the tables: see *tables*

turn-up for the books, a   ●   *piece of good fortune, usually unexpected*

The *books* are those in which bookmakers keep a record of bets. Something which happens (*turns up*) unexpectedly is welcome to bookmakers because few people will have bet on it and not many winnings will have to be paid out.

turtle, turn　●　*turn upside down*

Sailors originally invented this term when they learnt to overturn the turtle or marine tortoise, which is suitable for food, in order to immobilise it. They applied the expression to the capsizing of ships or boats, but its use has now spread to other things that accidentally overturn.

Tweedledum and Tweedledee　●　*two people or groups who are practically indistinguishable*

These characters are best known as two almost identical little fat men in Lewis Carroll's *Through the Looking-Glass* (1872) but the names were coined by John Byrom (1692–1763), the inventor of a system of shorthand and the author of the hymn *Christians, awake!*. In the 1720s there was a squabble in London musical circles about the rival merits of Handel and the Italian composer Bonacini, recently appointed as one of the resident composers at the newly founded Royal Academy of Music. Byrom wrote a comic jingle about this argument, rhyming 'Bonacini' with 'ninny' and ending:

Strange! That such high dispute should be
'Twixt Tweedledum and Tweedledee!

The names, satirically based on the now obsolete verb 'tweedle' (produce a shrill sound on a musical instrument), implied that there was nothing to choose between the two composers. Actually their musical styles were quite different, Handel is now regarded as an important composer and Bonacini has been forgotten.

twink; twinkling; twinkling of an eye　●　*very short time*

The first two are shortened versions of the third, which means 'the time taken to wink' and is best known from the Bible (see the quotation under **trump**) though it is first recorded much earlier, in about 1300.

two bites at the (same) cherry: see *cherry*

two-faced: see *Janus-like*

335

tycoon ● *exceptionally wealthy or powerful business executive*

The hereditary commander-in-chief of the Japanese army, and until 1867 the virtual ruler of Japan, was called the shogun, but the title by which he was described to foreigners was *tycoon*, from a Japanese word meaning 'great lord'. The Americans adopted the word as a jocular name for the boss of a large business empire and it has since become standard English.

U

ugly duckling   ● *somebody or something unpromising that becomes successful or admirable*

The title of a short story by the Danish writer Hans Christian Andersen (1805–75) which first appeared in English in 1847. In it the duckling, spurned and embarrassed because of its oddity when compared with its peers, is in fact a cygnet which grows into a beautiful swan.

umpteen   ● *an indefinite but fairly large number*

From First World War slang, in which *umpteen* meant merely an unstated number; it was used to disguise and keep secret the official number of a brigade, division, etc. for reasons of operational security. Its origin was 'umpty', signallers' slang for a dash when reading morse code; presumably the basis of this was 'um' as a noncommittal sound.

unacceptable face of   ● *unpleasant aspect of (something generally admirable)*

In May 1973 the then British Prime Minister, Edward Heath, commenting in the House of Commons about the business practices of a company which was alleged in the High Court to run a company-owned mansion and to have made payments into an offshore tax haven, said 'It is an unpleasant and unacceptable face of capitalism'. Coming from a politician whose party was generally sympathetic to capitalism, this statement was much commented on and remains much quoted both in its original form and with variations.

Uncle Sam • *personification of the government (or citizens) of the USA*

The popular story is that the original Uncle Sam was Samuel Wilson (1766–1854), variously referred to as a store-owner, meat-packer or government inspector, who was responsible for supplies of meat to the US army and accordingly stamped 'US' on the sides of the packing cases in which it was shipped. Because the abbreviation was unfamiliar to soldiers so soon after the country had won its independence from Britain, they assumed these letters stood for Uncle Sam, Wilson's alleged nickname. The starting-point for this story is that the first printed reference to the US government as *Uncle Sam* is found in the newspaper of the city of Troy in New York State—the *Troy News* of September 7, 1813—where Wilson lived.

However, it is unlikely that US troops would have known who had supplied (or packed or inspected) their meat or what his nickname was (if indeed he had one). The more plausible origin of *Uncle Sam* is therefore less colourful: it is simply a jocular expansion and personification of *US Am*erica from the initials widely seen on the sides of government wagons at the time.

Uncle Tom • *black person who is thought to have a deferential attitude towards white people*

A derogatory reference to the central character of Harriet Beecher Stowe's famous novel *Uncle Tom's Cabin* (1852) who is a faithful and dignified old black slave. His attitudes towards white people were regarded as servile by later black activists for whom the establishment of equal rights was incompatible with 'Uncle Tom-ism'. Others have argued that the book originally helped the US public towards a better understanding of the iniquities of slavery.

underhand: see *palm off*

Union Jack

Strictly speaking, a jack is a smaller version of a main flag or ensign and is flown at the bow of a ship to indicate nationality. In this sense it is probably related to the diminutive, affectionate and familiar uses of **jack**. In popular use, however, the *Union Jack* is the British flag in all its uses. *Union* refers to the three united crosses of St George (England), St Andrew (Scotland) and St Patrick (Ireland, added after the Act of Union 1800, now representing Northern Ireland).

unkindest cut of all • *most hurtful action or words*

A quotation from Mark Antony's famous funeral speech in *Julius Caesar*, III, 2, line 183. Speaking over Caesar's body he describes to the citizens of Rome how Caesar was murdered and points out the holes made in his mantle by the daggers of his assassins. The 'unkindest cut'—he means 'cut' literally—is that made by Brutus, whom Caesar trusted.

unwashed, the great • *the broad mass of people*

First found in Edward Bulwer-Lytton's novel *Paul Clifford* (1830), though this phrase is said to have been used earlier in speeches by Edward Burke at the time of the French Revolution and by Lord Brougham (1778–1868), a lawyer and politician. As a contemptuous term for the lower orders it was perhaps originally restricted to the private audiences of the upper ones. It is now jocular.

up to the ears: see *head over heels*

upset the apple-cart: see *apple*

upstage • *take away attention from*

Originally a theatrical term. An *upstage* position is in that part of the stage away from the audience; stages used to slope slightly from back to front, which explains 'up'. If an actor is speaking from such a position, other actors who are downstage have to face him or her, in order to be addressed. This obviously focuses attention on the speaker and *upstages* the others, putting them in a subordinate position with their backs to the audience.

In the days when this sort of thing was thought to matter to actors, anyone who unnecessarily upstaged others was guilty of

339

theatrical bad manners and excessive self-importance. Modern uses of the word still often imply petty manoeuvring.

Uriah Heep

In Dickens' *David Copperfield* (1849–50) Uriah Heep is a fawning clerk who tells everyone how "umble' he is. Actually he is a cunning villain, but it is his servile and hypocritical grovelling that is remembered in modern allusions to his character.

Utopia • *place or condition of perfection, usually social or political*

This was the title of an important and influential political fantasy (1516) by the English statesman Sir Thomas More (1477–1535) who coined the word from two Greek ones meaning 'nowhere'. It is the name of an ideal imaginary island whose inhabitants share everything in a spirit of Christianity and communism, enjoying toleration of religious differences, access to free education for all and a perfect social and economic system. In modern use the word is sometimes used sneeringly by those who feel that social improvement is impractical.

V

valentine • *card, greeting or gift sent, usually anonymously, to a real or imagined sweetheart on St Valentine's Day, February 14; person receiving such a present*

There are two St Valentines, both Italian, one a priest and the other a bishop, who were martyred (one of them on February 14) in the second half of the third century and are commemorated in the Roman Catholic calendar on the same day. They have no romantic associations, however, and the modern customs linked with their day arise from its coincidence with the start of the mating season for birds. As Chaucer wrote in his *Parliament of Fowls* (lines 309–10) as early as about 1382,

For this was on Saint Valentine's day,
When every bird cometh there to chose his mate.

This traditional link gave rise to a fifteenth century custom of choosing lots on February 14 for a sweetheart or special friend for the ensuring year. The modern observances go back only to the nineteenth century.

There may be a link with the older Roman festival of the Lupercal (February 15), a fertility ritual which included a ceremony for women wanting to become pregnant. Before its suppression by the pope in 494 and replacement with a festival honouring the Virgin, this ritual was exported to Roman Britain and might have merged, under Christian influences, into a rather chaster but related observance a day earlier.

Valhalla • *resting place of the great*

In Scandinavian mythology *Valhalla* was the court of Odin, chief deity of Norse belief. It was a vast hall glittering with gold, its framework formed of spears and its roof of shields, lit by great fires and the flash of swords, with 540 doors, each able to admit 800 warriors abreast. To this place Odin summoned warriors who had died in battle and whom he wished to honour. They passed their time in warlike games and lavish feasting.

vamoose • *go away; be off!*

The Spanish word *vamos* (let's go) crossed the border from Mexico into US slang. Its meaning, like that of some other adopted foreign words, was either misunderstood or jocularly misused.

vandal • *wantonly destructive person*

The original *Vandals* were members of a Germanic tribe which in the fourth and fifth centuries invaded western Europe and settled in France and Spain before moving on to north Africa. Their reputation for destructiveness comes especially from their sacking of Rome in 455, when they destroyed its artistic and literary treasures.

vaulting ambition • *extreme ambition*

A quotation from Macbeth's soliloquy at the beginning of I, 7:

> I have no spur
> To prick the side of my intent, but only
> Vaulting ambition, which o'erleaps itself
> And falls on the other.

The metaphor is from horse-riding: ambition is envisaged either as a horse that jumps too high over an obstacle and falls down on the other side of it, or as a rider who leaps too energetically into the saddle and falls off the other side of the horse. Thus the original sense was of coming to grief by being over-ambitious.

Vicar of Bray • *time-server: one who makes one's opinions or behaviour fit those of current fashion or of one's superiors*

The title of a well-known anonymous song (c. 1720) about a parson who boasts that he has accommodated himself to the very different religious emphases of the reigns of Charles II, James II, William and Mary, Anne and now George I, and

> That whatsoever king shall reign
> I'll still be Vicar of Bray, sir.

This is based on an actual sixteenth century Vicar of Bray, in Berkshire, named as Symon Symonds or Aleyn, who managed to retain the living during the reigns of Henry VIII, Edward VI, Mary I and Elizabeth I, being twice a Roman Catholic and twice a Protestant as the centre of power changed. When asked if he were not a turncoat he is quoted as replying 'I always kept my principle, which is this, to live and die the vicar of Bray' (Fuller, *Worthies of England*, 1662).

vicious circle ● *situation in which a difficulty leads to a further difficulty that leads back to the original one*

Not *vicious* in the sense of 'depraved or spiteful' but in its rather archaic sense of 'flawed, spoiled by some fault'. The expression was originally a technical term in logic for a fallacious mode of reasoning by which a proposition that has been employed to establish a conclusion is then proved by that conclusion—in simple language, a circular argument.

VIP ● *very important person*

First used by Compton Mackenzie (1883–1972) in his *Water on the Brain* (1933), this abbreviation was otherwise unknown until Second World War slang made it general. Its popularity is attributed to an RAF station commander who was responsible for the air transport of some high-ranking people to the Middle East in 1944. To preserve secrecy he referred to them only as Very Important Personages, and subsequently by the initials of those words, in the written movement orders he issued to his station staff. The usage caught on rapidly in military circles besotted—as they still are—by initials. It is not known whether the station commander had read Compton Mackenzie.

viper in one's bosom: see *snake*

voice crying in the wilderness • *person whose prophecies, warnings, opinions, etc. are ignored*

An approximation to the claim of John the Baptist to be 'the voice of one crying in the wilderness, Make straight the way of the Lord' (*John*, 1: 23; also in the other three Gospels) in fulfilment of a prophecy in *Isaiah*, 40: 3. The Baptist was an important and fearless preacher (see **head on a platter**) who recognised Christ as the Messiah prophesied in the Old Testament.

The modern meaning of the expression is a misrepresentation: John was not of course ignored. There has obviously been a popular presumption that a voice in the wilderness is bound to be unheard. This is to misunderstand the biblical meaning of 'wilderness', which is merely the countryside as opposed to the town and cultivated land. John lived and preached there because he was an ascetic, and his voice was actually heard by very many.

W

wages of sin

Now used of the consequences of wrongdoing or even jocularly of the results of over-indulgence, but the original is stronger: 'The wages of sin is death' (*Romans*, 6: 23).

Wagnerian

Richard Wagner (1813–83) was a German composer chiefly remembered for a series of operatic masterpieces that are mythological epics dealing with huge themes, such as the notion of redemption through love. Most of his work, musically, visually and thematically, is on a grandiose scale, emotionally highly charged, dramatically intense and overwhelmingly powerful (and rather long). The adjectival adaptation of his name is often applied to non-musical events having these qualities.

wagon, on the   ● *teetotal (having previously not been)*

Short for 'on the water-wagon' as a metaphor for the non-consumption of alcohol. In the USA, where the expression originated, water-wagons were used to spray dusty streets and to be a source of communal supply in times of drought.

wall, go to the: see *weakest to the wall*

Walter Mitty • *person who lives in his or her own dream-world*

'The Secret Life of Walter Mitty' is a story by the American humorist James Thurber (1894–1961) which first appeared in the *New Yorker* in 1932. It tells of a docile husband who has vivid escapist fantasies in which he imagines himself in various guises, roles and exploits far removed from his humdrum existence. A successful film based on the story helped to propel the name of the central character into more general use.

warhorse, old • *standard, familiar, slightly hackneyed play, piece of music, etc. that can be relied on to please; elderly person, especially military or political, in any field of conflict*

A *warhorse* was originally a strong charger used by a knight and later a cavalryman in battle. An *old warhorse* was therefore an experienced one or one that had been put out to grass at the end of a distinguished career. From this the expression came to mean a veteran warrior; the modern meanings carry on these ideas of age, dependability and survivability.

warmonger • *person promoting war or warlike ideas*

Monger is an Old English word for dealer or trader, as in fish-monger and ironmonger. It has become tacked on to other words (e.g. scandalmonger) with the same meaning, though not in the literal sense.

warm the cockles of one's heart: see *cockles*

warpath, on the • *angry, looking to take hostile action*

Warpath used to be the term for the route taken by a warlike party of North American Indians.

warts and all • *without any attempt to cover up (one's own) blemishes*

Oliver Cromwell (1599–1658), leader of the Parliamentary side in the Civil War, had **Puritan** religious beliefs which gave him a rigid honesty. He is reputed to have said to the painter of his portrait, Sir Peter Lely, 'Remark all these roughnesses, pimples, warts, and everything as you see me, otherwise I will never pay a farthing for it.'

wash one's dirty linen in public   • *reveal something discreditable that should be kept private*

Attributed to Napoleon in a speech on his return from Elba in 1815 after a period of exile: 'It is at home, not in public, that one washes one's dirty linen'.

wash one's hands of   • *have nothing more to do with; (publicly) disown responsibility for*

Accused of blasphemy by the chief priests, Christ was brought before the Roman governor **Pontius Pilate**, who was warned by his wife to have 'nothing to do with that just man' because of a dream she had had. The people demanded crucifixion: 'When Pilate saw that he could prevail nothing, but that rather a tumult was made, he took water, and washed his hands before the multitude, saying, I am innocent of the blood of this just man: see ye to it' (*Matthew*, 27: 24).

Waterloo, meet one's   • *encounter a final challenge and defeat, often after a period of success or strife*

At the battle of Waterloo, near Brussels, in 1815, Napoleon's army was defeated by Wellington's combination of British, German, Dutch and Belgian forces. It was important in that it ended the military and political career of Napoleon, during which he had conquered much of Europe.

weakest to the wall   • *the weakest are pushed aside, ignored, unable to survive, etc*

Together with *go to the wall* (be ruined), this expression is said to have originated in St Stephen's chapel, now the chapel in the Houses of Parliament. It was for centuries the meeting place of the House of Commons, but the only seating consisted of stone benches along the walls. When the chapel was crowded, the cry of 'the weakest [go] to the wall' was used so that the sick or elderly would be found somewhere to sit. The metaphorical meaning, considerably less charitable than the original, has been common since the fifteenth century.

wear one's heart on one's sleeve: see *heart on one's sleeve*

weasel words • *evasive or intentionally misleading words, especially spoken ones*

The origin, which is American, is well explained in Stewart Chaplin's short story *Stained-glass Political Platform* (1900), where the term made its first appearance in print: 'weasel words are words that suck the life out of the words next to them, just as a weasel sucks the egg and leaves the shell'. The expression was popularised in 1916 in a speech by Theodore Roosevelt attacking President Wilson.

weather, under the • *slightly unwell*

Originally, suffering from a minor or temporary complaint of the sort that may have been caused by bad weather, as cold, damp or fog may give one a cough, ache, etc. It is now sometimes a euphemism for having a hangover.

well-heeled • *rich*

A nineteenth-century Americanism, probably no more than an inversion of the earlier 'down at heel' (slovenly, shabby, like people who do not bother or cannot afford to have the worn heels of their shoes repaired).

wellingtons

Not invented by but named in honour of the Duke of Wellington (1769–1852), the British soldier and later prime minister. The name was originally given, shortly after his resounding victory at **Waterloo**, to a type of military boot that came up to the knee; it was later applied to the familiar civilian variety.

Welsh rabbit or **rarebit** • *melted cheese on toast*

The original was *rabbit*, apparently a jocular name for a dish that was obviously not rabbit and was perhaps a poor substitute for it; there may have been an implication that Welsh people would not know the difference. The later and now common *rarebit* (a word that exists nowhere else) seems to have been an affectation invented by people who thought it sounded better—or who could not see the joke.

west, go   • *be lost or destroyed; die*

This phrase was popularised by the First World War; because the Western Front generally ran north/south, with Briitsh troops facing east, a dead or injured soldier who was transferred from the scene of fighting to behind the lines would *go west*. But the idea is older than that and is based on a common literary comparison between death and the setting of the sun in the west. There are also references in literature to people *going west* to be hanged at Tyburn, which was used for executions from the twelfth century until 1783 and which in those days lay well to the west of London, near what is now Marble Arch.

wet behind the ears   • *immature, naive*

A reference to children's lack of thoroughness in sometimes not drying themselves behind the ears after washing. The expression seems to have originated in military slang, derisively applied to an incompetent young recruit or inexperienced officer who still needed his mother to check that he had dried himself properly.

wet one's whistle   • *take a drink*

Whistle has been jocular for the mouth or throat since medieval times. The whole expression is first found in Chaucer's 'Reeve's Tale' among the *Canterbury Tales* of about 1387.

wheel has come full circle, the   • *matters are back to where they started*

From Shakespeare: 'The wheel is come full circle' (*King Lear*, V, 3, line 174). The allusion is to the wheel of Fortune, a very ancient Roman goddess much depicted in Roman art as holding either a wheel as a symbol of the turning and changing movement of life or some revolving device enabling the goddess to select random changes in human affairs. This idea was a commonplace of literature but Shakespeare seems to have been the first to introduce the notion of things coming *full circle*.

wheels within wheels • *unseen or little-known workings within the controlling forces or methods of an organisation, system, etc.; complication of influences; intricately connected events*

The original image is in a vision of angels described by an Old Testament prophet: 'their appearance and their work was as it were a wheel within a wheel' (*Ezekiel*, 1: 16). It has been suggested that the image was suggested to Ezekiel by certain striking phenomena which are sometimes seen in the western sky after sunset over the plains of Mesopotamia (in present day Iraq), but modern applications of the image have more to do with the interconnecting parts of a piece of machinery.

whipping boy • *person punished for another's mistakes*

In some European royal families a prince was educated in the company of a commoner-boy who was whipped if the prince offended. Apart from preserving the royal hide, the boy kept for whipping was perhaps intended as an encouragement to the prince to behave well and so avoid manifestly unfair consequences, but nothing is known of the success rate of this curious educational practice.

whistle for it or **for the wind**

Used as a catch-phrase: 'You can whistle for it' means 'I won't give it to you' or 'You won't get it'. A person who whistles for the wind is hoping for the impossible.

The origin is an ancient superstition or saying among seamen that the wind could be brought to a becalmed sailing-ship by whistling for it, as if the wind would blow in sympathy with a mariner's 'blowing'.

white elephant • *something no longer wanted by its owner; something, often property, requiring so much expenditure and care as to be an encumbrance or give little profit*

The kings of Siam, now Thailand, used to give white elephants as gifts to courtiers who fell out of favour. The white elephant was not only rare but also sacred, and so could not be put to work to recoup the cost of its upkeep. Nor could it be got rid of, because like all white elephants it remained the property of the king. The gift was symbolic rather than ruinous, but the message was clear.

white feather: see *feather, (show the) white*

White Knight   • *person who comes to the rescue*

From stock exchange slang for a company that rescues another
which faces a takeover. This in turn comes from the general idea,
based on popular literature, of knights in armour being on the
side of the needy. White is traditionally associated with purity.
See **knight in shining armour**.

There is a White Knight among the fantasy figures of Lewis
Carroll's *Through the Looking-Glass* (1892). He may have added to
the currency of the expression but, being an ineffectual character,
is unrelated to the modern meaning.

white lie   • *a lie justified by praiseworthy motives*

From the traditional association of white with purity and innocence, as in 'though your sins be as scarlet, they shall be as white
as snow' (*Isaiah*, 1: 18) which dates from the eighth century BC.

whited sepulchre   • *hypocrite*

In denouncing the Pharisees (see **pharisaic**) Christ described
them as 'whited sepulchres, which indeed appear beautiful outward, but are within full of dead men's bones and of all unclean-
ness' (*Matthew*, 23: 27). Because of certain Jewish notions that
impurity could result from contact with a tomb, the stones
covering burial pits and the rocks at the mouths of burial caves
were whitewashed as a warning to passers-by.

whole hog: see *hog*

wide berth, give a: see *berth*

wide of the mark   • *wrong*

Mark is an old word for anything set up to be aimed at. The whole
expression is borrowed from target-shooting.

wild-goose chase   • *hopeless or foolish quest or pursuit of something unattainable or never found*

A chase in the manner of a wild goose, not a wild chase after a goose (i.e. 'wild goose-chase') which the normal pronunciation implies.

In the sixteenth century, *wild-goose chase* was the name given to a sort of cross-country horse-race; it was so called because the participants had to follow the course of the leader, as a flight of wild geese does. The basic idea is therefore that of pursuit over an erratic course.

wild oats: see *sow one's wild oats*

wilderness: see *voice crying in the wilderness*

will o' the wisp   • *elusive person or goal*

This was formerly the popular name of a phosphorescent light or flicker seen over marshes which is now supposed to have been caused by the spontaneous combustion of methane gas from decaying organic matter. The name was a personification, originally 'Will with the wisp', *Will* being an abbreviation of the common forename and *wisp* meaning a bundle of twisted straw used for burning as a torch. The expression used to be metaphorical for a guiding principle, hope, ambition, etc. that would lead one astray, but the modern meaning has more to do with elusiveness than delusion.

wimp   • *ineffectual, weak person*

Probably an abbreviation of 'whimperer', one who complains in a soft plaintive whine.

wind of change

Now a cliché but originally a striking metaphor, principally because of the circumstances in which it was first used. It occurred in a speech by Harold Macmillan when he was the British prime minister. He was referring to the strength of African national consciousness and he introduced the phrase when actually addressing the South African parliament (1960), which at the time was rigorously committed—as it was until 1991—to the policy of apartheid: 'The wind of change is blowing through this continent. Whether we like it or not, this growth of political consciousness is a political fact.'

It is not known whether the phrase was coined by the person who wrote the speech (David Hunt, a diplomat) or by one of the revisers (who included Macmillan himself), or whether it was a conscious echo of the words used in 1934 by Stanley Baldwin (a prime minister himself, though not at the time he said them): 'There is a wind of nationalism and freedom blowing round the world, and blowing as strongly in Asia as elsewhere'.

wind out of one's sails, take the   ● *disconcert, deflate or frustrate one; deprive one of an advantage*

A figure of speech derived from sailing. A boat under sail can be slowed down if the wind is prevented from reaching its sails. This can happen if another boat is positioned nearby in the direction from which the wind is blowing. This second boat is said to *take the wind out of the sails* of the first.

The expression is sometimes used of frustrating someone's intentions by doing in advance what he or she has already planned to do.

windfall   ● *unexpected acquisition or benefit*

Literally, anything—such as fruit or a branch—that falls from a tree as a result of being blown by the wind. The connection between this and the figurative meaning is obvious enough in that both come about without human effort, but the underlying idea of benefit originates from the old days when laws controlled tree-felling but allowed windfallen branches to be freely gathered for fuel.

windmills: see *tilt*

wing(s)

To *take under one's wing* is to give care, protection and guidance. The image is from young birds nestling under a parent's wing for warmth and security. To *clip one's wings* (restrict one's freedom to act as one wishes) is a reference to the literal cutting short of the long feathers of the wings of domesticated birds, such as ducks, to prevent them from flying away.

winter of discontent

A cliché ever since it was applied to the winter of 1978–9, a period of notorious disruption by strikes in Britain. It is still a newspaper favourite whenever a period of unrest coincides with winter. The original is the opening lines of Shakespeare's *Richard III*:

> Now is the winter of our discontent
> Made glorious summer by this sun of York . . .

The *winter* here is the reign of Henry VI, the Lancastrian king who has just been murdered; the *summer* is the succession of the Yorkist Edward IV, whose device was a *sun*, during the civil wars in England, 1455–85 (the Wars of the Roses).

wipe the slate clean: see *slate*

wives' tale, old   • *superstition; traditional belief or piece of wisdom, usually foolish*

Wife originally meant no more than 'woman'. The idea underlying the expression is that old people tend to live in the past, so that what they say is not always to be taken seriously. The Bible has 'refuse profane and old wives' fables' (*I Timothy*, 4: 7), but the expression was proverbial before English translations of the Bible became popularly known.

wolf

A wolf in sheep's clothing is somebody, occasionally something, hiding a hostile intention behind a friendly manner. The Bible has 'Beware of false prophets, which come to you in sheep's clothing, but inwardly they are ravening wolves' (*Matthew*, 7: 15). In one of Aesop's fables (sixth century BC) a wolf puts on a sheepskin in order to trick the shepherd and is duly locked up with the sheep for the night, but before it can profit from its ruse it is killed by the shepherd, who thought he was killing a sheep for his supper. As

Aesop predates St Matthew, either Aesop must take the credit for the idea or, more likely, it was common among Mediterranean cultures. Its use in English, however, is more likely to be from the scriptural allusion.

To *cry wolf* is to raise a false alarm. This too is in Aesop: a shepherd boy cried 'Wolf' for the fun of seeing people come running from the village to help stave off the danger; when a wolf actually did come, nobody took any notice of the boy's cry and his sheep were killed. To *cry wolf once too often* is thus to lose credibility after too much alarmism.

It is because of the wolf's ravenous appetite that hungry or greedy people are said to *wolf* their food. To keep starvation or other penury at bay is *to keep the wolf* (symbol of hunger) *from the door* (i.e. away from oneself).

wooden horse: see *Trojan*

wooden spoon ● *booby prize*

Traditionally presented to the candidate placed bottom in the mathematics degree examination at Cambridge University, perhaps in ironic contrast to the **silver spoon**, a customary and valuable baptismal gift from godparents to a child as a symbol of future plenty.

wool-gathering ● *daydreaming; absent-mindedness*

Literally, the collection of scraps of wool torn from the fleeces of sheep by bushes, etc. or as a result of sheep scratching or grooming themselves. It was an activity for poor people hoping to gather enough fragments to weave together, entailing a certain amount of haphazard rambling among hedgerows and fields by women and children. This rather random wandering has been a metaphor for dreaminess since the sixteenth century.

world is one's oyster, the ● *one has a chance to make one's fortune*

Invented by Shakespeare and put into the mouth of Pistol, a comic character in *The Merry Wives of Windsor*, as a flamboyant boast (II, 2, lines 4–5):

Why, then the word's mine oyster,
Which I with sword will open.

He means that he will use his sword to extract money from an unwilling world, a sense removed from the modern one which is that the world is simply waiting to be opened up to provide good things.

Pistol is also alluding to an old expression that drew a parallel between opening oysters with a dagger and keeping one's distance because of a smell. His proposed use of his sword to effect the opening—a comically cumbersome operation—implies an even greater degree of rottenness in the oyster/world. This colouring too is absent from the modern use of the expression.

writing is on the wall, the   ● *the warning (of approaching calamity) is plain for all to see*

When Belshazzar, the last king of Babylon, held a great feast during which wine was drunk from the vessels which his father Nebuchadnezzar had removed from the temple at Jerusalem, the fingers of a man's hand appeared and wrote on the plaster of the wall. As his own astrologer could not interpret the message he sent for Daniel, who had successfully explained Nebuchadnezzar's dream (see **feet of clay**). Daniel read the message as foretelling Belshazzar's overthrow because of his opposition to the God of the Hebrews and his defilement of the temple vessels. That night the king was killed and his kingdom divided. This famous story, demonstrating God's intervention in favour of the Jews, is in *Daniel*, chapter 5.

Y

yahoo • *brutal, rowdy, obscenely coarse lout*

A rather literary term of abuse. In the fourth part of Jonathan Swift's *Gulliver's Travels* (1726) the Yahoos are filthy and brutal beasts in human shape who inhabit the country of the Houyhnhnms, horses who possess reason and live in a simple and clean society. The Yahoos' vicious bestiality is so gross that it alienates Gulliver from his own species.

Yank, Yankee • *American*

Originally US slang for a citizen of New England, then for a citizen of the northern states generally: during the Civil War it was applied to the Federal Army of the north by the Confederates of the south. In Britain, however, these distinctions have not been observed and the word is used of any American.

The derivation is probably from the Dutch *Janke*, a diminutive of Jan (John) pronounced 'Yan', or from *Jan Kees* (John Cheese), both derisive nicknames used by New York Dutch settlers when speaking of English colonists in nearby New England, especially Connecticut.

yellow press • *popular newspapers*

As an early experiment in mass-produced colour-printing to increase circulation, the *New York World* produced in 1895 a cartoon in which the main character was a little girl in a yellow frock. One result of this was the coinage of the term *yellow press* to describe popular sensational newspapers as a whole.

yen   • *longing*

A comparatively recent importation (about 1930) from the USA, this was originally the Chinese *(in-) yan* or *ye(e)n*, an intense craving for opium smoke.

young Turk   • *young and rebellious or unmanageable member of an organisation*

The original Young Turks were a reformist political movement in the Ottoman Empire. It was founded in 1889, brought about constitutional changes in 1908 after a revolt, was successful in the Balkan Wars of 1912–13, but was dissolved at the end of the First World War when the Ottoman Empire, having fought in the German cause, was broken up. The name reflected both the desire to rejuvenate a declining empire and the youthfulness of its founders (young army officers) and some of its supporters (students). In modern English use, the implication of unreliable extremism owes less to the actual Young Turks than to the old-fashioned English view of Turks as rather hot-headed and violent people.

yuppy   • *ostentatious, aggressively thrusting and high-earning young person in business*

Acronym derived from 'young upwardly mobile professional person'.

Z

zap   ●   *use a remote-control device to switch from channel to channel while watching television, or to fast-forward through commercial breaks on a video-recording*

This word was invented in the drawings of American comic strips to represent the sound of a bullet, laser, ray-gun, etc. It passed into spoken and written vocabulary during the Vietnam War when American troops used it as a childish euphemism for 'kill' or 'strike'. Computer language then adopted it, in the related sense of 'erase', and this sense persists in its latest use.

zizz   ●   *sleep*

From the convention in cartoons, especially in children's comics, of depicting sleeping characters with 'zzzz' coming out of their mouths to represent the sound of snoring. This was turned into a word in RAF slang some time before the Second World War.

zombie   ●   *inactive person lacking mental or physical alertness*

A word from West African voodoo, transferred to the Americas by the slave trade and then into standard English. It may originally have been the name of a snake deity but is better known as the term for a soulless corpse allegedly revived by witchcraft; hence the idea of lifelessness.

OTHER TITLES AVAILABLE
IN TEACH YOURSELF

☐	0 340 42996 8	**Correct English**	£4.99
		B. A. Phythian	
☐	0 340 35873 4	**English Grammar**	£4.99
		B. A. Phythian	
☐	0 340 57494 1	**Concise Dictionary of English Idioms**	£6.99
		B. A. Phythian	
☐	0 340 57496 8	**Concise Dictionary of Correct English**	£6.99
		B. A. Phythian	
☐	0 340 58743 1	**Concise Dictionary of English Slang**	£6.99
		B. A. Phythian	
☐	0 340 28765 9	**Creative Writing**	£4.99
		Dianne Doubtfire	

All these books are available at your local bookshop or newsagent, or can be ordered direct from the publisher. Just tick the titles you want and fill in the form below.

Prices and availability subject to change without notice.

HODDER AND STOUGHTON PAPERBACKS, P.O. Box 11, Falmouth, Cornwall.

Please send cheque or postal order for the value of the book, and add the following for postage and packing:

UK including BFPO – £1.00 for one book, plus 50p for the second book, and 30p for each additional book ordered up to a £3.00 maximum.

OVERSEAS, INCLUDING EIRE – £2.00 for the first book, plus £1.00 for the second book, and 50p for each additional book ordered.

OR Please debit this amount from my Access/Visa Card (delete as appropriate).

CARD NUMBER ☐☐☐☐☐☐☐☐☐☐☐☐☐☐☐☐

AMOUNT £ . . . .

EXPIRY DATE . . . .

SIGNED . . . .

NAME . . . .

ADDRESS . . . .

. . . .